MW00595488

A+ PARENTING

PARENTING

THE SURPRISINGLY
FUN GUIDE TO RAISING
SURPRISINGLY SMART KIDS

Eva Moskowitz
with Eric Grannis

HARVEST
An Imprint of WILLIAM MORROW

FIRST EDITION

Library of Congress Cataloging-in-Publication Data

Names: Moskowitz, Eva S., author. | Grannis, Eric, author.
Title: A+ parenting : the surprisingly fun guide to raising surprisingly smart kids / Eva Moskowitz, with Eric Grannis.
Other titles: A plus parenting
Description: First edition. | New York : Harvest, an imprint of William Morrow, [2023] | Includes bibliographical references and index. |
Identifiers: LCCN 2023016681 (print) | LCCN 2023016682 (ebook) | ISBN 9780063310223 (hardcover) | ISBN 9780063310254 (ebook)
Subjects: LCSH: Early childhood education—Parent participation. | Early childhood education—Activity programs. | Parenting. | Child development. | Parent and child.
Classification: LCC LB1139.35.P37 M6 2023 (print) | LCC LB1139.35.P37 (ebook) | DDC 649/.124—dc23/eng/20230602
LC record available at https://lccn.loc.gov/2023016681
LC ebook record available at https://lccn.loc.gov/2023016682

ISBN 978-0-06-331022-3

23 24 25 26 27 LBC 5 4 3 2 1

Dedicated to our parents,
Martin and Anita Moskowitz and
Joseph and Alexandra Grannis,
from whom we learned so much about parenting

CONTENTS

INTRODUCTION

On August 20, 1998, my journey as a parent began with the birth of my first child, and it continued with the births of two more in the next six years, but it was on August 21, 2006, when I suddenly became responsible for 165 more children, that my understanding of parenting truly began to accelerate. Although these children weren't my own, but rather the students admitted to Success Academy, a school I'd just founded, I quickly learned that educating young children is a lot like parenting them. While the curriculum is ostensibly about reading, writing, and arithmetic, it's really about teaching children how to learn.

Take something as simple as paying attention. Adults know that they can't afford to let their minds wander when they are listening to a lecture or a story since they may miss information that is critical to understanding what follows. Kindergartners lack this discipline. They are easily distracted by a classmate's cool sneakers, a flickering lightbulb, or a dinosaur poster they've suddenly noticed. Figuring out how to control one's attention is just one of the many intellectual habits children need to develop to become good students and thinkers. They must also learn to be patient, inquisitive, and inventive; to review their work critically, overcome their fears, and exercise discipline; and perhaps most important, to enjoy and value learning—in other words, to become *enthusiastic learners*.

I was determined to teach these skills to our students at Success Academy to ensure they obtained a first-rate education. I also knew that this would be a big challenge since most of them came from disadvantaged families. Seventy-three percent were eligible for free or reduced-price lunch, and most came from a school district in Harlem in which only one in five eighth graders read on grade level and only one in a hundred gained admission to a four-year college. Nonetheless, we were determined to ensure that our students would have the same type of opportunities as children from more affluent families, and I believe we succeeded. As I write these words sixteen years later, 96 percent of our eighth graders are at or above grade level in reading and 93 percent are at or above grade level in math. As for our high school graduates, 100 percent of them have been admitted to four-year colleges. Moreover, we've managed to replicate these results across fifty schools serving more than 20,000 students.

I won't take credit for all of this success, much of which must go to the incredibly talented educators with whom I have had the privilege to work, but I will claim to have learned a lot in the process, particularly since my two younger children attended Success Academy from kindergarten through twelfth grade. My dual role as both a school leader and a mother gave me the perfect opportunity to understand how schooling and parenting come together to contribute to a child's intellectual development. Sharing that knowledge with you is the purpose of this book.

Given my role as a school leader, many parents seek my advice. I find that even people who are very confident and successful in every other aspect of their lives are often unsure about parenting. That isn't surprising when you consider that parenting is probably the most important thing we do for which we receive no training. Unlike becoming a doctor, a lawyer, or a hairdresser or even learning how to drive a car, there are no required courses or certifications for parenting. It's assumed that we know what we're doing because we were once parented ourselves, which is a bit like assuming that someone who has undergone heart surgery is qualified to be a heart surgeon.

Moreover, the challenges facing parents have changed over time. College admissions, for example, have become far more competitive in recent years. Many parents are torn between wanting to ensure that their children are prepared for this competition and wanting to let their children find themselves, pursue a variety of interests, and enjoy their childhoods.

When I founded Success Academy, I faced a similar conflict. I knew it would be challenging to prepare our students to compete with children from more affluent backgrounds, but I didn't want to give short shrift to sports, arts, and other "extracurricular" activities. These activities are important for children's development, and many children from disadvantaged communities don't have access to them. Take sports. In middle-class suburbs, many kids get the opportunity to play on soccer or Little League teams. These experiences are usually far better than conventional "gym" classes because the coaches for these teams take sports more seriously. As a result, the participants learn real skills and strive to improve them so that their team can compete successfully. This teaches children about effort and teamwork.

Since most of the families we serve don't have access to these types of opportunities, I believed that it was important we build them into our program. Beginning in kindergarten, our children learn soccer under the direction of coaches who have played soccer at a high level either in college or in professional clubs. This instruction occurs during the school day, but students can also join our afterschool programs if they want to play competitively. As a result, many of our students have become excellent soccer players. In 2021, our high school team was invited to represent North America in a competition organized by A.C. Milan, the most renowned soccer club in Italy.

We also teach every child chess beginning in kindergarten and encourage them to play competitively beginning in third grade. We have more than 11,000 children playing chess and more than 500 US Chess Federation–rated players. We routinely send over 150 of them to national tournaments.

I also encouraged my own children to pursue these opportunities and to engage in other enjoyable childhood activities. They acted in their school plays, competed on their school's debate and chess teams, played on their school's varsity soccer and basketball teams, spent much of their summers in camps or vacationing with us, and had good friends and serious romantic relationships. Nonetheless, all three of my children got into top-notch universities, as do most of the students at Success Academy.

How were these children able to achieve this level of success despite all these distractions? Because many of these "distractions" actually contribute to intellectual development. Take chess. I made chess part of Success's curriculum because my husband had taught chess to our older son, Culver, and I felt that he had benefited from it. I became even more convinced of this when my two younger children, Dillon and Hannah, learned chess as students at Success Academy. When Dillon was in third grade, he and about a dozen other Success students competed in a national tournament. To my astonishment, students were required to play three matches per day, each of which could last up to four hours. But despite playing up to twelve hours a day, Dillon hardly noticed the time passing. When he'd finished his final match one day, he asked me if it was dinnertime yet. It was 11 P.M.

A few years later, I got a call from Dillon's teacher on the day we were administering the state math test. That year, the State Education Department had decided that students should be able to take as long as they wanted on the state test, so we weren't supposed to pressure them to finish. The problem was that Dillon was taking an unusually long time, far more than any of the other students. It wasn't that he was having any problem with the math. On the contrary, he was quite strong in math. He was taking such a long time because he was triple-checking his work to ensure he didn't get a single question wrong. This intellectual stamina has proved very useful to Dillon as he has pursued very challenging studies in college including advanced math and computer programming courses. I'm convinced that his intellectual stamina is due in part to his experience playing chess and that this is also true of Success Academy's other students, who tend to do quite well on high-stakes tests and other activities that require long periods of concentration.

Another activity in which my children participated was debate. Like chess, debate can bring out a student's best efforts because it is competitive. When my children participated in a debate tournament, they would often work until midnight the night before to prepare for it. One summer, Hannah went to a debate camp at Harvard. When she returned, I found that she'd gone through an astonishing transformation. In a matter of weeks, all of the "ums" and "likes" had disappeared from her speech and she seemed to speak in paragraphs. I was also amazed at how much knowledge she and Dillon picked up from debating. At family dinners, we would regularly find ourselves stumbling onto some topic on which they were surprisingly knowledgeable, such as nuclear proliferation or the legal standards for conducting searches and seizures, and it was usually because they had debated it. As a school leader, I was humbled at times to realize how much of Hannah and Dillon's knowledge seemed to come from this extracurricular activity compared to Success Academy's formal curriculum.

There are many activities like these that will help children become nimble thinkers and enthusiastic learners. Moreover, most of them are enjoyable and can take place at home. These include playing board games, watching great films, visiting museums, having interesting dinner table conversations, telling jokes, solving logical puzzles, and listening to comedy albums, good songs, and short stories. Eric and I aren't alone in this—many families engage in some of these activities—but we did so more frequently and intentionally than most.

At first, we did so largely for fun and because these were things that our parents had done with us, but we came to realize that they were having an enormous impact on our children's intellectual development. When our children would talk about history, politics, or science, they would draw upon information they'd gleaned from a science program we'd watched, a museum we'd visited, or a dinnertime conversation we'd had. When they made a witty remark, we'd notice how it was a variation on a joke we'd told or a comedy album to which we'd listened. When we read their school essays on poetry, we saw how they picked up on double entendres they'd learned to recognize from listening to Tin Pan Alley songs or watching classic films. And when they took tests, we saw how they summoned the intensity, concentration, and competitive zeal they'd developed from playing chess, bridge, Blokus, Set, and dozens of other games. In all of the intellectual progress they made, we could see the fingerprints of the activities in which we'd engaged as a family.

We also began to notice how many of the highly successful people we knew had also engaged in these same activities as children. They, too, had grown up playing chess, Monopoly, or Clue; had enjoyed *Monty Python*, *The Hitchhiker's Guide to the Galaxy*, and the songs of Bob Dylan; had played charades, password, and other parlor games with their parents; and had been encouraged to participate in adult conversations at dinners and parties.

These activities have allowed our children to become confident and enthusiastic learners. They like reading, talking about serious topics, learning new things, solving logical puzzles, and engaging in intellectual competition, and this has carried over into their schoolwork. Instead of dreading writing essays, our children see them as an opportunity to express themselves. Instead of viewing standardized tests as unwelcome ordeals, they view them as a chance to compete. Instead of floundering in college because they can't motivate themselves, they are excited by the courses they are taking. In short, they have become lifelong learners.

You may be surprised that children can learn so much at home, but keep in mind that children only spend about 180 days in school each year. How your children spend the remaining 185 days is up to you. Moreover, you have far more time to engage in fun educational activities with your children than we do at school since we need to spend most of our time on more conventional academic activities. On a single Saturday, you can play chess with your child in the morning, take them to a museum in the afternoon, and watch a movie with them in the evening. And the truth is that if you can manage to do just one of these things every day that your child is out of school, it will have an enormous impact.

Of course, your child also needs to do their schoolwork, but one of the things I've learned from running schools is that if children are simply more purposeful when they study, they can learn far more without spending much more time on their schoolwork. When most children do their homework, they simply go through the motions instead of seeking to master the skills and acquire the knowledge that the homework is supposed to teach. When children take responsibility for learning rather than passively doing their homework, they can learn far more efficiently.

Running schools has also taught me a lot about disciplining children: that expressing disappointment is much more effective than expressing anger; that giving a child time to understand why their behavior was wrong is better than insisting on an apology in the heat of the moment; and that praise, when it has been earned, can be an even more effective motivator than criticism. Patient, thoughtful parenting can achieve terrific results and avoid much of the family conflict that arises when parents allow themselves to be ruled by their emotions.

Not surprisingly, running schools has also taught me about

some of the dangers of parenting in contemporary America. One of the biggest is the availability of video games and television, given the ubiquity of smartphones. I've seen the negative impact that getting addicted to these forms of entertainment can have on a child's ability to concentrate and enjoy more educational activities such as reading or engaging in creative projects. This is one of the areas in which parents must really exert their authority if they want their children to achieve their intellectual potential.

These are some of the most important aspects of our parenting, but there are others that I describe in this book. What my husband, Eric, and I found was that when we put all of these pieces together, they worked so well as a whole that we didn't have to put too much weight on any single piece of the structure. Because our children were learning so much at home through informal educational activities, it was easier for them to do well in school, which meant we didn't have to push them as hard as we otherwise would have. We weren't forced to nag them, ground them, or get into fights with them about doing their schoolwork or spending time with their friends. To be sure, we set some expectations for our children and leaned on them at times, but it wasn't often. Mainly, we shared with them our enthusiasm for life and learning by doing things with them that we enjoyed. And that is as it should be. Parents should be able to enjoy parenting. After all, why have children if they don't enrich your life with love, joy, and sense of purpose?

In the pages that follow, you will find carefully curated lists of activities that you can do with your children, or that they can do on their own, including games to play, movies to watch, puzzles to solve, books to read, music to listen to, and experiments to perform, but don't think that you need to do all of these things or do them in any particular order. The most important thing is to bring love, joy, and enthusiasm to your parenting. The more you do so, the more your children will learn to appreciate intellectual pursuits and become lifelong learners.

NOBODY IS A PERFECT PARENT

Before I dive into the details of this program, I want to address one more topic. While I hope that you will be excited to learn about the many ways in which you can help your children develop intellectually, I fear that some of you may have a different reaction. You may worry that you don't have time to do everything I suggest in this book, that it's "too late" because your kids are too old, or that you aren't equipped to do them. ("I never learned how to play chess!" "I don't know anything about science!")

These reactions are symptoms of what I would call "parental inadequacy syndrome." You feel that you are never doing enough for your kids, who will therefore be at a terrible disadvantage compared to children who had the good fortune to be born to more competent and devoted parents. If any of this sounds familiar, then I have some important messages for you: (1) nobody is a perfect parent; (2) you don't have a moral obligation to be a perfect parent; (3) your children can be happy and well educated without your being a perfect parent; (4) trying too hard to be a perfect parent can actually be counterproductive; and (5) if you are worried about whether you are doing enough for your children, then you are probably already doing a lot for them.

You may get the impression from this book that Eric and I spent endless amounts of time parenting our children. Trust me, we didn't, particularly when our children were young. The main barrier was our careers. Coming out of college, I planned to become a professor of history. In part, this was because I knew from my parents that this was a good profession for parenting. Although it requires a lot of work, your schedule is flexible outside of the dozen or so hours a week when you are actually scheduled to teach. However, I'd also learned from them that it was tricky to have kids before your career was well established. My brother and I were born before my father earned his graduate degree or my mother had even begun her studies. As a result, they were so poor that my father had to take out a $25 "emergency loan" from his department every month to pay his rent. Even when he got a position as an assistant professor, our financial situation was quite precarious. In addition, it was very hard for my parents to find time for their studies, particularly since they didn't have enough money to hire a babysitter or someone to help them with cleaning or laundry.

So I decided that while I would follow in my parents' footsteps by becoming an academic, I would delay becoming a mother until I was better established in my career, and Eric and I were more financially secure. I followed this plan by earning my Ph.D. in record time, and after a few temporary positions, I managed to get a position at a university that looked like it could become permanent. Meanwhile, Eric had graduated from law school and was at a big firm, so we were doing fairly well. My whole plan was working like clockwork, except for one thing: I found that my heart wasn't really into being a professor. Although I liked American history and enjoyed teaching it, I never really loved all the research and writing that being a professor required.

On December 1, 1995, I came across an article about an upcoming city council election and decided to volunteer for one of the candidate's campaigns. I discovered that I loved politics. I enjoyed organizing and dealing with people. It came much more easily to me than academia. Within weeks of entering the field, I got multiple job offers, including one that I accepted to run a congressional campaign. Two years later, I was elected to the New York City Council. I loved the work, particularly when I became chair of the council's education committee, a topic of particular interest to me.

I was happy to find something that I really loved and was good at, but in solving one problem, I'd created another. Just a year before I got elected to the council, I'd had my first child, and in the next four years, I had two more. I had been hoping that by the time I had children, I'd be well established in a flexible career that allowed me to spend a lot of time with them. Being a council member did not. Not only did most of my work require me to attend events in person, but these events were often in the evening. Moreover, I wasn't well established. To the contrary, I was just starting this new profession, so I felt I had to work hard to contribute and make a mark.

Let me make this even more concrete. Before I was elected to the city council, I served on a local community board. At this time, my first son was only a few months old, and since I didn't have childcare in the evening, I brought him to community board meetings. As the meetings usually lasted until the wee hours of the morning, I sometimes left before they ended. Unfortunately, that was exactly when many of the votes took place. When I subsequently ran for city council, my opponent mailed a flyer to tens of thousands of voters attacking me for missing these votes. It was a legitimate criticism, and I was mortified.

At moments like that, I felt despondent, that there was no way that I could be both a good mother and a good elected official. When I was working, I felt I should be parenting; when I was parenting, I felt I should be working. And right after I left politics, I founded Success Academy, which was just as important to me and even more demanding of my time.

You may be thinking that this is the part where I'm going to tell you how Eric and I figured out some magical solution to allow us to

NOBODY IS A PERFECT PARENT

be just as good parents as we would have been if we hadn't chosen highly demanding professions. I have no such magic solution. We didn't have enough time for parenting and our children suffered. Our oldest son in particular ended up having language and reading delays that I'm convinced were in part due to our absence. As for our two younger children, they fared better in their early years, perhaps in part because we sent them to nursery school earlier, but they didn't develop as quickly as the children of parents who were more involved in their children's upbringing.

But despite this slow start, our children ended up doing quite well academically. The reality is that you can be a quite imperfect parent and still have very capable children, particularly if you follow some of the advice in this book. Most people can't be perfect parents because they have other priorities in their lives that need to be balanced against their parenting responsibilities. In my case, I felt that the work I was doing both on the city council and then at Success Academy was very important. But you may also simply need to make time in your life for things that you enjoy. You are not under a moral obligation to sacrifice your happiness for that of your children. If you did, then your children would presumably have a moral obligation to sacrifice their happiness for their children, and it would go on and on, a parenting Ponzi scheme in which nobody actually gets to enjoy themselves!

So, while you may feel guilty that you don't have enough time for your children—I certainly did—try not to. Feeling an obligation to sacrifice yourself for your children can ultimately be counterproductive. Some parents think they owe it to their children to clean up after them, to entertain them every moment they get bored, and to let them whine and complain whenever they're unhappy. This may lead your children to think that the whole world revolves around them and that their needs should take precedence over everyone else's, including yours, which isn't a good way to start life. Moreover, if you sacrifice yourself for your children to the point that it makes you unhappy, you will become a worse parent.

For all of these reasons, the last thing I'd want is for this book to make any reader feel inadequate as a parent. Eric and I weren't at all perfect parents and didn't spend endless hours doing everything listed in this book. To the contrary, we did these things fleetingly and intermittently, especially since we didn't have this book when we started our parenting journey! If, like us, you can find *some* time to do *some* of the things in this book, it will have a huge positive impact on your children.

PART I

FUN AND GAMES

1

BOARD GAMES

When I talk to successful people about their childhoods, some predictable common themes emerge—reading, attending good schools, regular dinner conversations with well-educated parents—but there's another common theme that may surprise you: playing board games such as Monopoly, Risk, and Clue, and card games such as bridge, poker, and gin rummy.

Many very accomplished people played such games when they were young and have continued doing so as adults. Avid bridge players include Bill Gates and Warren Buffett (who has said that it is "the best intellectual exercise out there"). The roll of serious chess players is even more illustrious, including directors Stanley Kubrick and Mel Brooks, writers William Shakespeare and George R. R. Martin, investors Peter Thiel and George Soros, comedians Steve Martin and Chris Rock, presidents Abraham Lincoln and Teddy Roosevelt, actors Matt Damon and Robin Williams, philosophers Jean-Paul Sartre and Blaise Pascal, and polymaths Isaac Newton and Benjamin Franklin.[1]

As African American Grandmaster Maurice Ashley has written:

*Chess is an intellectual discipline masking as a game. . . .
All the skills we want our children to have, problem solving,
analytical reasoning, focus and concentration, are imbedded
in the game itself, in the playing of the game itself, so kids have
fun and learn at the same time and they don't even know it.*[2]

Similarly, Benjamin Franklin has written:

*The game of chess is not merely an idle amusement. Several
very valuable qualities of the mind, useful in the course of
human life, are to be acquired or strengthened by it, so as to
become habits, ready on all occasions.*

1. *Foresight, which . . . considers the consequences that may
   attend an action . . . "If I move this piece, what will be the
   advantages or disadvantages of my new situation? What
   use can my adversary make of it to annoy me? What other
   moves can I make to support it, and to defend myself from
   his attacks?"*
2. *Circumspection, which surveys the whole chessboard,
   or scene of action; the relations of the several pieces and
   situations, the dangers they are respectively exposed to,
   the several possibilities of their aiding each other, the
   probabilities that the adversary may make this or that
   move, and attack this or the other piece, and what
   different means can be used to avoid his stroke, or turn its
   consequences against him.*
3. *Caution, not to make our moves too hastily . . .*[3]

Franklin's explanation shows how much analysis even a single
move can require. Playing an entire game requires tremendous powers of concentration and patience.

Given the intellectual benefits of chess, we teach it to every student at Success Academy beginning in kindergarten. It isn't simply

an afterschool activity but part of our regular curriculum. When our students get to third grade, they can choose to play competitively on our teams.

In addition to helping with one's concentration, chess teaches you the self-discipline to search for the *best possible decision*. As Stanley Kubrick, who was a chess hustler in Washington Square Park before becoming a director, explains:

> *You sit at the board and suddenly your heart leaps. Your hand trembles to pick up the piece and move it. But what Chess teaches you is that you must sit there calmly and think about whether it's really a good idea and whether there are other better ideas.*[4]

The discipline of resisting hasty decisions is useful in many endeavors, including taking standardized tests, which typically require that students choose the best among several plausible answers. For example, suppose that a test asks for the main idea of the nursery rhyme "Humpty Dumpty":

> *Humpty Dumpty sat on a wall*
> *Humpty Dumpty had a great fall*
> *All the king's horses and all the king's men*
> *Couldn't put Humpty together again*

Suppose that one of the multiple-choice answers is: "One should be careful because things can break." An impatient test taker may select this answer since it certainly expresses part of what is implicit in this rhyme, but a better answer is that one should be careful because sometimes things that break can't be fixed. This answer is better because it gives meaning to the last two lines of the nursery rhyme about the king's men being unable to put Humpty together again, which the first answer doesn't.

Many children will get multiple-choice questions wrong because they are impatient. Just as Kubrick suggests happens in chess, when the student sees what seems to be a plausible answer, their heart leaps and they immediately select it because they like the feeling that they've figured out the answer. Even if they know they are supposed to look at all the answers before making their final decision, they prefer to believe that the answer they've already selected is so clearly correct that it would be a waste of time to look at the others. Chess teaches children to resist such urges, as Maurice Ashley has written:

> *The great thing about chess is that you are punished for bad thinking; you are punished for impatience. You have to stop and plan ahead before you move or else you are going to lose the game.*[5]

I believe it is this discipline learned from playing chess that accounts in part for why students at Success Academy do so well on standardized tests.

Since I've raised the dreaded topic of standardized tests, I should probably say something about them. I realize that many people despise standardized tests and bemoan the fact that they play such a large role in college admissions. Even if that's how you feel, your children will have to learn to do well on them if they wish to maximize their chances of getting into a good college or graduate program. Throughout this book, I will explain how various activities—fun, family activities that you can do after school or on the weekend—will enable your children to do well on standardized tests. If you really hate standardized tests, then think of these activities as a way to minimize the amount of time that your children will need to engage in more conventional test prep.

Games can also develop a child's mathematical skills and intuition. Take backgammon. Since its rules are fairly simple, a five-year-old can learn to play it, and it will help firm up their addition and counting skills, but as children get older, they can also develop an understanding of probability. Imagine a child playing backgammon who sees they can land on one of their opponent's pieces if only they can roll a 12, which requires double 6's. They roll the dice and one die lands on 3 while the other is still tumbling. No matter what happens to that second die, they realize there is no way to end up with a 12. A few turns later, the child is hoping for a 7 and again rolls a 3. This time they realize that they can still get a 7 if the other die comes up 4. Then the next time they need to get a 7, they roll a 1, and realize that they can also get a 7 if the other dies come up 6. Eventually, they come to realize that no matter what happens to the first die, they can still get a 7. Next, they realize that it is more likely that they will roll a 7 than a 12 because there are many more paths to this result. And from there, it is only a short jump to realizing that this has significance for the game: that if they want to minimize the chance that their opponent will be able to land on their piece, it is safer to leave it 12 places away than 7 places away.

If a child has strong mathematical intuitions, they may eventually realize that they can actually calculate that the odds of rolling a 12 are only 1 out of 36 since there are 36 possible combinations and only 1 that results in a 12. However, even if the child only gets as far as realizing that they're more likely to roll a 7 than a 12, that is an incredibly valuable experience because they have now learned that they can actually discover math for themselves, that this isn't something that can be obtained only from teachers and books. Moreover, discovering mathematical concepts for yourself leads to far more durable learning. It's hard to forget something you discovered yourself, and even if you do, you can just discover it again! That's why, at Success, we try to teach children in a manner that draws on their mathematical intuition. But you have an advantage that we don't. Children have lots of leisure time, particularly on weekends and on vacations. As a result, you can afford to let your child spend hours and hours playing backgammon until they discover the concept of probability. Schools don't have that luxury because of the amount of material we have to cover.

One reason children learn so much from playing games is that it taps into their competitive instincts. That's what motivated Dillon to concentrate on chess for such long periods of time. Similarly, Culver, who is perhaps the most competitive of all our children, has developed great powers of concentration from playing bridge. When he finishes a hand, he can tell you who won every one of the thirteen tricks played, which card won each trick, and which cards each player held at the beginning.

Some educators are uncomfortable with encouraging children's competitive instincts. I think that's silly. To be sure, children must be taught to compete in a mature fashion—to do so without cheating, gloating, or being a sore loser—but healthy competition can motivate a child to use their best efforts, which can result in greater intellectual achievement.

Games can be considered a modern implementation of John Dewey's theory that children learn by doing. "Give the pupils something to do," he wrote, and if "the doing is of such a nature as to demand thinking[,] learning naturally results."[6] The types of activities that Dewey had in mind were gardening, carpentry, and cooking, which made sense at a time when so many jobs involved manual labor, but these days there is a greater need for workers with higher-order thinking skills, and many board games are well suited to developing those skills. Monopoly, for example, is essentially a business simulation. Among the lessons it teaches are the advantages and dangers of leverage. By borrowing against your properties, you can buy more houses and hotels, which will increase your revenue, but you'll run the risk that if you land on an opponent's property, you'll be forced to sell your houses and hotels at half price. As a child, I tended to invest cautiously in Monopoly so I could hold on to my cash for a rainy day. I figured this was a wise strategy because it was safe, but I eventually learned that being too cautious was usually a losing strategy because my rental properties would grow too slowly. There is a lesson in that: The most conservative strategy isn't always best. As the head of Success, I have to weigh risks in a similar manner. On the one hand, opening up more schools allows us to serve more students and achieve certain economies of scale. On the other hand, it requires that we invest money that we might otherwise use as a safety cushion if we suffer some setback such as a cut in public funding.

If you are troubled by the idea that I might draw on a board game to run a school system serving more than 20,000 students, consider that John F. Kennedy and Henry Kissinger are said to have been avid players of the game Diplomacy. Indeed, the comedian Eddie Izzard joked that Hitler must not have played the game Risk as a child since he didn't appreciate the resources necessary to maintain control of Eastern Europe.

Another important business concept that Monopoly teaches is that people can engage in a mutually advantageous trade. Suppose that three people are playing Monopoly and that Player A has two red properties and one green property and Player B has two green properties and one red property. If Players A and B trade with one another, they can each get monopolies. This will increase both players' chances of winning since they have improved both of their positions relative to Player C. This teaches that an exchange isn't necessarily a zero-sum game, that trading can leave both parties better off when one person values an object more than another. That is a fundamental economic principle and an important business strategy, whether it's baseball teams trading players or companies selling technology to another company.

One of the best games for developing a child's mental agility is Set. It uses special cards with shapes that vary in four ways: (1) the number of shapes (one to three); (2) the color of the shape; (3) the pattern of the shape (e.g., striped); and (4) the type of shape (e.g., triangle). These cards are laid out one by one until a player identifies a set of three cards for which each of the four characteristics are either all the same or all different. So, for example, if three cards each showed two solid green triangles, that would be a set because all four characteristics on each of the cards are *the same*. It would also be a pattern if the triangles on one card were green, on the second card were red, and on the third card were blue because in that case, the colors on the shapes on each card are all *different*. It would not be a set if, say, the triangles on two of the cards were blue and on the third card were green because they would neither be all the same color nor all different colors.

Playing the game is somewhat like the old challenge of tapping your head and rubbing your belly at the same time. Doing one of these things isn't that hard but doing both of them at once is challenging. The same is true of Set. Making all four of these comparisons simultaneously requires a great deal of concentration.

The game Othello is advertised as a game that takes "a moment to learn, a lifetime to master." Games like this are good for young children since they can easily be learned but allow for intellectual development. Some other games that fall into this category are Connect 4, Blokus, and Gobblet.

By contrast, there are some games that aren't as intellectually stimulating and beneficial. The game Candy Land, for example, is fine for a child who is just learning to count since it develops that skill, but that's the only thing it teaches because it's a game of pure luck, as is the card game "war." You should encourage your children to graduate quickly from simple games of chance like these to ones that involve more strategy.

I've listed next the many games that I consider to be educational, by level of difficulty. You should encourage your child to play a variety of these games since they develop different intellectual skills.

+ Eyegamer—Memory Matching Game
+ Connect 4
+ Sorry!
+ Mancala
+ Uno
+ Gobblet Gobblers
+ Blokus
+ Monopoly Junior
+ Rummikub
+ Gobblet
+ Qwirkle
+ ThinkFun Laser Chess
+ Labyrinth
+ Sumoku
+ 24
+ Ticket to Ride

+ Apples to Apples
+ Boggle
+ Othello
+ Backgammon
+ Monopoly
+ Clue
+ Mastermind
+ Settlers of Catan
+ Yahtzee
+ Kismet
+ Prime Climb
+ Sequence
+ Set
+ Taboo
+ Chess
+ Scrabble
+ Bridge

Here are some board games that your children can play by themselves:

+ ThinkFun Gravity Maze Marble Run Logic Game and STEM Toy for Boys and Girls
+ ThinkFun Rush Hour Traffic Jam Logic Game and STEM Toy
+ ThinkFun Shape by Shape
+ ThinkFun Balance Beans Math Game
+ ThinkFun Clue Master Logic Game and STEM Toy
+ Educational Insights Kanoodle—Brain-Twisting Solitaire Game

2

PARLOR GAMES

Many years ago, Eric started playing a simple game with our children in which they'd form a circle in the shallow end of a swimming pool and try to hit a ball to one another as many times as possible without letting it fall into the water. Each time someone hit the ball, that person would say the next number. After a while, they got bored of that so they created a new version of the game based on the drinking game "sevens" (without the drinking obviously!). Every time a person reached a number that was either a multiple of 7 or contained a 7 (e.g., 7, 17, 27), that person would just hit the ball silently rather than saying the number out loud. Next, they developed a variation in which they would hit the ball silently when they reached a prime number. And after that, they developed a version in which they would start out hitting the ball clockwise around the circle and then change the direction in which they hit the ball every time they reached a prime number.

To some, this may sound like a case of an overzealous parent ruining a perfectly nice day at the pool, but nothing could be further from the truth. Our kids loved playing these games. For some reason, it usually led to hysterical laughter. I suspect it's in part because they were surprised at how often they made silly mistakes since it's surprisingly hard to simultaneously hit a ball and do even fairly simple mathematical thinking. Whatever the reason, they would laugh so much that other children who were engaging in more conventional pool activities would often look at our children with envy. I'm sure they would have been astonished to learn that the game our children were having so much fun playing involved prime numbers.

I would place this game in the category of what are known as "parlor" games, which tend to have more of a social element than board games. Since these games typically have teams, it's easy to include people of varying skills (such as young children), and since they usually involve cooperation, they are often better at developing a child's communication and verbal skills than board games are.

Here are a few of our favorites:

+ **FICTIONARY**: One player selects a real but obscure word from a dictionary, announces it, and writes the definition down on a piece of paper. Other players write down plausible definitions. The person who selected the words reads the definitions out loud and everyone guesses which one is real. You get points for either selecting the real definition or getting other people to think your definition is real. (For more information, see: en.wikipedia.org/wiki/Fictionary.)
+ **CHARADES**: The most famous parlor game. People silently act out phrases such as book titles and others have to guess. (For more information, see: en.wikipedia.org/wiki/Charades.)
+ **MALARKY**: A player writes down answers to questions such as "What does the 'Q' in Q-Tips stand for?" or "What is the 'cottage' in cottage cheese?" The other players then

have to guess which answer is real and which ones are fake.

+ **FISHBOWL/PASSWORD:** Similar to the TV game show in that players guess words using one-word hints provided by other players. This game has variations. Here is one: sarasfavoritethings.com/2012/12/17/the-fishbowl-game/.

+ **CODENAMES:** A game in which each side guesses the codenames of spies.

+ **WORD ASSOCIATION:** Hannah learned this game in an improv group. People sit in a circle. Let's imagine our players are Adam, Betsy, Camilla, and Darryl. A word is selected randomly and told to everyone. Let's say that word is "banana." Adam and Betsy simultaneously say a word that they associate with banana. If they say the same word (e.g., "split"), they've won (although it's not really a competitive game since no points are kept). However, if they say different words (e.g., "split" and "fruit"), then Betsy turns to Camilla and they both simultaneously say whatever words they associate with "split" and "fruit" (other than the word "banana" since words can never be repeated). If they both say the same word (e.g., "wedge"), then they've won. However, if they say different words, then Camilla turns to Darryl and they simultaneously say a word that they associate with the two words that Betsy and Camilla just said. This keeps going until two people simultaneously say the same word. The game is supposed to be played quickly with people saying whatever words pop into their heads.

3

MUSIC

When Eric and I drive somewhere for vacations or weekend getaways, we often play music. When our kids were younger, one of their favorite songs was "Broke Down House" by the folk singer Rachel Garlin. Here's an excerpt:

We got a broke down house
With a crooked porch
We got a rusty swing
A tiki torch
A shady tree, a barbeque, a freeway breeze and a valley view
A leaky sink, a creaky stair, a cracked-up window with a
*   curtain tear*
The roof's got rot, the gutter's shot, the fridge ain't cold and
*   the stove ain't hot*
A coupla chairs, a couple guitars
A couple stray cats who think they're ours
Our family is framed on the wall
Sometimes the wind goes whistling right through the hall
We got a broke down house but our hearts ain't broke at all

This song is chock-full of nifty turns of phrase and wonderful humor: its ironic praise of the house's "freeway breeze" and "creaky stair"; its lament that the "fridge ain't cold and the stove ain't hot"; its ambiguous attitude toward the stray cats who "think they're ours" but apparently aren't worthy of adoption. Of course, our children didn't pick up on these jokes right away, particularly as some of them are a bit subtle, but that's the great thing about songs: If one has a catchy tune, a child will listen to it over and over again until they do understand its lyrics. Songs are an educational Trojan horse with music on the outside and lyrics on the inside.

The best lyrics are really poetry set to music, which is why Bob Dylan was awarded the Nobel Prize in Literature. Consider this line from Dylan's anti-war song "Blowin' in the Wind":

> *How many ears must one man have*
> *before he can hear people cry?*

Imagine a young child thinking about Dylan's idea that one's ability to hear might depend upon the number of ears one has. Their first reaction may be one of bemusement. The idea that a person might have more than two ears, or that this would allow them to hear better, may intrigue a child. This leads the child to think each time they listen to the song and to realize that Dylan isn't being literal. Rather, he is pointing out how absurd it is that we should be unable to hear the evidence of war's harm with the two ears we already have.

A fascinating and surprising bookend to this song is Dylan's song "My Back Pages." Having lamented people's failure to see the obvious, Dylan now suggests that it was the hubris of youth that had led him to think the truth was so obvious:

> *Good and bad, I defined these terms quite clear, no doubt,*
> *   somehow*
> *Ah, but I was so much older then, I'm younger than that now.*

Dylan's point is that he used to be quite certain about his beliefs (and thus older despite being younger) and is now less certain of them (and thus younger despite being older). In just a few words, he communicates the message that younger people's inexperience can lead them to think they know more than they do and that good and bad may not always be obvious. And again, what makes a song like this so intellectually provocative is that Dylan starts with an idea that seems so paradoxical that it demands thought, namely that he was once older than he is now. You may not realize how much thought a song like this provokes in your child because children don't tell you everything they are thinking.

Musicals are often quite educational, none more so than Lin-Manuel Miranda's *Hamilton*. Take the song "You'll Be Back," in which King George III addresses American revolutionaries in the wake of the Boston Tea Party:

> *You say*
> *the price of my love's not a price that you're willing to pay.*
> *You cry*
> *in your tea which you hurl in the sea when you see me go by*
> *Why so sad?*
> *Remember we made an arrangement when you went away.*
> *Now you're making me mad.*
> *Remember, despite our estrangement, I'm your man.*
> *You'll be back, soon you'll see,*
> *you'll remember you belong to me.*
> *You'll be back, time will tell*
> *you'll remember that I served you well.*
> *Oceans rise, empires fall,*
> *we have seen each other through it all.*
> *And when push comes to shove*
> *I will send a fully armed battalion to remind you of my love!*

These few lines contain a plethora of jokes, observations, and wordplay. Miranda exposes the glaring contradictions in King

George's beliefs: that he "serves" the colonies but that they "belong" to him; that he is confident the colonists will see the value of his reign but will force them to do so if necessary; that he loves his subjects but is willing to wage war on them. Miranda examines these contradictions with language that is both subtle and witty. Take, for example, his use of the term "estrangement." It's amusing because the song is essentially a parody of a breakup song in which King George is cast into the role of a spurned lover. In addition, the obvious contrast between the term "estrangement," which is a rather intellectual word, and the more colloquial phrase "I'm your man" makes it apparent that this effete king is making a rather ham-handed attempt to be a populist.

Another instance of Miranda's subtle play on words is the line: "The price of my love's not a price that you're willing to pay." Here, "price" is used first in its narrower sense of a monetary amount (in this case, the tax on tea), and then in the broader meaning reflected in the phrase the "price of success" (which in this case refers to giving up the right to self-government).

Miranda has said that when he was writing *Hamilton*, he decided he was "not going to worry about everybody getting everything on the first take" but rather instead wanted his play to have "many layers" so people could "get stuff on repeated listenings." While books and poems also have many layers, children are more likely to appreciate these layers in songs because they listen to them repeatedly.

There is no greater example of the value of listening to songs than Miranda himself. Since Miranda's parents loved musicals, they owned hundreds of cast albums to which they'd listen frequently. As a result, Miranda was continually exposed to great lyrics from a young age. He has identified fifteen songs that most influenced his writing of *Hamilton*. Two of them come from my favorite musicals— *West Side Story* and *The Sound of Music*. I loved *The Sound of Music* so much that when I saw it for the first time, I sat through three consecutive showings. I loved *West Side Story* for its boisterous music and the comic lyrics written by the great Stephen Sondheim, such as these from the song "America" about the experience of Puerto Ricans on mainland America:

> GIRLS: I like to be in America / OK by me in America / Everything free in America
>
> BERNARDO: For a small fee in America.
>
> ANITA: Buying on credit is so nice.
>
> BERNARDO: One look at us and they charge twice. . . .
>
> ANITA: Lots of new housing with more space.
>
> BERNARDO: Lots of doors slamming in our face.
>
> ANITA: I'll get a terrace apartment.
>
> BERNARDO: Better get rid of your accent. . . .
>
> GIRLS: Free to be anything you choose.
>
> BOYS: Free to wait tables and shine shoes. . . .
>
> BERNARDO: I think I'll go back to San Juan.
>
> ANITA: I know a boat you can get on. Bye bye!
>
> BERNARDO: Everyone there will give big cheer!
>
> ANITA: Everyone there will have moved here!

Sondheim manages to use humor to address an important concept: that poverty, prejudice, and limited career prospects may render America's promise of "freedom" illusory for some. Notice, also, the subtlety of the way Sondheim acknowledges the tension between wanting to be loyal to Puerto Rico ("Everyone will give big cheer!") and the need to seek better opportunities on the mainland ("Everyone there will have moved here!").

Musical influences were also important in Eric's upbringing. He grew up listening to the comedian Tom Lehrer, who wrote songs satirizing political and cultural issues. He listened to these songs so often that, decades later, he can still recite many of them from memory. He now plays them for our kids, who love them almost as much as he did. Here's an excerpt from one of their favorites, "Who's Next?"—a song about nuclear proliferation:

> *First, we got the bomb and that was good,*
> *'cause we love peace and motherhood.*
> *Then Russia got the bomb, but that's O.K.,*
> *'cause the balance of power's maintained that way!*
> *Who's next?*
>
> . . . .
>
> *Egypt's gonna get one, too,*
> *Just to use on you know who.*
> *So, Israel's getting tense,*
> *Wants one in self-defense.*
> *"The Lord's our shepherd," says the Psalm,*
> *but just in case, we better get a bomb!*

These lyrics are incredibly rich and informative. In just the excerpt I've included here, Lehrer manages to include an important political concept (balance of power), a reference to the Bible ("The Lord's our shepherd"), subtle irony (the sardonic references to peace and motherhood), and several important facts (that we got the bomb first, that Russia got it second, and that Egypt and Israel were enemies). Our children were able to pick up on some of these ideas just from listening to the context, but they also asked us to explain things that they knew from the audience's laughter were supposed to be funny but didn't understand.

To help your child appreciate music, just start playing it. You don't need to sit your child down and say, "Now we are going to listen to the lyrics of Nobel Prize winner Bob Dylan and analyze their meaning." Rather, just play music when your child is eating, playing, or traveling in the car with you. At some point, you may want to say something you like about the lyrics or ask a question about them, but listening alone is of great value.

Some music for young children is painfully insipid. If you don't mind listening to it, there is no harm in your children doing so, but there is plenty of great music with melodies children can appreciate including folk tunes by Simon & Garfunkel and Peter, Paul and Mary, classical music by Bach or Mozart, and jazz music by Scott Joplin and Louis Armstrong.

When your children get a bit older, you should expose them to the great "Tin Pan Alley" songwriters such as Irving Berlin, Harold Arlen, and George and Ira Gershwin, whose songs combine catchy melodies with witty lyrics. Take, for example, Ira Gershwin's lyrics for "Let's Call the Whole Thing Off":

You like potato and I like potahto
You like tomato and I like tomahto
Potato, potahto, tomato, tomahto.
Let's call the whole thing off

Like so many songs, this one has a deeper meaning. On its surface, it's about some couple that is so silly that they nearly break up over a disagreement over the pronunciation of words. At a deeper level, however, it's about how lovers' quarrels are often about silly things. Later in the song, the singer has second thoughts and suggests that they "better call the calling off off." Exposure to this type of witty double negative will help a child understand double negatives in other contexts such as the idea that subtracting –2 is the same as adding +2.

There is no better way to introduce your child to America's great songwriters than listening to the eight "song books" recorded by Ella Fitzgerald, each of which is devoted to the music of a particular composer. Ira Gershwin once observed that "I never knew how good our songs were until I heard Ella Fitzgerald sing them." Frank Sinatra also has done many covers of excellent songs.

A good way to introduce your children to classical music is to have them listen to the Classical Kids albums, which can be found on streaming platforms such as Spotify and YouTube Music. These albums set dramatic storytelling against classical music. For example, in *Mozart's Magic Fantasy*, a girl who visits the opera "falls into" the opera *The Magic Flute*, while in *Song of the Unicorn*, Jeremy Irons narrates a fairy tale against a background of medieval music. The stories are so well acted and move so quickly that they won't try the patience of young children.

You may also wish to have your children listen to performances by Peter Schickele, who does parodies of classical music under the stage name P. D. Q. Bach. These provide a very enticing way for your child to be exposed to some classical music while enjoying the comedy. Schickele's best work is a performance of the first movement of Beethoven's Symphony No. 5, which Schickele narrates as if it were an athletic competition complete with a referee, injuries, slow motion replays, and contested calls, while slyly working in informative observations about classical music. You can find this on YouTube. You may also consider watching Leonard Bernstein's famous Young People's Concerts on YouTube.

Below is a list of recommended music for your children. When your child starts talking, I'd recommend you begin to play songs with simple lyrics. For very young children, the following albums specifically for children are good and, unlike some children's songs, kind on adult ears:

+ *The Singable Songs Collection* (Raffi)
+ *Children's Concert at Town Hall* (Pete Seeger)
+ *Abiyoyo and Other Story Songs for Children* (Pete Seeger)
+ *Birds, Beasts, Bugs & Fishes Little & Big: Animal Folk Songs* (Pete Seeger)
+ *Burl Ives Sings Little White Duck and Other Children's Favorites* (Burl Ives)
+ *Peter, Paul and Mommy* (Peter, Paul and Mary)

+ *Songs to Grow On for Mother and Child* (Woody Guthrie)
+ *The Johnny Cash Children's Album* (Johnny Cash)

Here are some terrific records that combine classical music with the spoken word:

+ *The Bernstein Favorites: Children's Classics* (Leonard Bernstein). Includes *Peter and the Wolf, Carnival of the Animals,* and *The Young Person's Guide to the Orchestra*
+ *Stories in Music: The Sorcerer's Apprentice* (London Philharmonic Orchestra and Yadu & Stephen Simon)
+ *Stories in Music: Mike Mulligan and His Steam Shovel* (London Philharmonic Orchestra and Yadu & Stephen Simon)
+ *The Messiah*: The music and lyrics are wonderful, and they can easily become part of your family tradition if you celebrate Christmas.
+ *Gershwin's Magic Key* (Classical Kids): Step into the streets of 1920s New York, where a young newspaper boy meets the famous composer George Gershwin. While learning about his life and music, listeners explore the many sights and sounds of the city and the vast melting pot of American music.
+ *Mr. Bach Comes to Call* (Classical Kids): Bach drops in on a little girl practicing his famous Minuet in G Major. He tells her about his life and music while her house fills up with a boys' choir.
+ *Beethoven Lives Upstairs* (Classical Kids): When Beethoven moves in above Christophe, the boy writes letters to his uncle complaining about the noise and eccentricities of their new boarder. But gradually he comes to realize that something extraordinary is happening upstairs.

+ *Vivaldi's Ring of Mystery* (Classical Kids): Young Katarina searches for her grandfather with the help of Giovanni the gondolier and a magic violin. Set in Venice around Mardi Gras, this is a fascinating mystery of Vivaldi, violins, and Venice.
+ *Mozart's Magic Fantasy* (Classical Kids): When Elizabeth comes to find her mother singing the Queen of the Night aria, she "falls into" the opera. There she meets Prince Tamino, Princess Pamina, Papageno, Sarastro, and a cowardly dragon. Delightful lyrics and music bring alive one of Mozart's most well-loved operas.
+ *Mozart's Magnificent Voyage* (Classical Kids): Mozart's seven-year-old son Karl joins three boys from *The Magic Flute* in their flying boat.
+ *Tchaikovsky Discovers America* (Classical Kids): While on a train to Niagara Falls, Tchaikovsky talks to two children about his life in Russia, the *1812 Overture*, and the three great ballets of *Swan Lake*, *Sleeping Beauty*, and *The Nutcracker*.
+ *Hallelujah Handel* (Classical Kids): Katarina from *Vivaldi's Ring of Mystery* reappears in Georgian London, where she meets Handel and a poor orphan who sings but won't speak. Music includes *Water Music*, operas, and of course, the immortal *Messiah*.
+ *Song of the Unicorn* (Classical Kids): When a medieval queen falls ill, her children set out to find a cure. Along the way, they meet Merlin, magically speaking animals, evil Morgan, and even unicorns on the Isle of Avalon. An enchanting fairy tale illuminated with medieval music, children's choirs, and riddles. The story is narrated by Jeremy Irons.
+ *Daydreams and Lullabies* (Classical Kids): Classical music, rounds, poems, and lullabies.

+ *A Classical Kids Christmas* (Classical Kids): Children
  recite poetry and sing carols from around the world.
  Along the way, they pass "scenes" depicting Christmas
  from Advent to Epiphany.

As your children get older, they'll be increasingly able to understand songs written for adults. Here are some albums you can share
with them:

+ Bob Dylan: *Highway 61 Revisited*; *Bringing It All Back
  Home*; *The Freewheelin' Bob Dylan*
+ Simon & Garfunkel: *Bridge over Troubled Water*,
  Bookends
+ Arlo Guthrie: *Alice's Restaurant*
+ Cat Stevens: *Tea for the Tillerman*, *Teaser and the Firecat*,
  Mona Bone Jakon
+ Joan Baez: *Joan Baez in Concert*; *Farewell, Angelina*
+ Judy Collins: *Wildflowers*, *The Very Best of Judy Collins*
+ Joni Mitchell: *Clouds*
+ Joe Turner: *Greatest Hits*
+ Rachel Garlin: *Hello Again*, *Big Blue Sky*
+ The Beatles: *Sgt. Pepper's Lonely Hearts Club Band*
+ Aretha Franklin: *Amazing Grace*
+ Sammy Davis, Jr.: *Sammy Davis, Jr.: Greatest Hits*,
  Sammy Davis Jr. Sings, *Laurindo Almeida Plays*
+ Frank Sinatra: *In the Wee Small Hours*, *Come Fly with Me*

In the category of musicals, there are a plethora of choices:

+ *It's a Bird . . . It's
  a Plane . . . It's
  Superman!*
+ *Something Rotten!*

+ *You're a Good Man,
  Charlie Brown*
+ *Once Upon a Mattress*
+ *Grease*

+ *A Chorus Line*
+ *Spamalot*
+ *Young Frankenstein*
+ *Wicked*
+ Julie Andrews and
  Carol Burnett: *The*
  CBS Television Specials
+ *Chicago*
+ *My Fair Lady*

+ *Man of La Mancha*
+ *Fiddler on the Roof*
+ *Godspell*
+ *Les Misérables*
+ *1776*
+ *Hamilton*
+ *The Pirates of Penzance*
+ *Into the Woods*
+ *Dear Evan Hansen*

Finally, here are some wonderful Peter Schickele albums:

+ *An Hysteric Return: P.D.Q. Bach at Carnegie Hall*
+ *The Jekyll and Hyde Tour*

4

LOGIC PUZZLES

When Eric was young, someone gave him a logical puzzle that has fascinated him ever since:

You are in a room with two doors, behind one of which is a pot of gold. In front of each door is a guard, one who always tells the truth, another who always lies, and you don't know which is which. The guards are omniscient—they know everything. You have to choose one door to open. How can you find out which door leads to the pot of gold by asking only one question to one guard?

Most people quickly realize that they can figure out which guard tells the truth by first asking a question to which they know the answer (e.g., does 2 + 2 = 4). The problem, however, is that you get only one question, so most people try to think of a question that will both require the guard to say where the gold is and reveal whether that guard is telling the truth. However, no such question exists. After wrestling with that, the next stage is often denial: The person throws up their hands and insists that it must be a trick question, that the answer is something like simply asking a guard to open a door so they can see whether there is gold behind it. But no, that isn't allowed, and it isn't a trick question. A solution exists, but finding it requires that you reject the very assumption that most people make from the very start, an assumption that seems self-evident, which is that determining the gold's location requires figuring out which guard is telling the truth. It isn't. Surprisingly, there is a question you can ask that allows you to determine where the gold is without knowing whether the guard you ask is telling the truth.

I would encourage you to try to figure out the answer to this question because there is value in the struggle, but I'm going to give you the answer in the next paragraph. SPOILER ALERT!

The answer is that you need to ask one guard what the other guard would say if you asked him where the pot of gold is. No matter which guard you ask, you will get the wrong answer. If you ask the truthful guard, he will truthfully tell you what the lying guard would say, which will be incorrect because the lying guard will lie. If you ask the lying guard what the truthful guard would say, the lying guard will tell you the opposite of the correct answer that the truthful guard would give you, so you will again get the incorrect answer. Since you know that you will get the wrong answer either way, you simply choose to open the door that the guard tells you doesn't have gold behind it. The fascinating aspect of this solution is that you figure out where the gold is even though you never know whether the guard you asked was being truthful or not.

Very few people can figure out the solution to this logical puzzle but that doesn't matter. Even understanding the solution is quite educational.

Lest I discourage you by giving you the hardest problem first, let me assure you that most logic problems are easier to solve. Here are several classic logical puzzles that are challenging but not impossible to solve:

THE HIKER'S DILEMMA: A hiker comes across an intersection where three roads cross. He looks for the sign indicating the direction to his destination city. He finds that the pole carrying three city names and arrows pointing to them has fallen. He picks it up, considers it, and pops it back into place, pointing out the correct direction for his destination. How did he do it?

DUCK, WOLF, AND CORN: A farmer wishes to carry a wolf, a duck, and corn across a river but his boat is only big enough to carry one of these items at a time (plus the farmer himself). In addition, if left unattended, the wolf will eat the duck and the duck will eat the corn. How can the farmer safely transport the wolf, duck, and corn across the river?

THE THREE HATS: Three wise men are standing in a straight line, one in front of the other, and a hat is put on each of their heads. They are told that each of these hats was selected from a group of five hats: two black hats and three white hats. The first man, standing at the front of the line, can't see either of the men behind him or their hats. The second man, in the middle, can see only the first man and his hat. The last man, at the rear, can see both other men and their hats. None of the men can see the hat on his own head but they are asked to deduce its color. Some time goes by as the wise men ponder the puzzle in silence. Finally, the first one, at the front of the line, says: "My hat is white." How did he know?

BURNING ROPES AS TIMERS: You need to measure exactly forty-five minutes. You have two identical ropes and an unlimited supply of matches. When you light one end of a rope, the fire will take exactly 1 hour to travel to the other end. Between the two ropes, you have four ends and you can light those four ends in any sequence you wish. You cannot measure or fold the rope.

SCALES AND THREE BALLS: You are given twelve identical-looking balls and a two-sided scale. One of the balls is of a different weight, although you don't know whether it's lighter or heavier. How can you use just three weighings of the scale to determine not only which ball is different but whether it is lighter or heavier?

COIN WEIGHING PROBLEM: You are given a precise scale and ten stacks of coins. Nine of the stacks contain 10 gold coins, each of which weighs 10 grams. One of the stacks consists of 10 silver coins that weigh 9 grams each but which look identical to the golden coins as they are painted golden. How can you identify the stack containing the silver coins by only weighing once?

ONE MILE SOUTH, EAST, AND NORTH: How many points are there on the earth from which you could travel one mile south, then one mile east, then one mile north and end up in the same spot you started, and where are these points? (Note: This is a problem that Elon Musk said he'd ask job candidates in interviews.)*

Working on problems like this can allow your child to develop an important intellectual skill that schools rarely teach. Teachers generally focus on teaching specific skills. In math, for example, the teacher will show children how to figure out the quantity of chocolate chips that will be necessary to double a chocolate chip cookie recipe and the student will then be asked to figure out the quantity of raisins that will be required to triple an oatmeal cookie recipe. Essentially, it's the same problem but with raisins instead of chocolate chips and tripling instead of doubling. Teachers prefer to show children how to solve problems rather than just throw them

---

* *If you want the answers to all of the puzzles listed, you can look them up on the internet, but don't give up too quickly!*

into the deep end of the pool and ask them to figure it out. That's understandable since teachers are under pressure to get through a prescribed curriculum, but the problem is that, in real life, you sometimes do get thrown into the deep end of the pool. When your boss needs you to solve a problem, they won't teach you exactly how to solve it because they may not know themselves; if they did, they wouldn't need you.

Take the iPhone. You might think that Apple's engineers tackled all of the iPhone's technical problems by simply applying the scientific and engineering skills they'd been taught. They didn't. There was a lot of plain old creativity. For example, one of the biggest technical challenges was solved with an idea that anybody could have come up with but only one person did. Relatively late in the design process, Apple was still having trouble figuring out how to make a virtual keyboard work. The virtual keys were so small compared to people's thumbs that people were making lots of typos. Since the team working on the virtual keyboard had been unable to solve this problem, Steve Jobs asked several other engineers at Apple to try. One succeeded. He simply accepted the fact that people were going to miss the keys but figured out a way to deal with that. He observed that when people made a typo, their finger was usually off by a little bit. For example, if a person typed a "k" instead of an "l," it was typically because the center of their thumb was just a bit closer to the "k" than the "l." He realized that this could be addressed with predictive typing. For example, if you type "bel," the iPhone predicts that the next letter you type is more likely to be an "l" (to make "bell") or a "t" (to make "belt") than a "k." The iPhone, therefore, increases the virtual size of those keys you probably intend to type and shrinks the size of the neighboring keys. Your iPhone doesn't display them differently, but if the center of your thumb touches about halfway between an "l" and "k," the iPhone will assume that you intended to press "l" since that is more likely than "k." It's still possible to type a "k" if you hit it right on the nose, but touches centered between keys will be treated as an "l." Using this approach dramatically increases typing accuracy.

Learning how to solve a problem can be hard but it's even harder if you have no experience with trying to solve difficult problems. You may underestimate your ability to solve a problem, or you may get so frustrated with the time it takes that it inhibits your creativity, or you may panic. If you encounter a problem in a work context, you may worry, fearing that you'll lose your job if you can't figure it out, which may lead you to focus your intellectual energy on proving to your boss that the problem can't be solved rather than on actually trying to solve it.

In one of Eric's first jobs, he had a problem that was so like a logical puzzle that it could have been one. He was setting up a local area network when these were quite new. He'd had cable installed through the floor ducts and then needed to put jacks on the ends of the cables. The way the cables worked was that you put them in a daisy chain from computer to computer and you put the jack on one way at one end of each cable and then the opposite way on the other end of that cable. But when Eric showed up, all he saw were two cables coming out of the floor at each computer location. He couldn't tell which cable was going in one direction and which cable was going in the other direction so there was no way to ensure that he installed the jacks the opposite way on the end of each cable. At first, he panicked, fearing he'd look incompetent because he hadn't thought to have the cables labeled. However, he sat down to think it through and eventually came up with a solution. If you imagine each cable as having an "A" jack and a "B" jack, Eric had originally thought that the daisy chain would go like this: $A \mapsto B, A \mapsto B, A \mapsto B, A \mapsto B, A \mapsto B, A \mapsto B$. However, he realized that it could go $A \mapsto B, B \mapsto A, A \mapsto B, B \mapsto A, A \mapsto B, B \mapsto A, A \mapsto B, B \mapsto A$. This meant that at every location, he would just install two "A" jacks and at each of the neighboring stations he could install two "B" jacks, and so on around the circle. He didn't need to know which cable went which way, just as in the pot of gold problem, he didn't need to know which guard told the truth.

There is no recipe for solving novel problems but there are some good habits one can develop. One is to closely examine the parameters of your problem to make sure you understand them. For example, like the three balls puzzle above, the coin weighing puzzle also involves a scale, but while the three balls problem specifies a "two-sided scale," meaning a scale that simply tells you which of two objects is heavier, the coin weighing problem involves a regular scale that tells you precisely how much something weighs. If you don't notice that, you won't be able to solve the problem.

Another good habit is to question all of your assumptions about how a problem can be solved. For example, in the pot of gold problem, it seems self-evident that one must figure out which guard is the liar, but one doesn't need to figure that out. This lesson of questioning your assumptions came in handy when Eric and I were on a bike trip with a friend and the rear derailleur on their bike broke. Without a rear derailleur, the chain just hangs loose and so it won't stay on. For about ten minutes, Eric racked his mind as to how we could fix the rear derailleur and he concluded that it just wasn't possible, which was a real problem because we were on the backroads in the French countryside. But then Eric realized he'd been making an incorrect assumption. He didn't have to fix the derailleur. If he shortened the chain by removing some links, it would stay in place. Without a derailleur, the gears couldn't be changed, but since the bike worked, we could at least keep on cycling until we got to a bike shop where we could buy a new derailleur.

The most important good habit to learn is simply to keep on trying. When faced with a problem they don't know how to solve, many people quickly give up. They figure that if they are no closer to a solution after five minutes than they were at the start, then they aren't making progress and will never succeed. That isn't necessarily true. If you try to open your mind to new possibilities, you may eventually think of something. But to do that, you need to get comfortable with floundering and the feelings of frustration and self-doubt that can come with that. A while back, our son Dillon gave Eric a famously difficult problem known in some quarters as the Chessboard Problem. Every now and then Eric works on it. He still hasn't solved it but he hasn't given up!

One of the most delightful things I've ever heard an educator say was said by a chess instructor at Success Academy. He was looking over the shoulder of a second grader who was trying to figure out her next move. When the girl quietly said, "It's hard," the instructor responded sympathetically, "Yeah, it's supposed to be hard." Which is exactly right. If you find that a logical puzzle is hard, don't despair: *It's supposed to be hard.* The trick is not minding. If you can tolerate flailing around for twenty or forty minutes or even an hour and come up with the solution anyway, then you've really accomplished something. And that is why logical puzzles are such great intellectual preparation.

The following books by Bonnie Risby are good for introducing children to logic:

+ *Logic Safari: Book 1, Grades 2–3*
+ *Logic Safari: Book 2, Grades 3–4*
+ *Logic Safari: Book 3, Grades 5–6*
+ *Logic Countdown: Grades 3–4*
+ *Logic Liftoff: Grades 4–6*

Here are books with a plethora of logical puzzles:

+ *Of Course!: The Greatest Collection of Riddles & Brain Teasers for Expanding Your Mind* (Zack Guido, 2014).
+ *My Best Mathematical and Logic Puzzles* (Martin Gardner, 1994)
+ *Perplexing Puzzles and Tantalizing Teasers* (Martin Gardner, 1988).

+ *Math Puzzles Volume 1: Classic Riddles and Brain Teasers in Counting, Geometry, Probability, and Game Theory* (Presh Talwalkar, 2015).
+ *The Colossal Book of Short Puzzles and Problems* (Martin Gardner, 2005)
+ *The Moscow Puzzles: 359 Mathematical Recreations* (Boris A. Kordemsky, 1992)
+ *Puzzle Baron's Logic Puzzles: Hours of Brain-Challenging Fun!* (Puzzle Baron, 2010)
+ *Logitica: Learn Logic and Math Together* (Neelabh Kumar, 2019)
+ *Mind Your Decisions* (YouTube channel) (Presh Talwalkar, n.d.)

The late Raymond Smullyan was a mathematician who wrote popular books on logic that I'm listing separately as they are more advanced than those above:

+ *To Mock a Mockingbird: Including an Amazing Adventure in Combinatory Logic* (2012)
+ *A Beginner's Guide to Mathematical Logic* (2014)
+ *The Gödelian Puzzle Book: Puzzles, Paradoxes and Proofs* (2013)

Finally, this a good book on spotting logical fallacies in arguments:

+ *Don't Get Fooled!: How to Analyze Claims for Fallacies, Biases, and Other Deceptions* (Ray Givler, 2012)

5

MOVIES AND TELEVISION

When my daughter's friend came over for dinner one night, it quickly became apparent that he was quite knowledgeable about science. When we asked him where he'd learned all this science, he explained that he'd gotten it from the National Geographic channel because that was the only television channel his mother had allowed him to watch. This doesn't surprise me. Television—a term I'm going to use to include streaming video and movies as well—can be quite educational for children, as long as it's good television and they don't watch too much of it (a topic I'll address later in this book).

Nature documentaries in particular have gotten better and better over the years. Much of the credit for this goes to David Attenborough, whose documentaries are famous for their visual accomplishments but are groundbreaking in other ways, too. First, the intellectual content of these documentaries is stronger. For example, the second episode of *A Perfect Planet* explores a big idea: that the angle of the sun determines the amount of life on different parts of our globe. Dense rain forests exist near the equator because that's where the sunlight hits the earth head-on, which allows it to transmit enough energy to support dense foliage. By contrast, since the sunlight only glances off the earth at the poles, it doesn't convey much energy and therefore can't support as much foliage. This big idea holds together the whole episode.

In addition to conveying these big ideas about nature, Attenborough's documentaries also use rich language such as the following:

> *Out on the open plains, life must await the chance arrival of rain. When it does fall, it has an extraordinary effect. Each sporadic downpour may only last minutes but it can bring life—and in spectacular numbers.*[1]

This passage includes both wonderful vocabulary ("sporadic," "plains," "downpour") and the interesting phrases ("chance arrival," "spectacular numbers").

Similarly, here is a wonderful introduction in a National Geographic video from the series *Savage Kingdom*, in which hyenas compete for food with lions, which are characterized as "kings and queens":

> *For generations, kings and queens have reigned well over Mombo, a bountiful Eden far south of Savute. But they now face the greatest threat to their long rule. A rebel army is rising from the shadows led by Mmamotse, commander of the damned. The abundant land fuels her savage ranks. She now has enough soldiers to lay siege to the kingdom. No more hiding in the darkness, eating scraps. Mmamotse wants the lion's share.*[2]

Again, we find rich language such as "bountiful," "rebel," "abundant," "savage," "siege," "rule," and "kingdom." Notice also the nifty way in which the phrase "the lion's share" is used both in its figurative sense (the largest share) and its literal sense (the share that is currently being eaten by actual lions).

By contrast, here is an excerpt from a nature documentary from the 1970s:

> *Many kinds of spiders build homes. You've all seen big ground spider webs but here's a different kind, one with a tunnel to hide in. The spider spins a flat web out in front of the tunnel to trap food. Spiders are helpful because they kill so many of the insects that bother us.*[3]

This language is simple and uninventive, so it won't increase a child's vocabulary. In addition, it's rather boring compared to the language of the National Geographic and Attenborough documentaries.

Children can also learn about history from the growing collection of excellent historical films such as *The Crossing*, about George Washington's crossing of the Delaware River, and *Gettysburg*, about this historic Civil War battle. Of particular note is *John Adams*, a docudrama about our second president that is phenomenally written and acted. Here is a scene in which Hamilton and Jefferson debate the merits of establishing a national bank:

JEFFERSON: And how would you propose to establish international credit?

HAMILTON: Our first step would be to incur a national debt. The greater the debt, the greater the credit. And to that end, I am recommending that Congress adopt all the debts incurred by the individual states during the war through a National Bank.

JEFFERSON: If the states are indebted to a central authority, it increases the power of the central government.

HAMILTON: The greater the government's responsibility, the greater its authority.

JEFFERSON: The moneyed interest in this country is all in
the North so the wealth and power would inevitably be
concentrated there to the expense of the South.

HAMILTON: If that is the case, it is unavoidable if the Union is
to be preserved.

JEFFERSON: I fear our revolution will have been in vain
if the Virginia farmer is to be held in hock to a New
York stock jobber, who in turn is in hock to a London
banker.[4]

The issues at stake are expressed in a remarkably cogent fashion
and the actors bring this scene alive. Hamilton is portrayed as brilliant and brash while Jefferson is portrayed as sly and skeptical. One
gets the feeling that one is a fly on the wall witnessing intellectual
fencing at the highest level.

In addition to docudramas, there are also many wonderful documentaries, particularly those of Ken and Ric Burns. Although Ken
is the better known of the Burns brothers, I particularly enjoyed Ric
Burns's documentary on Coney Island.

Watching fictional films can be quite educational if the films
themselves are good. Unfortunately, many are rather predictable.
They return to the same old themes: that people who are good and
hardworking win out in the end; that you should marry for love and
follow your instincts; that people will succeed when they learn how
to work together; that all people can be divided into bad people
(terrorists, Nazis, racists, big corporations) and good people (un-
derdogs, environmentalists). People are attracted to films like this
because we like to see the good guys win and the bad guys lose and
to have all of our beliefs reaffirmed, but they remind me of this passage by Henry Fielding:

*There are a set of religious, or rather moral writers, who
teach that virtue is the certain road to happiness, and vice*

to misery, in this world. A very wholesome and comfortable doctrine, and to which we have but one objection, namely, that it is not true.[5]

Films with simple messages and heartwarming outcomes often bear little relationship to the real world. People are complex. Thomas Jefferson drafted the Declaration of Independence but owned slaves. Winston Churchill led the fight against Nazi Germany but was an avid colonialist. Henry Ford was a great inventor but an inveterate antisemite. To teach children that people can easily be sorted out into good and bad is to ignore the complexity of human nature. Moreover, films with complex or even ambiguous themes are more likely to provoke thought and interesting conversations. Here are some examples:

+ **AMADEUS:** This film rejects the idea that we are always rewarded for our hard work. Mozart is shown as a rather dissolute childish character who succeeds simply because he is brilliant. By contrast, his colleague Salieri is more devoted to his task and is painfully aware that he will not be able to equal Mozart's achievements no matter how hard he tries.

+ **SENSE AND SENSIBILITY:** In this film, based upon Jane Austen's great novel, Marianne is humiliated and heartbroken when her love for Willoughby leads her to be too trusting and open, but her sister Elinor's romantic desires are thwarted by her excessive reticence. Each approach seemingly has its dangers.

+ **STEVE JOBS:** This film explores Steve Jobs's many contradictions: that he could be an inspirational leader while often being mean and ungenerous; that he was a visionary but could be astonishingly petty; that he was an incredible innovator in computers despite lacking any technical abilities; and that he was one of the most successful businessmen in history despite practically bankrupting Apple.

+ **IN THE HEAT OF THE NIGHT:** In this film, a black detective (played by the great Sidney Poitier) helps a white detective in a Southern town solve a murder. This is the type of film that could be completely predictable and banal if it weren't so brilliantly written and acted.

+ **THE FOG OF WAR:** In this documentary, Robert McNamara observes that if America had lost World War II, he would have been tried as a war criminal for his role in firebombing Japan. He asks, "What makes it immoral if you lose, and not immoral if you win?" This challenges a more conventional view of American morality during World War II and raises important questions about what conduct can be justified in war.

The appeal of more complicated films like these is that they lead you to think about the film after it is done. Could Steve Jobs's virtues have existed without his flaws, or were they inextricably bound together? Does the fact that Japan was the aggressor in World War II justify America's firebombing of its cities? Was Marianne merely the victim of Willoughby's flawed nature, or did she bear some responsibility for her predicament?

The great thing about watching films together as a family is that you can talk about them after you watch them and everyone will be on the same footing since everyone has seen the film. For this reason, Eric and I often watch films with our children on weekend afternoons so that we can talk about them at dinner.

Page 216 has a list of films I recommend. I've included films from which your children can learn about topics such as history, science, law, and politics, as well as films that are classics or that are based upon certain literary classics.

6

ART

Shortly after dropping out of college, Steve Jobs began auditing a calligraphy class in which he "learned about serif and sans serif typefaces, about varying the amount of space between different letter combinations, about what makes great typography great." As Jobs later explained:

> *None of this had even a hope of any practical application in my life. But 10 years later, when we were designing the first Macintosh computer, it all came back to me. And we designed it all into the Mac. It was the first computer with beautiful typography. If I had never dropped in on that single course in college, the Mac would have never had multiple typefaces or proportionally spaced fonts.*[1]

While few adults grow up to be artists, many adults will find themselves in situations in life in which, like Jobs, aesthetic abilities may become relevant. In my case, I'm in the middle of building a large school building. Although I'm not designing it, I'm being presented with a lot of decisions that involve aesthetic judgments. I think I'm at an advantage from having spent a lot of time traveling around the world looking at buildings since my mother is an art historian.

Children should be exposed to great art from a young age. A good place to start is with coloring books such as these:

+ *Start Exploring: Masterpieces: A Fact-Filled Coloring Book* (Steven Zorn)
+ *Medieval Tapestries Coloring Book* (Marty Noble)
+ *Art Masterpieces to Color: 60 Great Paintings from Botticelli to Picasso* (Marty Noble)
+ *Architecture Coloring Book* (Peter Dobrin)

You may also want to buy art books that your children can peruse. Here are some suggestions:

+ *Through the Lens: "National Geographic" Greatest Photographs* (National Geographic)
+ *The Art Museum* (Phaidon Press)
+ *"National Geographic" 125 Years: Legendary Photographs, Adventures, and Discoveries That Changed the World* (Mark Collins Jenkins)
+ *Ansel Adams: 400 Photographs* (Ansel Adams)
+ *On This Earth: Photographs from East Africa* (Nick Brandt)
+ *Bruegel: The Master* (Elke Oberthale)
+ *World Architecture: The Masterworks* (Will Pryce)
+ *The Arts: A Visual Encyclopedia* (DK)
+ *Art That Changed the World: Transformative Art Movements and the Paintings That Inspired Them* (DK)

Here are two books that help children use art as a launching point for their own art projects:

+ *Discovering Great Artists: Hands-On Art Experiences in
  the Styles of Great Masters* (MaryAnn F. Kohl and Kim
  Solga)
+ *Great American Artists for Kids: Hands-On Art
  Experiences in the Styles of Great American Masters*
  (MaryAnn F. Kohl and Kim Solga)

Making art is a terrific opportunity for children not only to develop their artistic abilities but to learn how satisfying it can be to
create things. Children particularly like making objects that can be
used. When I was young, I made cups and bowls on a pottery wheel,
and my brother and I would also make our own Halloween costumes
with my mother's assistance. We would create tablecloths for dinner
using table-size pieces of paper that we decorated with crayons. We
really liked the idea of making something that our family would use
for dinner, even if it was for one night.

There are plenty of art kits that will allow your children to create usable objects such as flowerpots, wind chimes, bird feeders,
jewelry, night lamps, water bottles, and key rings. You can also
encourage your children's artistic efforts by displaying their artwork
in your home.

Visiting museums is another great way to expose your children
to art. I strongly recommend the audio guides that are often available at these museums. They are quite informative, and it's much
easier to listen to a narrative while you are looking at art than to
switch back and forth between reading and looking at art.

In the first draft of this book, I wrote, "I have to confess that
Eric and I never got our children to enjoy art museums." However,
in my daughter's senior year in high school, we belatedly celebrated
her sixteenth birthday with a trip and she got to decide where we'd
go. She chose Paris and among the things that she wanted to do was
to visit art museums. Then, the following summer, our family took a
trip to Vienna and we visited the Kunsthistorisches art museum. At

the end of the visit, Culver commented that he'd enjoyed visiting the museum more than he'd expected.

The moral of this story, one that I will return to many times in this book, is that you shouldn't be discouraged by a lack of apparent progress. Don't get so frustrated that you give up or, even worse, berate your children for failing to enjoy the museum, which will only leave a bitter taste in their mouths that will make it even harder for them to come around. Just explain to your children that even if they don't enjoy museums, you have a responsibility to expose them to art so neither you nor they have a choice in the matter. In addition, you can pair visiting an art museum with something they do like, such as going to a movie or having lunch at a favorite restaurant. Eventually, the seeds you plant will grow.

7

ASKING QUESTIONS

The scientist Randy Pausch, who gave a famous "Last Lecture" when he got cancer, wrote about how he learned to be inquisitive:

> [M]y dad had this infectious inquisitiveness about current events, history, our lives. . . . Most every night, we'd end up consulting the dictionary, which we kept on a shelf just six steps from the table. "If you have a question," my folks would say, "then find the answer." The instinct in our house was never to sit around like slobs and wonder. We knew a better way: Open the encyclopedia. Open the dictionary. Open your mind.[1]

It can seem intimidating to take responsibility for teaching your kids because you may not feel you know that much. However, as Pausch's father illustrates, it's more important to model curiosity and inquisitiveness than to have all the answers.

One way to encourage your children to be curious is to look at the world around you and ask yourself if there is anything you can see that you know something about that your child doesn't. Particularly when your children are young, that's a lot. Take storm drains. Even if a child understands that their purpose is to allow water to drain from the street, they probably don't know that the streets are sloped to ensure that water flows into the drain rather than puddling in the middle of the street; that drains lead to sewers; that large cities have thousands of miles of sewers; that waste from apartments also flows into these sewers; and that this water goes into sewage treatment plants and then into rivers.

You can teach your children an enormous amount just by talking about the things you see around you. You'll be amazed at how many things you can find, at how much you know that your child doesn't. To illustrate this, suppose that you walk out of your apartment with your child one day to take a bus. Here are some things you can ask your children about in the short distance between your apartment door and the bus:

+ Why does the door have a lock?
+ Why do you need a key to get into your apartment but not to get out of your apartment?
+ How does the door lock automatically when you close it?
+ What makes the elevator go up and down?
+ Why is there a cable that pulls the elevator up but not one that pulls it down?
+ What stops the elevator from moving when the door is open?
+ Why do some buildings have more than one elevator?
+ Why is there both an up and a down button for the elevator? Why not just have one button that tells the elevator to stop?
+ Why do you need stairs in the building if there is an elevator?

+ Why is there a door to the stairway?
+ Why are the doors from the lobby to the street closed?
  Why not leave them open all the time? Why even have
  doors?
+ Why are there painted lines in the street?
+ Why are streets higher in the middle rather than flat?
+ Why is there a curb for the sidewalk?
+ Why do sidewalks slope downward toward the street?
+ Why are sidewalks divided into squares with lines
  between them?
+ How do you make a sidewalk? What is it made of?
+ Why are there curb cuts at the corners?
+ Why are there parking meters? Why are they on some
  streets and not others?
+ What's the purpose of the sewer? What happens to the
  water that goes down into it?
+ What are all the signs on the street?
+ Why are the streetlights only on sometimes? What makes
  them turn on and off?
+ Why do people sometimes tear up the street? What's
  underneath the street?
+ What's the purpose of the red and green traffic signals?
  What is the purpose of the yellow light?
+ Why does the DON'T WALK sign sometimes blink?
+ What are the signs on the street for? Why aren't you
  allowed to park your car on the street at certain times on
  certain days?
+ Why are the wheels on the bus bigger than the wheels on
  a car?
+ Why is a bus taller than a car?
+ Why do some buses "kneel" when the door opens? What
  makes the bus go lower?
+ Why do you need to pay for the bus? Where does the
  money go?

+ What makes buses go?
+ Where do buses go at night?
+ How do bus drivers change the direction of the bus? How do they make it go faster? Slower?

You should encourage your children to see if they can figure out the answers to these questions by themselves before you answer them. Figuring out how things work is a useful skill. The more your children understand how things work, the more they will be able to invent new things.

8

EXPOSING KIDS TO
ADULT CONVERSATIONS

When I was six years old, I wrote a letter to President Nixon expressing my opposition to his bombing of Cambodia. His staff responded with a cheery portrait of his family. I felt this suggested that he hadn't fully appreciated my concerns, so I called the White House and spoke to an operator, who dutifully if somewhat impatiently took down my message for the president that I hadn't been satisfied with his response.

This might seem silly, but it's good for kids to be concerned about the world and to believe their opinion matters. To be sure, a child's views may be foolish and naïve, but so are those of many adults. The earlier someone begins thinking about serious things, the more opportunity they'll have to develop their ability to think more subtly and to develop a base of knowledge that will allow them to have informed opinions.

I became interested in politics early on because my parents involved my brother and me in their conversations. They were very active in the social protest movements of the late '60s and early '70s and assumed that we would be interested in these topics as well. Adults often assume their children won't be interested in adult topics. These notions of childhood can become self-fulfilling prophecies.

To get kids interested in a topic, it's helpful to explain it to them in terms they'll understand. Take immigration. I would explain to a child that there are people from other countries who want to live in the United States because their countries are dangerous or poor. Some people say we shouldn't let them in because sharing with them would make people in this country poorer. Other people think that admitting more immigrants will actually improve America's economy because they are hard workers and that even if it won't, we should be willing to make a sacrifice to help those who are less fortunate than us.

As children tend to be obsessed with fairness, they are interested in any topic that involves it, and most political issues do. Suppose, for example, that you and your spouse are having a conversation on whether the latest tax cut should have included wealthy people as well as middle-class people. You might think that children won't be interested in this topic. Wrong! Since this topic is related to fairness, most kids will be quite interested in it if you explain it to them. Explain to your child that the government needs money to pay for things that we all need—such as roads, firefighters and firetrucks, and schools—and so the government takes money from people to do this and it generally does so based on how much money you have. Imagine, you can say to your child, that when they grow up, they end up very rich and have two houses and three cars and a lot of money in the bank and one of their friends isn't rich and has just one house and one car and much less money in the bank. Should they each pay the same amount of taxes, or should your child pay more taxes because they have more money? And if they should pay more money, is it enough to do that by requiring that everyone pay a pro- portion of the money they make (say 25 percent) or should the rich person pay not only a larger *amount* but a larger *proportion* of their money? Once you explain that, you can now discuss the issue with your spouse, and your children can now understand what they are hearing, which will make it interesting.

When children have trouble participating in an adult conversation, it's usually because they lack relevant knowledge. You can remedy that by making an effort to provide your children with the background information they need to participate in a conversation. If your child does express an opinion, try to treat it respectfully and engage with it. If you communicate to your child that their opinion doesn't matter, it will discourage them from participating.

Children are naturally curious, and you should use every question as an opportunity to convey as much information as your child is willing to receive. If your child asks how someone becomes president, explain not only that there is an election in which people vote for their preferred candidate, but also that anybody who is over the age of eighteen and is a citizen of the United States can vote if they haven't been convicted of a crime; that this wasn't always the case because women and African Americans weren't always allowed to vote; that there are two major parties that each choose nominees who run for the position of president; and that anybody who was born in the United States and is at least thirty-five years old is allowed to run for president. In short, it's best if you treat every question as an opportunity to spill out every relevant fact you know about a topic. Often explaining one fact will lead to your child asking another question. If you don't know the answer to a question, a smart speaker such as those made by Google and Amazon can be a real boon to the discussion. Eric and I often turn to a smart speaker to answer questions that arise at dinner.

Conversations with your children are also good opportunities to discuss what interests you. Try talking about your work since that is something that you know about. You may be surprised at how much this interests your child. Try to share your enthusiasm with your children. If they see that something interests you a great deal, they are more likely to be interested. Don't assume that because your children are uninterested in your work when they are young, they won't become interested later on. When our children were young, they couldn't appreciate Eric's legal work, but as they've gotten older, it has become more interesting to them.

You should also use conversation to expand your child's vocabulary. Understanding vocabulary isn't just about being able to express yourself better but about understanding ideas. In his novel *1984*, George Orwell imagines a totalitarian government that has created an official language called Newspeak that is intended to ensure that everyone in this society subscribes to its political ideology, which is known as "Ingsoc":

> *The purpose of Newspeak was not only to provide a medium of expression for the world-view and mental habits proper to the devotees of Ingsoc, but to make all other modes of thought impossible. It was intended that when Newspeak had been adopted once and for all and Oldspeak forgotten, a heretical thought—that is, a thought diverging from the principles of Ingsoc—should be literally unthinkable, at least so far as thought is dependent on words.[1]*

As Orwell suggests, language is inextricably intertwined with conceptual thinking. You can't understand the word "democracy" unless you understand the idea of democracy, and conversely, it's hard to talk about democracy if you don't have a word for it. A person who develops a broader vocabulary is, therefore, not only better at expressing themselves but also at thinking. To advance both of these skills, you should help your children develop their vocabulary.

One battle I'm constantly fighting at Success Academy is the tendency of teachers to dumb down their vocabulary so their students can understand them, which prevents children from learning new words. At the height of language acquisition, a child learns about seven new words every day. If a teacher only uses words their students already know, they won't learn new ones. For this reason, we tell our teachers to consciously use more advanced vocabulary and you should, too. Instead of saying "very big," say "enormous," "humongous," or "gargantuan." Instead of saying "angry," say "apoplectic." Instead of saying a defendant "got off," say that they were "acquitted." Instead of saying that someone "doesn't do what they say," say that they are "hypocritical." Encourage your children to ask the meaning of words they don't understand. If you suspect that your child doesn't understand a word you've used, ask them if they do. If a child doesn't know the meaning of the word, it's sometimes good to ask your smart speaker for a definition. While you may be readily able to define simple words, it's harder to define subtler words such as "ironic" or "perplexed."

Understanding words is often just a starting point for a more informative discussion. If your child asks what the word "dictator" means, you can explain that a dictator is a ruler who does whatever they want and that this is different from a constitutional democracy like the United States in which the president has to obey the limits on their power imposed by the Constitution.

In addition to including your children in your conversations, you should also encourage them to talk to other adults such as guests at your home. For example, if you know that one of your guests has an interesting career or just took an exciting vacation, tell your child about that before the guest arrives and encourage them to ask your guest about it.

If you hire babysitters, try to find ones that are interesting. Eric and I hired college students, actors, and other interesting adults because they were more likely to provide a good educational experience for our children.

Another way that kids can learn from adults is to spend more time in adult settings. Children once spent far more time in adult settings. Nowadays, children spend most of their time with other children. They go to school with other children, hang out with other children after school, and attend camps with other children in the summer. Although it means that they get more education, which is good, it also means that they spend less time with adults, which isn't. To understand why, think about how you learn a foreign language. The best way to do so is to become immersed in that language by spending time with native speakers. Learning a language in a large class doesn't tend to work as well because you spend a fair amount of time listening to other students who don't speak the language well either. The same applies to children who spend all of their time with other children. When we educate children, we are in large measure trying to teach them how to be adults. To accomplish this, we try to equip them with the intellectual skills, knowledge, and habits they need to become happy, productive, and self-sufficient. An important way to learn how to behave like an adult is to spend time with them: to experience how they think, resolve conflict, solve problems, and act responsibly.

Take the actor and director Ron Howard. Since he began his acting career on *The Andy Griffith Show* at the age of six, he spent a lot of time with adults. It was a full-time job for much of the year. Howard recalls hearing Andy Griffith and Don Knotts talking about tax shelters and the fact that the marginal tax rate then was 91 percent as well as about problems in their marriages and seeing psychotherapists. These are topics that few children knew about in the early 1960s.

Howard was also exposed to the world of adult work. As he writes:

> *In the Renaissance era, the artisan class put its children*
> *to work as apprentices young, enlisting their help to create*
> *devotional frescoes and sculptures. The kids started out at*
> *age five or six, cleaning brushes and tools, and slowly took*

*on greater responsibilities as they began to better understand
the craft, which in turn fostered a better understanding of
the artistry involved. That parallels my trajectory on* The
Andy Griffith Show, *as I gradually figured out how and why
television worked.*[2]

While I'm not suggesting that we go back to apprenticing out
children at the age of five, Howard clearly learned a great deal from
his early exposure to adult work. He saw the hard work that was
required to produce a quality product in a limited amount of time.
He heard discussions in which writers and actors talked about how
scripts could be improved. It's hard not to think that this early exposure to adults accounts in part for his later success as a director.
Your children can also learn a lot by spending time both with you
and with other adults.

9

TRAVEL AND SUMMERS

As a child, I loved attending "living history museums," such as Colonial Williamsburg in Virginia and Old Sturbridge Village in Massachusetts, which have historical buildings and people within them who perform activities of the time such as making shoes or spinning yarn. These places made history come alive for me. I was fascinated by how different life was back then, particularly how much harder everything was. If you wanted pants, you didn't just go out and buy them. Instead, you had to spin the wool, turn it into cloth with a loom, and then stitch the pants together. When you wanted to cook a chicken, you had to kill the chicken, pluck it, clean it, and then start a fire to heat up the oven. And instead of children learning in separate grades, all of the children would learn together in a one-room schoolhouse.

Eric and I brought our own children to these sites, and while they didn't fall in love with them as much as I had, they certainly enjoyed them. I loved explaining to our children what these museums teach us about history. Eric was most interested in old technology such as the water-wheel-powered sawmill at Old Sturbridge Village. He studied the machine carefully, read the explanations, and then, when he understood how the whole thing worked, explained it to our kids. Eric was equally fascinated by how the Tower Bridge in London used what is called "potential energy" to lift the drawbridge. A steam engine lifted six enormous weights that effectively stored the energy produced by these engines for later use. When a ship needed to pass, the bridge operator would let one of these weights fall, which would push water that turned gears that raised the bridge. Eric took the kids through every step and pointed out the mechanism's use of a "centrifugal regulator," an ingenious device that was critical to the development of the steam engine because it could regulate the engine's speed by automatically decreasing the flow of fuel as the engine sped up.

Our kids also enjoyed visiting forts, churches, and other historical locations such as Churchill's underground headquarters in London. They were particularly fascinated by castles and their moats, drawbridges, and arrow slits, which permitted archers to shoot the enemy without danger to themselves.

In addition to historical sites, we took our kids to natural history museums, science museums, aquariums, and zoos. What you get out of these places depends on what you put into them. The trick is to dig deeper. While it's fun to marvel at the animals at the zoo ("Wow, isn't that elephant big!"), there is so much more you can learn if you read all the informational materials, watch the demonstrations that most zoos have, and most important, encourage your child to ask questions of the presenters or other zoo personnel. You can model the behavior you want from your children by asking questions yourself. The trick is realizing that all those things that you take for granted have explanations.

For example, when most people see an elephant, they don't wonder why it has big ears because they're so used to the idea that elephants have big ears. Not surprisingly, there is a reason that elephants have big ears: to keep them cool. As the blood flows through an elephant's ears, it is cooled down by the air. That's why an elephant flaps its ears when it is hot. This wouldn't work well if an elephant's ears were small like ours. Just as there's a reason that elephants have big ears, there's a reason that zebras have hooves and lions don't; that squirrels have big tails and pigs have small ones; that dogs have canine teeth while cows have only incisors and molars. Once you get into the habit of asking questions, you'll realize how many things you don't know and have just taken for granted.

Eric and I also took our children on several bicycle touring trips, something that Eric and I have been doing ever since we started dating in high school. On our first couple of trips with our kids, Hannah rode on a tandem with Eric. Traveling by bicycle allows you to have many interesting interactions with people. In addition, it often leads to unplanned adventures when, for example, you have a bike problem that can't easily be fixed. For many people, this will be more stress than they want on their vacation, but it allows your child to see firsthand what you do when you run into problems.

As a child, I traveled a lot with my parents in Italy and France, and it was quite fascinating to learn about the customs of different countries. We found the rigidity of the French to be a source of endless amusement. One time, when my dad asked for chocolate sauce on cassis ice cream at a restaurant, the waiter responded, "Not possible!" "Not possible?" my dad repeated, bemused and slightly irritated. "*Non!*" replied the waiter firmly, who apparently regarded the matter as culinary sacrilege. From his reaction, you'd have thought that my father had proposed burning the French flag.

I would also recommend that you take your children on vacations where they can experience nature. One of my children's most lasting memories was a trip we took mountain biking "hut to hut" in the wilderness of Colorado. Another was a hike we took in the White Mountains in New Hampshire.

Assuming you won't travel with your children all summer long, you'll need to figure out what your children should do with the rest of their summer. For several years, my children attended sports-oriented day camps virtually all summer long. While they read in the evenings and on weekends, there wasn't as much time for that as I'd have liked. In retrospect, I wonder whether that was the best decision. Summer is so long that it's unfortunate if a child doesn't make any intellectual progress during that time. Thus, I'd suggest that at least some of your child's summer be focused on activities that will advance their nonathletic skills or interests. As our children got older, they went to programs for drama, debate, improvisation, chess, and coding, and they enjoyed them just as much as they did their sports-oriented day camps.

Irrespective of what camp your children attend, they should do independent reading during the summer. I've found that the books I read while on vacation have made a particularly large impression on me because I don't have much else on my plate intellectually. I suspect that the same is true for kids: They will get more from independent reading during the summer than during the school year precisely because they aren't in school. For this reason, a half-day program that allows your child some reading time may be preferable. Some summer camps also set aside time each day for quiet activities such as reading.

10

COMEDY

The term "witty" means "full of clever humor," but it once meant simply "intelligent." I doubt that this implicit link between intelligence and humor is an accident. I believe not only that humor is linked to intelligence but that one's intellectual capacity may be increased through humor. Like other intelligent animals, children have an instinct to play games such as tag or catch that develop their physical abilities. I suspect that humor plays a similar role in developing our intellect—that comedy is an instinctive form of intellectual play that sharpens our minds.

I should specify that I'm not talking about all types of humor but rather a particular form of humor that draws upon and celebrates intellectual inventiveness. Take the famous comedy routine "Who's on First?" in which Costello tells Abbott the names of the players on a baseball team. The first baseman's name is "Who," which leads to confusion when Costello asks, "Who's on first base?" and Abbott simply answers "Yes" since that is the name of the first baseman. Costello then makes a series of futile efforts to get past this confusion:

COSTELLO: When you pay off the first baseman every month, who gets the money?

ABBOTT: Every dollar of it. And why not, the man's entitled to it.

COSTELLO: Who is?

ABBOTT: Yes.

COSTELLO: So who gets it?

ABBOTT: Why shouldn't he? Sometimes his wife comes down and collects it.

COSTELLO: Who's wife?

ABBOTT: Yes. After all, the man earns it.

COSTELLO: Who does?

ABBOTT: Absolutely.

COSTELLO: Well, all I'm trying to find out is what's the guy's name on first base?

ABBOTT: Oh, no, no. What is on second base.

COSTELLO: I'm not asking you who's on second.

ABBOTT: Who's on first![1]

This insanity keeps going on for perhaps ten minutes as Abbott and Costello introduce the names of other players including "I don't know," "Why," "Because," "Tomorrow," "Today," and "Naturally." It's amusing in part because Abbott gets frustrated, but the real satisfaction of listening to this routine comes from appreciating the ingenuity with which it is constructed. Abbott and Costello take a basic premise and then they spend ten minutes developing it much like a talented musician playing variations on a theme.

Another example of such ingenuity is a monologue by Jackie Mason in which he makes fun of the pop-psychology concept of searching for the "real me":

I went to a psychiatrist. It's because I didn't know who I was.
He took one look at me and said right away, "This is not you."

I said, "If this is not me, then who is it?"
He said, "I don't know either."
I said, "Then what do I need you for?"
He said, "To find out who you are."
I said to myself, "If I don't know who I am, how do I know who to look for? Besides why do I need him? Ten years ago, I'd be glad to look for anybody. Now I'm doing good. Why should I look for him? He needs help? Why doesn't he look for me?"
He said, "The search for the real you will have to continue. That'll be a hundred dollars, please."
I said to myself, "If this is not the real me, why should I give HIM a hundred dollars? I'll look for the real me. Let him give ME a hundred dollars. But what if I find the real me and he doesn't think it's worth a hundred dollars?"
Then I said, "For all I know the real me might be going to another psychiatrist altogether. Might even be a psychiatrist himself. Wouldn't it be funny if you're the real me and you owe me a hundred dollars?"
I said, "I'll tell you what. I'll charge you fifty dollars and we'll call it even."[2]

One could say that this routine is a form of observational humor, that Mason is making fun of the psychological concept of searching for the "real me," but Mason makes that point in the first half of the skit. The only justification for the second half is simply to enjoy the inventiveness of watching Mason turn this concept on its head in many ways. It's like watching someone juggle seven balls or multiply large numbers in their head.

That's why exposing your children to intelligent humor will develop not only their sense of humor but also their general intellectual skills. This is perhaps best illustrated by Lewis Carroll, who, in addition to being an author, was also a mathematician and logician, which is quite evident from his books. Consider this scene from *Through the*

Looking-Glass in which Alice expresses her surprise that she and the Queen haven't gotten anywhere despite running quickly:

> *"[I]n our country," said Alice, still panting a little, "you'd generally get to somewhere else—if you run very fast for a long time, as we've been doing."*
>
> *"A slow sort of country!" said the Queen. "Now, here, you see, it takes all the running you can do, to keep in the same place. If you want to get somewhere else, you must run at least twice as fast as that!"[3]*

In the form of a joke, Carroll is introducing the concept that speed isn't an absolute but is always relative to some other object, a fundamental concept in modern physics.

Another example of Carroll taking delight in mathematical concepts is Alice's interaction with the March Hare:

> *"Take some more tea," the March Hare said to Alice, very earnestly.*
>
> *"I've had nothing yet," Alice replied in an offended tone, "so I can't take more."*
>
> *"You mean you can't take less," said the Hatter: "It's very easy to take more than nothing."[4]*

In this passage, Carroll is exploring both the mathematical concept of "nothing" as well as making a rather interesting observation about the subtleties of language.

Perhaps the ultimate celebration of logical absurdity is Joseph Heller's *Catch-22*, whose title derives from this passage in which the narrator explains why pilots can't get out of flying dangerous missions by claiming they're crazy:

> *Catch-22 . . . specified that a concern for one's safety in the face of dangers that were real and immediate was the process of a*

COMEDY   **65**

*rational mind. Orr was crazy and could be grounded. All he
had to do was ask; and as soon as he did, he would no longer
be crazy and would have to fly more missions. Orr would be
crazy to fly more missions and sane if he didn't, but if he was
sane, he had to fly them. If he flew them, he was crazy and
didn't have to; but if he didn't want to, he was sane and had to.
Yossarian was moved very deeply by the absolute simplicity of
this clause of Catch-22 and let out a respectful whistle.*

   "That's some catch, that Catch-22," he observed.

Yossarian's awe at Catch-22 is amusing in part because it mirrors
the reader's own awe at Heller's intellectual ingenuity.

Another example of Heller's obsession with logic is a scene in
which a colonel claims that a character named Clevinger has said
he can't be punished. When Clevinger denies doing so, the colonel
demands to know *when* he hasn't said it:

   *"I'm sorry, sir. But I don't know how to answer it. I never
   said you couldn't punish me."*

   ". . . I'm asking you to tell us when you didn't say it."

   *Clevinger took a deep breath. "I always didn't say you
   couldn't punish me, sir."*

   "That's much better, Mr. Clevinger."

The joke here is that the statement "I always didn't say you
couldn't punish me" is logically equivalent to "I never said you
couldn't punish me." The requirement that Clevinger rephrase his
answer in a form that is literally logically identical fits right in with
Catch-22's theme that war is irrational.

This connection between humor and logic is also illustrated
by one of my kids' favorite comedy sketches, Monty Python's "Argument Clinic," in which a man pays to engage in a five-minute
argument with a professional arguer. After just a few minutes of argument, the professional arguer says the session is over:

CLIENT: That was never five minutes!

ARGUER: I'm afraid it was.

CLIENT: It wasn't.

ARGUER: I'm sorry, but I'm not allowed to argue unless you've paid!

CLIENT: Oh, all right. (*Pays money.*)

ARGUER: Thank you.

CLIENT: That wasn't really five minutes, just now.

ARGUER: I told you, I'm not allowed to argue unless you've paid.

CLIENT: I just paid!

ARGUER: No you didn't.

CLIENT: If I didn't pay, why are you arguing? I got you!

ARGUER: No, you haven't.

CLIENT: Yes, I have. If you're arguing, I must have paid.

ARGUER: Not necessarily. I could be arguing in my spare time.[5]

The client is seeking to invoke a classic principle of logic, that of contraposition. This principle states that "If P, then Q" is logically equivalent to "If not Q, then not P." In symbolic logic, this would be represented as: $P \mapsto Q = -Q \mapsto -P$. An example of this would be "If it is snowing, then it is cold" is logically equivalent to "If it is *not* cold, then it is *not* snowing." If one of these statements is true, then the other statement must also be true.

Here, the Arguer has said, "I'm not allowed to argue unless you've paid." To fit this more in the pattern of the contrapositive, we would rephrase this as "If you have *not* paid, I will *not* argue" or $-P \mapsto -A$. The Client then turns this around and says that this is logically equivalent to the contrapositive, $A \mapsto P$, which is "If I am arguing, then you have paid." It looks like the Arguer has been cornered but then he takes the position that the rule prohibiting him from arguing without payment applies only when he is working and that he could be arguing recreationally.

While a child who listens to this sketch won't consciously realize that they are being introduced to these formal logical propositions, they will nonetheless become familiar with these modes of thinking by listening to this sketch repeatedly.

Humor can also teach kids how to use language inventively. Take *Monty Python and the Holy Grail,* a film that combines broad slapstick humor with quite sophisticated language. In one scene, King Arthur happens upon a group of peasants who refuse to acknowledge his authority, one of the multitude of humiliations and frustrations to which Arthur is subject in his fruitless efforts to recruit people to his quest to find the Holy Grail:

ARTHUR: How do you do, good lady? I am Arthur, king of the Britons. Whose castle is that?

WOMAN: Didn't know we had a king. I thought we were an autonomous collective.

ARTHUR: I am your king.

WOMAN: Well, I didn't vote for you.

ARTHUR: You don't vote for kings.

WOMAN: Well, how'd you become king, then?

ARTHUR: The Lady of the Lake, her arm clad in the purest shimmering samite, held aloft Excalibur from the bosom of the water, signifying by divine providence that I, Arthur, was to carry Excalibur. That is why I am your king.

MAN: Listen. Strange women lying in ponds distributing swords is no basis for a system of government. Supreme executive power derives from a mandate from the masses, not from some farcical aquatic ceremony.

ARTHUR: Be quiet!

MAN: You can't expect to wield supreme executive power just 'cause some watery tart threw a sword at you!

ARTHUR: Shut up!

MAN: I mean, if I went around saying I was an emperor just because some moistened bint had lobbed a scimitar at me, they'd put me away![6]

On the surface, this skit is about King Arthur's increasing frustration at his inability to get an answer to his simple question ("Whose castle is that?") or to command the respect he believes he deserves, but at a deeper level, it is a kind of tour de force in using the richness of the English language to ridicule the concept of monarchial rule. Riffing on the king's reference to the noble-sounding "Lady of the Lake," the peasants demote her first to a "strange woman" lying in a "pond" participating in a "farcical aquatic ceremony," and then even further to a "moistened bint" and "watery tart."

Python uses a similar technique when the actor John Cleese demands a refund because he has been sold a dead parrot. When the shop owner obstinately refuses to acknowledge the obvious fact that the parrot is dead, Cleese protests:

> *This parrot is no more! He has ceased to be! He's expired and gone to meet his maker! This is a late parrot! He's a stiff! Bereft of life, he rests in peace! He's off the twig! He's kicked the bucket, he's shuffled off his mortal coil, run down the curtain and joined the bleedin' choir invisible!! THIS IS AN EX-PARROT![7]*

What is particularly amusing in this scene is that Python takes the most mundane and absurd consumer transaction—a refund for a dead parrot—and dresses it up with formal language ("expired," "bereft") and references to both George Eliot (the "choir invisible") and Shakespeare ("shuffled off his mortal coil," which is drawn from Hamlet's famous "To be or not to be" speech).

What makes Monty Python so great for kids is that it works on different levels. An eight-year-old can laugh at Cleese's frustration that he can't get the shop owner to admit that the parrot is dead, while an older child can pick up on the subtleties of the language employed and the deeper ironies of these scenes.

Although quite different in style, Douglas Adams, author of *The Hitchhiker's Guide to the Galaxy*, also has a wonderful ability to turn a phrase. He has observed, for example, that "A common mistake that people make when trying to design something completely foolproof is to underestimate the ingenuity of complete fools." The joke is that while foolishness suggests stupidity, some people are so incredibly foolish that it seems to rise to the level of ingenuity.

Here is a beautifully ironic passage from *The Hitchhiker's Guide to the Galaxy*:

> *"You know," said Arthur, "it's at times like this, when I'm trapped in a Vogon airlock with a man from Betelgeuse, and about to die of asphyxiation in deep space that I really wish I'd listened to what my mother told me when I was young."*
> *"Why, what did she tell you?"*
> *"I don't know, I didn't listen."*

Good jokes often play on subtle aspects of the English language. For example, in the Oscar Wilde play *The Importance of Being Earnest*, Lady Bracknell remarks to Ernest, who is an orphan: "To lose one parent, Mr. Worthing, may be regarded as a misfortune; to lose both looks like carelessness." In the first instance, this is about the ridiculousness of blaming someone for being an orphan but it's also an observation about how curious it is that the term "lost," which often means actively misplacing ("I've lost my keys") and usually applies to things, also applies to the death of one's relatives ("I'm sorry for your loss.").

Many jokes demand that you think precisely because it's the joke's subtext that makes it funny. That's why people talk about "getting" jokes. Take, for example, the putdown "This book fills a much-needed gap." On its surface, it seems complimentary: There was a gap that needed filling and this book did it. However, upon closer examination, one sees that the speaker is saying not that it is the *filling* of the gap that is much-needed but rather that it is the *gap itself*– i.e., that no book should fill it.

Or take these witticisms:

> *"Some cause happiness wherever they go; others, whenever they go."*
> —OSCAR WILDE

> *"Advice is what we ask for when we already know the answer but wish we didn't."*
> —ERICA JONG

> *"A narcissist is someone better looking than you are."*
> —GORE VIDAL

> *"We all agree that your theory is crazy, but is it crazy enough?"*
> —NIELS BOHR

> *"If you haven't got anything nice to say about anybody, come sit next to me."*
> —ALICE ROOSEVELT LONGWORTH

> *"I am not young enough to know everything."*
> —OSCAR WILDE

> *"The covers of this book are too far apart."*
> —AMBROSE BIERCE

> *"I'd challenge you to a battle of wits, but I see that you are unarmed."*
> —UNKNOWN

The humor of these jokes is their "subtext": their implicit and unstated meaning. The subtext of "The covers of this book are too far apart" is that there are too many pages in between because the author is verbose. The subtext of "I am not young enough to know everything" is that young people foolishly think they know everything. The subtext of "A narcissist is someone better looking than you are" is that the person saying it just resents anyone who looks better than they do.* Jokes like these are pedagogically useful because they challenge you to make an intellectual leap and reward you with a laugh if you do.

Besides the effect that humor has on one's intelligence, comedic ability is a great asset in virtually any career. Take politics. Many political figures have used their sense of humor to great advantage. Ronald Reagan used it not only to make himself more likable but also to convey his political beliefs. He particularly liked using jokes to highlight the problems with communism. Here is one of them:

> *Only one out of seven families in the Soviet Union own automobiles. There is a ten-year wait, and you go through quite a process when you are ready to buy, and then you put up the money in advance.*
>
> *This man laid down the money, and the fellow in charge said to him, "Come back in ten years and get your car." The man answered, "Morning or afternoon?" and the fellow behind the counter said, "Ten years from now, what difference does it make?" The man replied, "Well, the plumber is coming in the morning."*[8]

Many people would criticize communism by comparing the GDP or poverty levels of communist and capitalist countries, but Reagan knew that jokes would be more effective. It is said that a picture is worth a thousand words. It might also be said that a joke is worth a thousand statistics.

John F. Kennedy was another president who used his wit to great

---

* *There are many collections of witty quotes. One of the best belongs to Gabriel Robins, a professor of computer science, which illustrates the theme of this chapter that humor is linked to general intelligence. It can be found online at https://www.cs.virginia.edu/~robins/quotes.html.*

advantage. His jokes were often self-deprecating. For example, when a child asked him how he'd become a war hero, he responded: "It was absolutely involuntary; they sunk my boat." Kennedy understood that through the use of self-deprecating humor, he could convey the impression that he was so accomplished that he felt no need to brag. Golda Meir famously took note of this ploy when she said to one of her colleagues, "Don't be so humble—you are not that great."

Kennedy also used jokes to defuse criticism. At a campaign event, he responded to claims that his father was bankrolling his campaign by pretending to read from a telegram his father had just sent him:

Dear Jack:

Don't buy a single vote more than necessary. I'll be damned if I'm going to pay for a landslide.

Love, Dad[9]

By making light of the issue, Kennedy suggested that it couldn't be all that serious. Similarly, Reagan used humor to defuse concerns about his age. When asked about it at a debate, he said: "I will not make age an issue of this campaign. I am not going to exploit, for political purposes, my opponent's youth and inexperience."[10] On the surface, Reagan was suggesting that his experience could be seen in a positive light, but the real point of his joke was to demonstrate his mental faculties, which he did by constructing and delivering his joke perfectly. Since Reagan began with his very serious "commander in chief" tone, nobody suspected he was about to make a joke. Moreover, he constructed his words carefully so he could wait until his final words to lower the boom. Instead of finishing his sentence with the most natural construction—which would be "I won't exploit my opponent's youth and inexperience for political purposes"—he stuck the clause "for political purposes" in the middle of the sentence so that his joke isn't revealed until the last three words when he refers to his opponent's "youth and inexperience." Reagan's artful construction and masterful delivery of this riposte reassured listeners that he still had his wits about him.

To develop your child's sense of humor, there are many terrific comedy routines you can listen to or watch on Youtube together. Here are some that I particularly recommend:

+ For young children: "Free to Be . . . You and Me" (Marlo Thomas)
+ "Who's on First," "Stolen Oranges," "The Car," "Lend Me 50 Cents" (Abbott and Costello)
+ "Number One Hits (and Others, Too)" (Allan Sherman)
+ "The Button-Down Mind Strikes Back" (Bob Newhart)
+ "Behind the Button-Down Mind of Bob Newhart" (Bob Newhart)
+ "Peter and the Commissar" (Arthur Fiedler, Boston Pops, and Allan Sherman)
+ "Victor Borge: Comedy in Music," "Live!" (Victor Borge)
+ "Improvisations to Music," "An Evening with Mike Nichols and Elaine May" (Mike Nichols and Elaine May)
+ "Tom Lehrer: That Was the Year That Was," "The Tom Lehrer Collection 1953–60" (Tom Lehrer)
+ "The World According to Me" (Jackie Mason)
+ Mike Birbiglia: one of Culver's favorite comedians and one of the few modern comedians who doesn't use much profanity
+ Gary Gulman: a sophisticated and fairly clean comedian who manages to make even topics like punctuation quite funny
+ "Dress to Kill" (Eddie Izzard) Note: contains profanity; likely inappropriate for children not yet in high school.

Here are some books your child would benefit from reading (in addition to the comic strips I list in Chapter 12, "Reading"):

+ *Laugh-Out-Loud Jokes for Kids* (Rob Elliott)
+ *Sideways Stories from Wayside School* (Louis Sachar)
+ *MAD's Greatest Artists: Dave Berg: Five Decades of "The Lighter Side of . . ."*
+ *MAD's Greatest Artists: Don Martin: Three Decades of His Greatest Works*
+ *The Hitchhiker's Guide to the Galaxy* (Douglas Adams)
+ *The Best Short Stories of Mark Twain*
+ *Alice's Adventures in Wonderland* and *Through the Looking-Glass* (Lewis Carroll)
+ *The Princess Bride: S. Morgenstern's Classic Tale of True Love and High Adventure* (William Goldman)
+ *The Complete Cartoons of the New Yorker*
+ *Carry On, Jeeves* (P. G. Wodehouse)
+ *Hyperbole and a Half: Unfortunate Situations, Flawed Coping Mechanisms, Mayhem, and Other Things That Happened* (Allie Brosh)
+ *Good Omens: The Nice and Accurate Prophecies of Agnes Nutter, Witch* (Terry Pratchett, Neil Gaiman)
+ *Essays of E. B. White*
+ *Catch-22* (Joseph Heller)

In addition to reading and listening to comedy, you should also encourage your child to tell jokes and create skits. When Culver was in high school, he got interested in improvisation and took some classes. Now, he, Dillon, and Hannah regularly go to improv clubs both to perform and to listen to others perform. When Eric's mother had her eightieth birthday party, Eric and our children did a skit in which they made fun of the disagreements that Eric and his mother sometimes have about politics.

PART **II**

LET'S GET SERIOUS

To this point, I've been focusing on fun family activities. If you do nothing more than these activities, it will have an enormous impact on your child's intellect. Part II goes beyond that and delves into more traditional academic activities, but even these can be approached with a focus on the joy to be derived from them.

11

CHEAP THRILLS

Raising kids in twenty-first-century America reminds me of Dickens's famous opening lines from *A Tale of Two Cities*:

> *It was the best of times, it was the worst of times, it was the age of wisdom, it was the age of foolishness, it was the epoch of belief, it was the epoch of incredulity, it was the season of Light, it was the season of Darkness, it was the spring of hope, it was the winter of despair.*

Let's start with the best of times. Parents have advantages that families couldn't even have imagined a few hundred years ago. Take something as simple as books. Since a single book cost more than the weekly wages of an average laborer in 1787,[1] most families owned only one: the Bible. Moreover, lending libraries weren't widespread or free. Benjamin Franklin established the first American library, which was funded by dues. As he wrote:

*So few were the readers at that time in Philadelphia, and
the majority of us so poor, that I was not able, with great
industry, to find more than fifty persons, mostly young
tradesmen, willing to pay down for this purpose forty
shillings each, and ten shillings per annum.*[2]

Today, books are much more affordable and easily obtained from
the library. Moreover, there are far more books written specifically for
children than ever before. People also have more time to read to their
children and engage in parenting than they had in the past. My great-
grandfather Samuel Ehrenreich, who pressed clothes in a garment
factory, worked twelve hours a day, six days a week, a common work-
load then. Moreover, people then didn't have time-saving devices
such as dishwashers, washing machines, and microwave ovens.

For these reasons, this should be a golden age for parenting, education, and family life, but it plainly isn't, and the primary reason for
this, in my opinion, is the ubiquity of videos and video games.[3] Many
children spend so much time on these activities that they have little
time for anything else. In 1984, 35 percent of children in the United
States said they read for fun almost every day. By 2020, that number
had fallen to 17 percent, while their screen time had increased by
four to six hours per day.[4]

The impact of this was recently brought home to me when I
had dinner at my parents' house with one of the most knowledgeable people I've ever met. No matter what topic was raised—ancient
Judaism, the Roman Empire, American history—he was an expert. I
figured that he must be a professor of some kind, although even that
wouldn't fully explain the breadth of his knowledge. It turned out
that he edited scientific journals and books. How, I asked him, did
he know so much about, well, everything? "I don't have a television,"
he answered, quite seriously. Not watching television had opened up
so much time in his schedule, he explained, that he was able to read
prodigiously.

In addition to gobbling up time that children could be spending on more educational activities, watching videos and playing video games have a terrible impact on their minds. We see this at Success Academy all the time. Children are so used to the rapid pace and constant stimulation of video games and streaming video that they can't sit still, focus on their work, or listen to a story. To overcome this, we have to train them to pay attention for long periods of time. We require them to sit up straight, look at whoever is speaking, and be prepared to answer questions if we pick on them randomly. Over time, they manage to develop their powers of concentration but it's like weaning someone off an addictive drug.

In the book *Homeschooling Odyssey*, Matthew James explains the impact of not allowing his children to watch videos.[5] Remarkably, although all four of his children got into Stanford, their homeschooling consisted of only an hour a day of formal academic study and they were largely allowed to do what they pleased the rest of the time. Here is Mr. James's description of how one of his children, Adrian, spent his time:

> *There was plenty of work to be done on the mountain, but most of it seemed like fun to Adrian. The chickens and goats were full of monkey business and created farm crises which required innovative solutions. Fences needed mending, as the cows liked to break through the weak spots and wander away. An old outhouse had to be transformed into a chicken coup* [sic]. *Tree forts had to be built, according to Adrian's reckoning. These were the sorts of projects which could be done by an eight-year-old with a hammer, nails, and a saw. . . . He would get so involved that we often had to search for him at mealtimes and after sundown.*
>
> *In the evening, however, Adrian would read and he became more academically focused as he became older and he ended up studying mechanical engineering in college. Adrian's siblings were more academically inclined, so they tended to spend more of their time reading.*[6]

Mr. James allowed his children enormous amounts of freedom to do as they pleased, but the one thing they couldn't do was watch videos. As a result, explains Mr. James, they learned how to amuse themselves by playing, reading, building things, and engaging in art projects:

> *Compare this to the passivity of television viewing, in which the child's consciousness slavishly follows the programming. Real-life experience engenders curious, creative, and busy children who learn to interact and cooperate with others in order to make their lives more interesting. Habitual television viewing develops lazy, bored, impatient, and self-indulgent creatures who expect to be constantly stimulated through the expenditure of minimum effort, such as pushing buttons on remotes.*[7]

This statement rings true and is consistent with my own experience. My family didn't have a television so I had to find other ways to amuse myself: reading, baking cakes, and doing projects. I even enjoyed homework, which my parents never had to nag me about doing.

As for Eric, while his family did have a television in their apartment, they would spend summers at a house where they didn't. Like me, Eric found other ways to amuse himself. One summer, he wrote and put on a play. Another summer he made a film. And of course, he read a lot, as did I.

While both television and video games have been around for a while, recent advances have increased children's use of these technologies dramatically. In 1950, a family would have one black-and-white television with a relatively small screen, and there wasn't much interesting programming outside of prime-time television. Nowadays, children have computers, smartphones, and an endless fare of streaming video from which to choose. They can watch what they want when they want where they want.

Moreover, just as the tobacco companies deliberately manipulated the level of nicotine in their cigarettes, television producers have made their products ever more addictive. You can see this if you show a child a film from the 1950s such as the Western *Shane* or the science fiction film *Forbidden Planet*. Kids loved these films when they came out, but many kids today find them boring because they've gotten used to the pace of modern films, which now average 38 cuts per minute, compared to 12 in the 1950s.[8]

These changes not only cause children to watch more television, but increase the harmful impact of doing so. Since old films were slower, you had time to reflect on what was happening. If the guy was in love with the girl, you wondered whether those feelings were requited and whether they'd end up as a happy couple. If someone had been murdered, you'd be curious about who the real murderer was and whether so-and-so might be lying about the defendant's alibi. This thinking led you to become emotionally and intellectually involved with the film so you kept on watching it. Nowadays many films are so quick that you don't have time to think. Lest viewers feel unentertained for one second, movies feature a steady stream of action sequences and witty rejoinders. Kids get so addicted to this that it makes it harder for them to appreciate anything else. Imagine how hard reading a book will be for a child who finds a 1940s film with 12 cuts per minute too slow to enjoy.

Now I need to add a caveat here. I'm not saying that all films and videos are bad. There is some brilliant work being done in streaming video, and there are opportunities to use good films and videos to advance your children's intellectual interests, which I discuss elsewhere. The problem, however, is that children often watch the worst videos and watch them far too much.

And video games are even more harmful because they're interactive and wholly lacking in the content that is a redeeming quality of at least some television. When I see a five-year-old kid on a bus playing a videogame on a Nintendo Switch or a smartphone, it makes me want to cry. Playing these games is incredibly addictive and damaging. Indeed, there is evidence that children's increasing consumption of video games and television may be contributing to the increase in attention deficit/hyperactivity disorder (ADHD).[9]

I think that we are in the same position today with respect to video games and television that we were in 1963 with respect to cigarettes. In that year, annual cigarette consumption had grown to a peak of 4,345 cigarettes per person from 54 cigarettes per person in 1900. There had already been several studies linking smoking to lung cancer, including a 1950 study suggesting that smoking increased the risk of cancer fifty-fold, and in 1964, the United States Surgeon General published a report about the health dangers of smoking that led to warning labels on cigarettes. In that year, more than 100,000 Americans a year were dying from lung cancer compared to only around 10,000 per year in 1930. But incredibly, while we put warning labels on cigarettes, it wasn't until thirty years later that we really started taking aggressive measures to fight smoking by, for example, prohibiting smoking in public places and really cracking down on sales and advertising of cigarettes to young people. While the tobacco companies certainly deserve some blame for this, so do we. We just didn't want to face up to reality, to make the dramatic changes that needed to be made in our personal behavior and in our society.

I believe the same thing is happening today with respect to excessive watching of videos and playing of video games. It's obvious that it's bad for our children, but we don't want to face up to it. Just as with cigarettes, we'll no doubt be blaming the entertainment industry for tricking kids into watching videos too much, but the truth is that the responsibility lies with us. We are turning a blind eye to the damage it is doing because we don't want to face the fact of how much damage it is doing.

And because of that, parents today are faced with a problem that prior generations of parents weren't. Abraham Lincoln's parents didn't have to say to him, "Abe, enough with the television; it's turning your brain to mush." Thomas Jefferson's parents didn't have to say to him, "Tom, stop playing those damn video games already and write a declaration of independence or something." You are facing a problem that no prior parents have had to deal with in the five thousand or so years since mankind became literate, and if you ignore it, it will severely impede your children's ability to thrive intellectually. Failing to limit your children's consumption of video games and television will make everything else I suggest in this book much harder to achieve. When you suggest your child play a game of Monopoly, they'll decline and a half hour later you'll find them playing video games. When you ask how they're coming along in the book they're reading, you'll learn that they're still on page 7 but they did manage to squeeze in three more episodes of their favorite television show while you were having your morning coffee.

Now I realize that all this may sound like a bait and switch. To this point, I've been emphasizing how your child will learn from things they naturally enjoy and how much fun parenting can be. I'm now telling you that you need to be the disciplinarian who prohibits your child from engaging in what may be his favorite activities. Guilty as charged. This is the one big exception, the one area where you really need to put down your foot, because excessive television and video games will make it very difficult for your child to engage in more educational activities.

Think of it like this. Imagine putting a bunch of five-year-olds around a table with plates of roast chicken, rice, hamburgers, and French fries and telling them, "Just take whatever you like." Most kids will eat the hamburgers and French fries not because they dislike roast chicken and rice but because they like hamburgers and fries more. By putting hamburgers and fries on the table, you've made it harder to get the kids to eat roast chicken and rice. The same is true for television and video games. Children can enjoy intellectually worthwhile activities such as reading, board games, and playing with blocks but they are easily distracted from such activities by videos and video games, which are cheap thrills that provide instant gratification with no effort.

So that's the bad news. But the good news is that if you can deal with this one concededly difficult problem, there's a good chance that most of the rest of what I suggest in this book will fall into place pretty easily. Often when a child says that they hate reading because it's boring, what they really mean is that they'd prefer to watch television or play video games. Take away the television and video games, and reading starts to look a lot more attractive. Before smartphones, some kids would violate their bedtime by reading under the covers with a flashlight.

I recommend you forbid video games altogether. Given how addictive they are, you'll find that easier than trying to limit how much time your children play them. Eric and I forbade our children from playing video games in our house except during one period when Culver was ten years old. He promised that if he was allowed to play video games, he would only play them for a half hour per week. We agreed but Eric soon noticed that Culver seemed to be playing them more often than this so Eric confronted Culver, who tearfully confessed that Eric was right. Recognizing that he simply couldn't control himself, Culver promised never to play them again and didn't. Several years later, Dillon asked to be able to play video games. Just like Culver, Dillon insisted that he'd limit the amount he played. Eric and I didn't even have to deny this request because Culver shot it down for us. He explained to Dillon that he'd tried this and that it just wasn't worth it because Dillon would inevitably want to play more and more video games.

Denying one's child video games may not be easy. I'm sure it's wonderful to see one's child's eyes light up when they get an Xbox for their birthday. I'm sure it can be hard when one's child bitterly complains that all their friends are allowed to play video games. You need to trust that your children will thank you one day. I have yet to encounter an adult who said, "I had a horrible childhood because my parents wouldn't let me watch video games."

What to do about videos is a tougher question. Most parents watch videos themselves so it's difficult for them to prohibit their children from doing so. Moreover, videos, unlike video games, have the redeeming quality that they can be educational. The advantage of nonetheless outlawing videos completely is it can actually be easier than letting your child watch some television and then constantly having to fight his desire to watch more. If you don't want to go that far, however, then I'd suggest you consider the policy that Eric and I took with our children, which was to let them watch videos only on Friday, Saturday, and Sunday evenings. Enforcing a rule like this is far easier than setting a total allowance of hours for the week. Another possibility is that you only watch television together as a family. There are many good films, which I've included in a list in the back of this book, that are both educational and enjoyable for adults and children alike.

I would particularly urge you to avoid letting your preschool child watch television, even educational television. I'm sure that educational television is, in fact, educational: that children can learn shapes, letters, numbers, and other useful information. I nonetheless believe those benefits are outweighed by the potential harm to a child's intellect from getting used to the passive stimulation that television provides. I realize that television is an awfully convenient babysitter, but remember that for the 300,000 years that people have existed, children amused themselves without television until just recently. As long as your child has some toys to play with, they'll be able to amuse themselves.

If your child has already gotten addicted to video games or television, consider a summer detox. Many summer camps have a strict policy against using electronic devices. You might also combine this with a family vacation on which you don't watch television.

If you cut back or eliminate your child's video consumption, they will say they're bored. That is both inevitable and good. It is boredom that leads children to find something interesting to do. Given time, your child will eventually find a way to amuse themself, particularly if you've given them access to some of the games, books, and toys I recommend in this book. Like any withdrawal, it will be hard at first, but it will become easier with time.

Be prepared for the fact that if your child wants to watch videos and you suggest they do something like reading or even playing a board game, they'll probably say "No, that's boring." They'll say this not because they suddenly hate reading and board games but because they've gotten fixated on watching videos at that moment and know that their best chance of convincing you to allow them to do so is to claim that doing anything else would be sheer torture. Hang tough and your child will eventually get past their fixation and enjoy doing something else. Before television was invented, children didn't just mope around all day being bored.

To help children transition away from television, I would especially recommend audiobooks. As I discuss later, many audiobooks these days are astonishingly well read. Many are even "full cast" recordings.

One of the traps you want to avoid is dividing activities into two mutually exclusive categories of (1) educational and (2) fun. Some parents, for example, say that their kids can do whatever they want after they finish their homework. Given that many children get very modest amounts of homework, the result is that the child will spend many hours engaging in intellectually worthless activities. Moreover, this suggests to the child that there is no overlap between educational activities and fun activities. Rather than dividing all activities into "educational" and "fun," recognize the sweet spot of activities that are both educational and fun or at least *pretty fun* even if they are not the *most fun* activities. If you ask your child what they'd most like to do, they may well say that they'd prefer to go to an amusement park or watch the latest superhero film rather than play Monopoly or listen to a book. However, the activities in this book are nonetheless pretty fun and that is what you should be focused on as parents. If you can get your child to engage in such activities through a combination of poking, prodding, and inspiring, your children will develop intellectually without your being an overbearing parent. The first step is limiting your child's consumption of video games and television. Once you do that, everything else becomes much easier.

12

READING

I n his autobiography, Malcolm X observed:

> *Many [people] think I went to school far beyond the eighth grade. This impression is due entirely to my prison studies. [I]n every free moment, if I was not reading in the library, I was reading on my bunk. You couldn't have gotten me out of books with a wedge. [M]onths passed without my even thinking about being imprisoned. In fact, up to then, I never had been so truly free in my life. . . .*
>
> *I have often reflected upon the new vistas that reading opened to me. I knew right there in prison that reading had changed forever the course of my life. . . . Not long ago, an English writer telephoned me from London, asking questions. One was, "What's your alma mater?" I told him, "Books."[1]*

Similarly, Elon Musk has said, "I was raised by books. Books, and then my parents." Abraham Lincoln had only a year of formal education and learned by reading books such as *Aesop's Fables*, the Bible, *The Pilgrim's Progress*, *Robinson Crusoe*, Shakespeare, poetry, and British and American history. Similarly, Ben Franklin only had two years of formal education and learned by reading.

In school, there are all sorts of activities that we add on to reading to help children get more from it, such as writing essays and having class discussions. Those are helpful, but the truth is that your child can learn a lot just by reading.

To begin with, books teach children how language works. Many schools are forced to teach children grammatical rules that they would learn automatically and better if they just spent more time reading. Take the following sentence: "I would have caught the train if I'd woken up on time." Although most adults could come up with such a sentence, few would be able to identify the tenses in it, and nobody actually thinks about the tenses they use when they speak. People learn most grammar unconsciously through listening or reading. It's also how children learn to understand more complex sentences and increase their vocabulary. Children generally learn most of their vocabulary not by studying words on index cards for the SATs or doing vocabulary homework but simply by being exposed to words through listening and reading.

The best way for children to be exposed to more language is to read more. If your child reads a good book for an hour, they will read about 10,000 words of high-quality writing. Compare this to a class discussion. First, given the stops and starts in the conversation and the halting speech of many students, there will be many fewer words spoken. Second, the language will be of far lower quality. Much of it will be spoken by other students who are no more advanced than your child so they are unlikely to speak in grammatically intricate sentences or use advanced vocabulary. Even teachers, while undoubtedly more proficient speakers than students, are hardly likely to spontaneously speak as well as a gifted author can write.

Most teachers would probably be more effective if they talked less and gave their children more time to read. Indeed, if I had to choose between a teacher without a book and a book without a teacher, I'd take the book every day because reading allows you to hear the words of extraordinary intellects such as Shakespeare, Jane Austen, or for children, Dr. Seuss and Roald Dahl. While it's great to have a teacher to help you learn to "think critically" about a text, you can get a lot from reading a book if you merely understand it.

Take, for example, the following passage from *Northanger Abbey*, in which Jane Austen suggests that dancing is like marriage:

> *In both, man has the advantage of choice, woman only the power of refusal; that in both, it is an engagement between man and woman, formed for the advantage of each; and that when once entered into, they belong exclusively to each other till the moment of its dissolution; that it is their duty, each to endeavor to give the other no cause for wishing that he or she had bestowed themselves elsewhere, and their best interest to keep their own imagination from wandering towards the perfections of their neighbors, or fancying that they should have been better off with anyone else.*[2]

Austen makes several interesting points in this passage. The first is that while men and women have superficial equality in marriage in that the agreement of both is required, only men have the power to propose the agreement in the first place. Austen is also suggesting that marriage, like a dance, is not so much a romantic or a sacred arrangement as a practical one: It is "formed for the advantage of each" with specified terms (that the parties "belong exclusively to each other till the moment of its dissolution") and that each party thereafter has a mutual interest in ensuring that neither of them regrets their decision.

Children who read such a passage carefully will come to understand that words and ideas such as "choice" and "consent" have subtle relationships. They will also come to understand the power of making analogies such as the one that Austen makes between marriage and dancing. Of course, a teacher may help a child understand this passage at an even deeper, more critical level, but a child can get a lot just from understanding the words on the page. Indeed, a common mistake that teachers make is to have students jump immediately to give their critical opinions of texts they don't even understand.

Reading also helps a child with their imagination. When you watch a film, it provides you with images and sound. By contrast, when you read, all you get is words that convey meaning and then you imagine the world in your head like a dream. Kids are often better at this than adults, which is why so many children are such great readers.

I believe that there is something very special about reading that makes it unlike any other activity. Consider the opening lines from J. D. Salinger's *The Catcher in the Rye*:

> *If you really want to hear about it, the first thing you'll*
> *probably want to know is where I was born, and what my*
> *lousy childhood was like, and how my parents were occupied*
> *and all before they had me, and all that David Copperfield*
> *kind of crap, but I don't feel like going into it, if you want to*
> *know the truth. In the first place, that stuff bores me, and in*
> *the second place, my parents would have two hemorrhages*
> *apiece if I told anything pretty personal about them.*

There can be an incredible intimacy when you read a book, particularly a good one like *The Catcher in the Rye*. Although you are separated from the author by time and place, there is an outpouring of thoughts from the writer's head into yours through the medium of language that I find even more intimate than speaking to someone because you aren't distracted by their physical presence or the complications of your social interaction. Instead, you're left with nothing but their disembodied words and thoughts. Reading is as close as you can get to being inside someone else's head, which, when the author is brilliant, is an extraordinary opportunity.

Reading can have an incredible impact on a person's intellect. I have yet to meet a poorly educated voracious reader. If you can get your child to become an avid reader of good books, that alone will virtually ensure that they become well educated.

So how can you get your child to become an avid reader? The first step is to read to your children when they are young. Children love being read to by their parents both because they enjoy hearing a story and because they enjoy the intimacy of your reading it to them. Some of my most cherished memories are of my mother reading to me. Among the many books she read to my brother and me were *The Secret Garden*, *Heidi*, *The Call of the Wild*, and *The Wise Men of Chelm and Their Merry Tales*, a book of Jewish folktales that never failed to send my brother and me into hysterics.

Many parents have trouble finding the time to read to their children and are too tired to read them bedtime stories. To create more time for reading, I always had a book with me when I was with my children to read to them in my spare time. You may have time sitting on the bus, waiting in the doctor's office, waiting in line at the supermarket, sitting in the car (if you aren't driving!), or eating breakfast. Even if it's just five minutes here and there, it all adds up.

You may also want to encourage your child to read "wordless" books, which tell stories through pictures alone. Having children "read" these books helps them begin the process of constructing stories in their head from information on a page. Here are some terrific wordless or nearly wordless books:

+ *Tuesday* (David Wiesner)
+ *Flotsam* (David Wiesner)
+ *Creepy Castle* (John S. Goodall)

+ *Unspoken: A Story from the Underground Railroad* (Henry Cole)
+ *Quest* (Aaron Becker)
+ *Sector 7* (David Wiesner)
+ *Journey* (Aaron Becker)
+ *Good Dog, Carl* (Alexandra Day)
+ *The Arrival* (Shaun Tan)
+ *The Snowman* (Raymond Briggs)
+ *Chalk* (Bill Thomson)

Classic picture books have helped generations of children learn to read. Although it's important to understand that the quality of picture books can vary greatly, there are still great books for children at every level such as those of Dr. Seuss. For beginning readers, there are books that are more basic such as *Green Eggs and Ham* or *The Cat in the Hat* and for higher-level readers there are more text-heavy books such as *The 500 Hats of Bartholomew Cubbins* or *How the Grinch Stole Christmas!* Often, children have a level of sophistication that greatly exceeds their ability to read so it's terrific when an author manages to achieve a level of subtlety with fairly basic vocabulary. For example, in *Click, Clack, Moo: Cows That Type*, a bunch of cows find a typewriter and start leaving notes for their owner such as this:

Dear Farmer Brown,

The barn is very cold at night. We'd like some electric blankets.

> *Sincerely,*
> *The Cows.*

When I read this story to my children, I think that I laughed even more than they did! I also loved *The True Story of the 3 Little*

Pigs! (as told to Jon Scieszka), from the perspective of the wolf. As our protagonist Alexander T. Wolf explains:

> *I don't know how this whole Big Bad Wolf thing got started,*
> *but it's all wrong.*
>   *Maybe it's because of our diet.*
>   *Hey, it's not my fault wolves eat cute little animals like*
> *bunnies and sheep and pigs. That's just the way we are. If*
> *cheeseburgers were cute, folks would probably think you were*
> *Big and Bad, too.*

Stories like these are great for kids who like more interesting and sophisticated texts but aren't yet fluent readers. Even though *The True Story of the 3 Little Pigs!* has a subtle sense of humor and features an unreliable narrator, it has a Lexile score—a measure of reading difficulty—of only 510, which is a second-grade level. The Lexile score for *Click, Clack, Moo* is even lower (470).

Here are a few other books in the same spirit:

+ *The Three Pigs* (David Wiesner)
+ *The Frog Prince, Continued* (Jon Scieszka and Steve Johnson)
+ *Duck for President* (Doreen Cronin and Betsy Lewin)

I would invest in a large number of picture books when your children are young. Keep in mind that children enjoy having picture books read to them over and over again, which is a good thing because they understand the books better each time.

As your child develops their ability to read on their own, you may want to encourage them to read high-quality comic books and graphic novels. The visual elements of these books help children enjoy reading when they aren't yet fluent readers.

Here are some terrific graphic novels and graphic novel series.

+ *The Adventures of Tintin*
+ *The Adventures of Asterix*
+ *Amulet*
+ *Bone*
+ *The Invention of Hugo Cabret*

I should also mention *Classics Illustrated*, which are comic books based on classic literature. These comics were once very popular but have fallen out of favor. This is unfortunate because they are a terrific tool for encouraging middle school students to read since they incorporate relatively sophisticated vocabulary into a comic book format. The pictures and dialogue allow a child to follow the story despite the challenging text.

In the category of humorous comic strips, I'd recommend the following:

+ *Peanuts*
+ *Calvin and Hobbes*
+ *The Far Side*

Comic books can be quite sophisticated, far more than you might realize if you know them only from images on T-shirts and coffee cups or a few isolated strips or frames. Take *Peanuts*. When you read a collection of *Peanuts* comic strips, you begin to understand individual episodes against the personality of each character and the history of interactions between them. Lucy, for example, opens a psychiatry booth offering sessions for five cents each. The conceit that a child would open a psychiatry booth rather than a lemonade stand is itself funny, but what makes it more so is that a reader who has become familiar with Lucy's temperament will realize that she is uniquely ill suited to the psychiatric profession as she doesn't have an empathetic bone in her body. As a result, she often fills her sessions with admonitions such as "Snap out of it! Five cents please."

Another long-running theme is Lucy's unrequited love for Schroeder, who cares only for music and is typically pictured playing his toy piano as Lucy looks on with adoration. One day, the incurably ill-tempered Lucy asks Schroeder, "Do piano players ever marry crabby girls?" When Schroeder answers, "Never!" Lucy immediately responds, "WELL, NO WONDER WE'RE SO CRABBY!" On a surface level, it is amusing how Lucy turns the tables on Schroeder by blaming her ill temper on his indifference after first appearing to concede that she might have a crabby disposition, but the episode has even deeper humor if you know Lucy's character. Since Lucy tends to be independent, critical, and strong-willed, her reaction to Schroeder's indifference tends to be anger and impatience rather than hurt and self-doubt. Thus, Lucy's initial question leads the reader to sympathize with her, to suspect and perhaps even hope that an inner vulnerability lies underneath Lucy's crusty exterior—a hope that is utterly and comically dashed when Lucy turns on Schroeder with such verbal ferocity that he tumbles backward.

If you think I'm reading too much into *Peanuts*, I'd encourage you to read it yourself, and when you find something funny, ask yourself why. I think you'll find that the answer isn't always obvious: that you'll sense that the comics are funny but that you don't know quite why because there is a subtlety to the humor that makes you think.

Another way to help your child improve their reading is to take turns doing so; you read one page and your child reads the next. This will make reading a little less taxing for your child. Another trick is to read the first chapter of a book and then announce that you need to start making dinner or something. If your child likes the book, there is a good chance they'll continue reading it on their own.

You can also listen to recorded books with your children or encourage them to listen to such books on their own. For young children, a particularly appealing option are picture eBooks with audio. These books allow children to hear the book read as they turn the pages. They can be found on various platforms: Amazon Audible;

Google Play; and the iPhone App Store. There is a particularly good collection of iPhone apps put out by Oceanhouse Media that are essentially audible picture books by Dr. Seuss with some nifty features thrown in that allow children to touch objects and see how they are spelled.

You might think that once your child begins learning how to read, it wouldn't make sense for them to listen to books because it isn't really reading. While that's true in the literal sense of the word, listening to audiobooks develops skills that are important to reading. When parents think of a child learning to read, they typically think of what educators call "decoding," which is turning the printed letters into words. Decoding seems very important when your child is first learning to read because it's a gateway skill, but once a child learns it, their ability to become a strong reader is determined by their ability to understand sentences with complex structure, their vocabulary, their general knowledge, and their ability to think about a text's meaning. All these skills can be learned just as well by listening to books as by reading them. Moreover, listening to books has some advantages. Particularly when your child is just learning to decode, it can be hard for them to really enjoy reading because it's difficult to simultaneously do the work of decoding the words and understanding what those words mean. Listening to a book allows the child to focus only on understanding the words, which lets them to enjoy it more and to get more from it. And this isn't just true in the very early grades. Even in middle school, children can still find it hard to decode books that have advanced vocabulary and irregularly spelled words.

Listening to audiobooks also helps children develop their understanding of English as a spoken language, which is an important skill in and of itself and also helps them become better readers. There are many idioms in the English language that are easier to learn by hearing than by reading. Take this passage from Roald Dahl's *Fantastic Mr. Fox*:

"I therefore invite you all," Mr. Fox went on, "to stay here with me for ever."

"For ever!" they cried. "My goodness! How marvelous!" And Rabbit said to Mrs. Rabbit, "My dear, just think! We're never going to be shot again in our lives!"

You can't understand idioms such as "My goodness!" and "How marvelous!" by assembling the words they contain in the way that you can understand "The boy went to the zoo" by simply knowing what each word means individually. "My goodness" means something like "That surprises me"; "How marvelous" means essentially "That is surprisingly marvelous"; and "just think" means "If you just think about this for a moment, you'll realize what I'm about to tell you." It's easier to learn phrases like this when you hear them spoken because you hear their emotional content. For example, most people raise their voice when they say something positive such as "How marvelous!" or "How wonderful!" but they lower their voice when they say something negative like "How dreadful!" or "How annoying!"

Listening to audiobooks can also make it easier for children to read higher-level books because the narrator's expression of emotions provides a helpful guidepost for understanding what is going on in a scene. If a character says "you nitwit" angrily, a child can understand that this character is displeased with the person to whom he is speaking even if the child doesn't know the meaning of the word "nitwit."

Obviously, children need to engage in conventional reading as well, particularly as they get older. Nonetheless, it's incorrect to think of audiobooks as simply a temporary crutch for children who have trouble reading. All of my children continue to listen to audiobooks as adults, as do I.

When audiobooks were known as "books on tape," the primary goal was to allow people to enjoy books when they were engaged in other activities such as driving or exercising. Although narrators at this time were sometimes quite good, the advent of digital audiobooks has raised the narration of books to a true art form. Among the many brilliant narrators who are setting a new standard for this work are Katherine Kellgren (*The Incorrigible Children of Ashton Place*; *Bloody Jack*), Davina Porter (*Princess Cora and the Crocodile*); Guy Lockhard (*Ghost*; *As Brave As You*), and Jim Dale (*Harry Potter*; *Peter and the Starcatchers*).

Some publishers are even producing "full cast" readings of books. If you want to get a sense of how radically the quality of audiobooks has been transformed, take the example of *Charlotte's Web*. For many years, the only available *Charlotte's Web* audiobook was narrated by the author, E. B. White. Although White was a brilliant writer and there is some charm to hearing him read his own work, his recording doesn't hold a candle to the full cast recording of *Charlotte's Web* that was released in 2019 featuring Meryl Streep and nearly two dozen other actors. This recording is astonishingly good.

Here are a few suggestions of particularly wonderful audiobooks to get you hooked:

+ *The Three Billy Goats Gruff*, narrated by Stephen Mangan
+ *How the Grinch Stole Christmas!*, narrated by Walter Matthau
+ *The One and Only Shrek! Plus 5 Other Stories*, narrated by Meryl Streep and Stanley Tucci
+ *Peter and the Wolf*, narrated by Jim Dale
+ *Fantastic Mr. Fox and Other Animal Stories*, narrated by Quentin Blake, Hugh Laurie, Stephen Fry, and Chris O'Dowd
+ *How to Train Your Dragon*, narrated by David Tennant

I've listed dozens of additional audiobooks beginning on page 243. Audiobooks are much better and easier to access now than when my children were young. I envy parents who are bringing up children today with this incredible resource.

Many audiobooks can be borrowed from public libraries online through the Overdrive app. However, if you can afford it, many audiobooks are a bargain. Audiobooks for older children are often quite long. You can purchase *Harry Potter and the Order of the Phoenix*, which is 26 hours and 29 minutes long, for a $13.33 credit on Audible. And while audiobooks for younger children are shorter, children will listen to them repeatedly, which is good for them since they understand more each time they do.

As your children become more proficient at reading, they will hopefully become hooked. This often happens around eight years of age. Children have an incredible ability to become totally absorbed in a book. Culver became such an avid reader that when he'd come home with us from a day at the beach, he'd read in the car and get so absorbed in his book that he would just stay in the car for a half hour after we got home rather than interrupt his reading to get out.

Once your child begins to enjoy reading, the trick is to continually nurture this interest. To do this, make sure they always have books available. I would often just scatter the books I got for our kids in the back seat of our car so that they'd pick them up.

The quality of the books your children read matters. Just as the works of Shakespeare, Dickens, and Austen are better than romance novels, some children's books are better than others. Fortunately, the best ones are often the ones they like the most. When teachers at Success Academy read aloud from certain books such as *Charlotte's Web* and *My Father's Dragon*, the students are so quiet, you can hear a pin drop.

Children once learned to read with "readers" such as the classic Dick and Jane readers, which had scintillating text like this:

See Dick.
See Dick run.
Run, Dick, run!

At the time, these books were a useful innovation because they used repetition and short simple words to make them easy to read. Then along came Dr. Seuss, who transformed everything by writing books that were easy to read but were also amusing and inventive. When Dr. Seuss's publisher challenged him to write a best-selling children's book that contained fewer than a hundred unique words,[3] he wrote *Green Eggs and Ham*, a favorite of generations of children. Similarly, *The Cat in the Hat* contains only 236 unique words, but it is fun and subtler than you may realize at first glance. Take this stanza:

> *I know it is wet*
> *And the sun is not sunny.*
> *But we can have*
> *Lots of good fun that is funny!*

On the surface, this sounds like just a cute little rhyme, but there is a lot of instruction Dr. Seuss is packing into it. First, he is teaching children that many nouns have adjectival forms which are created by adding a suffix such as "y" onto the end of them. He is also making a rather subtle play on words here because "fun" and "funny" don't have quite the same meaning in the way that, say, "grass" and "grassy" do.

There is also more psychological depth to Seuss's books than you might appreciate at first glance. For example, as soon as the Cat in the Hat shows up, he declares:

> *A lot of good tricks.*
> *I will show them to you.*
> *Your mother*
> *Will not mind at all if I do.*

The fact that the Cat in the Hat spontaneously reassures the children that their mother will not mind his tricks despite their not having raised this concern is a warning sign that the Cat knows full well that he is going to engage in tricks that their mother will mind. Indeed, some have argued that the Cat represents the children's Freudian ids (their desire) and the fish who objects to the Cat's games represents their superegos (their conscience). While kids don't understand psychoanalytic theory, they absolutely understand the underlying theme that children often want to do things that will get them in trouble.

The last sixty years have been a golden age for children's literature. We have classics such as *Where the Wild Things Are, Stuart Little, Charlotte's Web, James and the Giant Peach, Where the Sidewalk Ends, A Wrinkle in Time,* and more recent additions such as *The Giver, The Book Thief,* and the Harry Potter books. Books like these are great because they are both fun to read and well written. Take this passage from *Harry Potter and the Sorcerer's Stone*:

> *Mr. Dursley was the director of a firm called Grunnings, which made drills. He was a big, beefy man with hardly any neck, although he did have a very large mustache. Mrs. Dursley was thin and blonde and had nearly twice the usual amount of neck, which came in very useful as she spent so much of her time craning over garden fences, spying on the neighbors.*

Notice how inventive J. K. Rowling is with her physical descriptions. Instead of saying that Mr. Dursley has a short neck and Mrs. Dursley has a long one, she describes them as having different amounts of neck, which is a rather curious way to think of necks. In addition, she throws in some interesting vocabulary ("beefy," "craning") and word choices ("director" rather than "manager," "firm" rather than "company"). And finally, the text is elegant and compact.

Or take this passage from *James and the Giant Peach*:

*"Poor Earthworm," the Ladybug said, whispering in
James's ear. "He loves to make everything into a disaster. He
hates to be happy. He is only happy when he is gloomy."*

Here, Roald Dahl is raising an interesting psychological conundrum, which is whether someone who tends to see the negative side of things may actually enjoy being unhappy.

Good books are full of these nuggets: interesting vocabulary and word choices, subtle plays on language, observations that make you think. That's why I can't stress enough that you should have your child read good books. Every time they read a mediocre book, they are wasting time that they could have spent on a really good book, so don't have them read books just because you inherited them, picked them up at a yard sale, or chose them randomly from the library. Educators often like the idea of having children pick out their own books. This works well if the child is selecting books from a collection of high-quality books, but I wouldn't encourage doing this at a library, where many of the kids' books may be quite mediocre.

I've included a list of recommended books (see page 223) because it's hard to find a reliable source of good books. Although Amazon may be a good bet for selecting many products, it's not ideal for picking children's books because people can enjoy books that aren't particularly good for developing a child's intellect. Although children tend to enjoy good books, that doesn't mean that all books that children enjoy are good. I have also found "best of" lists to be uneven and sometimes political in their choice of books. I think the most reliable recommendations can be found in the list of books on Goodreads.com, such as "Best Young Adult Fiction" or "The Next Generation of Children's Classics."

Once your child learns to read, it's important for them to read books at the right difficulty level. Books that are too hard will frustrate them; books that are too easy won't help them advance their ability to read texts with more sophisticated vocabulary and sentence structure. Your child will need these skills in order to enjoy great literature, do well on the standardized tests that will get your child into a good college, and do well in college once there. (Now, there I go again, mentioning the unpleasant topic of standardized tests, but reading good books is a much more enjoyable way to learn vocabulary than memorizing words for the SATs or writing out the definitions of words for homework, which is how vocabulary is typically taught in school.)

When your children get to high school, they should start reading adult literature so they can get used to more complex sentences and subtle ideas. For example, take this passage from George Orwell's *1984*, in which the book's antagonist explains his theory of politics:

> *The German Nazis and the Russian Communists . . .*
> *pretended, perhaps they even believed, that they had seized*
> *power unwillingly and for a limited time, and that just*
> *around the corner there lay a paradise where human beings*
> *would be free and equal. We are not like that. We know that*
> *no one ever seizes power with the intention of relinquishing*
> *it. Power is not a means; it is an end. One does not establish*
> *a dictatorship in order to safeguard a revolution; one makes*
> *the revolution in order to establish the dictatorship. The*
> *object of persecution is persecution. The object of torture is*
> *torture. The object of power is power.*

Reading passages like this can teach children a great deal about writing without their realizing it since much of learning is unconscious. Just as we learn to speak by listening to people speak, we can learn to write by reading other people's writing. Here, the reader is exposed to some quite interesting rhetorical techniques. Notice not only the parallelism of the last three sentences but of the two sentences before that in which negative propositions are followed closely by an associated positive proposition. This is the same technique that Kennedy used in his famous statement "Ask not what your country can do for you; ask what you can do for your country." Once a child becomes familiar with these rhetorical techniques, they can use them in their own writing.

Twentieth-century classics such as *1984*, *The Great Gatsby*, and *Catch-22* are excellent for high school students because they are well written but more easily readable than older classics. However, if your child can eventually stretch themselves to read some of the great classics, they will be exposed to some exceptionally rich prose. Take, for example, the following sentence from Jane Austen's *Northanger Abbey*:

> *It would be mortifying to the feelings of many ladies, could they be made to understand how little the heart of a man is affected by what is costly or new in their attire. . . . No man will admire her the more, no woman will like her the better for it. Neatness and fashion are enough for the former, and a something of shabbiness or impropriety will be most endearing to the latter.*

Not only is there density of challenging vocabulary ("mortifying," "attire," "shabbiness," "impropriety," "endearing"), but the text requires the reader to unpack the meaning of several sentences that are linked together in a rather complicated fashion. One must recognize that the word "it" in the second sentence refers to "costly and new attire" in the first sentence and that "former" and "latter" in the third sentence refer to men and women in the second. In addition, the reader is expected to understand points that are implicit. For example, Austen presumably believes that women prefer that other women appear a little shabby because it makes them feel more fashionable by comparison, but she nowhere expressly states this.

The trick is to get your child to move along the path from Dr. Seuss to Jane Austen gradually enough to avoid frustration but steadily enough to achieve the desired level of mastery. Educators consider an appropriately challenging book—which is called a "just right book"—to be one that has two or three words per page that the child either doesn't know or has trouble decoding. Once you find such a book, then you can determine its level and purchase books at that level or slightly higher. There are several systems for determining reading level, including Fountas & Pinnell, Lexile, and Reading Recovery, and there are various websites that can help you determine the reading level of particular books. It doesn't matter which system you use nor should you become obsessed with making sure that every book your child reads is at exactly the right level. The point, rather, is to keep your child moving in the right direction without pushing them to read books that are so hard that they don't enjoy reading.

Once kids read a book they like, they often like to read more and more books from the same series because they know what they'll get and it's easier for them to understand such books, given that the characters and themes are familiar. It's not a bad thing for a child to read a few books in a series, but it isn't ideal if your child spends six months plowing through all fifty-five volumes of the Magic Tree House series, even though they are good books. They'll benefit more from reading a variety of books.

Finally, you can help your children become better readers by talking to them about the books they read. For example, you might have a conversation like this about Dr. Seuss's famous book *Green Eggs and Ham*:

> **YOU:** Why doesn't Sam want to eat the eggs and ham?
> **CHILD:** Because they look yucky, and Sam thinks that if they look yucky, they will taste yucky.
> **YOU:** And what does he learn?
> **CHILD:** Even though something looks yucky, it could taste good.

YOU: Very good. Sometimes people say that you can't judge a book by its cover. What do you think that means?

CHILD: That something can be good even if it doesn't look good.

At Success Academy, teachers talk about a book not only after they have read it to their students but while they are reading it. Teachers do this to help students become *active readers*: readers who don't just passively take in the words they are reading but think about what is happening in the book they are reading and what they expect to happen. Much of the enjoyment of reading comes from being an active reader, from watching the story unfold against the background of the expectations, hopes, and fears you are forming. When you begin to suspect that one character is falling in love with another, you wonder whether they will and, if they do, whether their love will be requited. When you see that a protagonist has fallen in with bad company, you fear they will be led astray. When a hardworking employee comes up with an idea, you hope that they will get credit for their contribution but fear that a conniving rival may do so.

Since forming these kinds of expectations is critical to becoming a good reader, you should help your children learn how to do so. Here's an example of a conversation you might have with your child after a scene in which a boy named Ben has slammed a door shut after his sister gets a brand-new bike:

YOU: How do you think Ben feels?

CHILD: He's angry.

YOU: Why?

CHILD: Because his sister got a bike.

YOU: Why does that make him angry?

CHILD: Now her bike's better than his and he thinks that's not fair.

YOU: I wonder what he's going to do now.

CHILD: I bet you he takes his sister's bike and hides it.

YOU: Well, let's see.

Once you encourage your children to become active readers when you read to them, they'll start to do it on their own.

13

SCIENCE

The science educator Neil deGrasse Tyson gives parents the following advice for encouraging children's interest in science:

> *Get out of their way. Kids are born curious. Period. I don't care about your economic background. I don't care what town you're born in, what city, what country. If you're a child, you are curious about your environment. You're overturning rocks. You're plucking leaves off of trees and petals off of flowers, looking inside, and you're doing things that create disorder in the lives of the adults around you. And so then, so what do adults do? They say, "Don't pluck the petals off the flowers. I just spent money on that. Don't play with the egg. It might break. Don't . . ." Everything is a don't. We spend the first year teaching them to walk and talk and the rest of their lives telling them to shut up and sit down.*[1]

As a parent, I've definitely experienced that sense of uneasiness as my kids were attracted to whatever seemed the ickiest—worms, caterpillars, frogs—but it's important not just to tolerate your children's curiosity about such things but to encourage it.

Children are natural scientists in part because, unlike adults, they don't take things for granted. So many things happen to us every day that are pretty miraculous but that we've just gotten used to. Take the fact that a 747 with a total weight of just under 1 million pounds can be held up by the air under its wings. I know it's true since I've flown in 747s and they didn't plummet to the ground, but it still seems incredible to me. How can something so light and insubstantial as air hold up a million-pound airplane? Or take the fact that a single gallon of gasoline can push a one-ton car about 30 miles. Where does all of that energy come from? Or if you want something even closer to home, take a look at your hands. They seem solid, but in fact, they are mostly empty space. They consist of atoms which in turn consist of protons and neutrons (which are very small) and electrons (which have no size at all). If you could take all of the protons, neutrons, and electrons in your hands and pack them together as closely as possible as if you were making a snowball, that snowball would be so small that you couldn't even see it. In other words, our hands are just empty space with the barest traces of matter. Given that, why do they seem so solid and why doesn't light just shine through them? And for that matter, why does light shine through glass?

Albert Einstein once observed that there are two ways to live your life: "One is as though nothing is a miracle. The other is as though everything is a miracle." Children and scientists take the latter approach. Scientists do so because they work at the cusp of human knowledge. As a result, they are profoundly aware of what is unknown and sometimes even unknowable. Take gravity. Physicists know objects are attracted to one another and that the force of this attraction can be calculated by multiplying the mass of these objects and dividing that product by the distance between them squared. However, scientists have no idea what causes gravity, why it exists, or where it comes from. Neither do they know whether space goes on infinitely, what dark matter is, or why light travels at 186,000 miles per second rather than, say, 185,000 miles per second or 187,000 miles per second. Some hypothesize that there are parallel universes in which the laws of physics are different.

Children take the attitude that everything is a miracle because, unlike most adults, they haven't gotten so used to things that they take them for granted nor have they accepted the proposition that there may be a limit to what they'll be able to understand about science. As a result, many children have an insatiable curiosity to understand everything. They want to know why water freezes when it gets cold, why blowing on fire makes it hotter, and why magnets stick to refrigerators. When children are trying to understand these things, they are engaged in the same fundamental enterprise as an astrophysicist who is trying to understand black holes. America's greatest physicist, the late Richard Feynman, once observed that he felt "like someone who was given something wonderful when he was a child, and he's always looking for it again. I'm always looking, like a child, for the wonders I know I'm going to find."[2]

One easy way to nurture your child's natural curiosity is simply to answer their questions, which is what Feynman's father did. One day when Feynman was quite young, he noticed that when he pulled on his toy wagon, a ball inside of it rolled toward the back, so he asked his father why this happened. Feynman's father explained to him that the ball was actually just staying in the same place as a result of inertia. Feynman tested this explanation by looking from the side of the wagon while moving it and saw that his father was right, that the ball was staying in the same place relative to the ground.

Feynman's father wasn't a scientist nor did he have a college degree. What he did have was an encyclopedia and a willingness to help his son understand it, as Feynman lovingly recounts in an interview he gave toward the end of his life:

> *He used to sit me on his lap when I was a kid and read out of the [*Encyclopedia Britannica*]. [H]e would read . . . "the dinosaur" so and so "attains a length of so and so many feet." He would always stop and he would say, "You know what that means? It means, if the dinosaur's standing on our front yard, and your bedroom window . . . is on the second floor, you'd see out the window his head standing looking at you.*[3]

Nowadays, it's much easier for you to answer your children's scientific questions. Rather than having to wade through an encyclopedia, you can simply type them into Google or even ask your smart speaker. When you do this, you are modeling what you want your children to do, which is to learn how they can answer their own questions and to understand how a single observation can set them on a scientific journey in which they learn far more than the answer to the question they posed at the outset.

If you fear you won't enjoy helping your children understand science, I urge you to give it a chance. You may find that learning science of your own volition, without the pressure of knowing you will be tested on it, is far more enjoyable than it was when you last studied it in school. Moreover, there are so many incredible scientific resources available today. Take a few minutes to watch Brian Cox's YouTube video on black holes, Professor Chris Bishop's video on rocket science, or the video by Dianna Cowern (AKA "Physics Girl") about gravitational waves.

You don't need lots of scientific equipment to teach your children about science. It simply requires looking around and wondering why things work the way they do. Albert Einstein discovered the theory of relativity by engaging in what he called "thought experiments." For example, he imagined that he was standing next to train tracks when two bolts of lightning struck a moving train simultaneously, one of which struck the front of the train and one of which struck the back of the train. He realized that if someone was standing on the train, that person would see that lightning bolt that struck the front first because they would be moving toward the light. From this thought experiment, he realized that space and time are relative to your position and motion, the core of his Special Theory of Relativity.

Like Einstein, your children can learn a lot about science simply by thinking about the world they see around them. For example, most children notice that some things float while others sink. If your child asks you why, you may want to help them figure it out for themselves by giving them a collection of objects to test, such as a baseball, a tennis ball, a basketball, a Ping-Pong ball, and a golf ball. You might ask your child to guess which ones will float before testing them. If your child concludes that heavier things sink, you might ask whether the golf ball is heavier than the basketball. Your child may then figure out that what determines whether an object floats is not just its weight but rather its density, the ratio of its weight to its volume. Even if your child can't express the concept of a "ratio," they may nonetheless develop a more intuitive concept of density. What's important is that your child starts thinking.

Another everyday experience you can talk about with your child is why rubbing one's hands together makes them warmer. It's because, just as hitting a bell with a hammer makes it vibrate, rubbing your hands together makes the atoms in them vibrate. The vibration of the atoms in an object are what makes it hot. You can also see this effect by bending a paper clip or a metal hanger back and forth. You will find that it quickly becomes hot because your bending causes the atoms to knock into each other.

Of course, atoms are too small to see them move but there are various ways in which we can tell they are moving. For example, if you put drops of food coloring into two glasses of water, one of which is hot and one of which is cold, the food coloring will spread more quickly in the hot water than the cold water because the atoms in the hot water are moving much more than those in the cold water.

Kids are particularly fascinated by things that seem counterintuitive since these things challenge their conception of the world. For example, take the question of where a tree's nutrition comes from. You may think the answer is the soil, but it isn't. Ninety-five percent of a tree's matter comes from the carbon atoms that trees extract from the air. Trees take in carbon dioxide, strip off the carbon atoms, and emit oxygen. If you explain this to your children, they are likely to remember it because it's counterintuitive that a tree can be made from a substance as light as air. A few days later, you'll probably hear your child say to some friend, "Do you know that trees are made of air?"

When a child asks questions about the sun or digs up worms, it is easy to think that their childish curiosity has little to do with the practice of science by adults but nothing could be further from the truth. Like Peter Pan, most scientists are children who refuse to grow up.

Although your child will have many questions of their own, you may want to spur their scientific interest by suggesting some yourself:

+ Where does the sun go at night?
+ Why do snowflakes fall more slowly than raindrops?
+ What are shadows? Why do shadows disappear when the sun goes behind the clouds?
+ Why does a golf ball sink in water but a tennis ball float?
+ How is your thumb different from your big toe, and why is that important?
+ Why do you sink to the bottom of a pool if you blow as much air out of your lungs as possible? (Try it!)

+ Why do the pupils in your eyes get smaller if you look at something bright?
+ Why do people blink their eyes?
+ Most people naturally float in water, but if they swim deep enough, they'll sink. Why?
+ Why does a baseball go farther than a tennis ball when you throw them?
+ Why do your hands have the lines that give you fingerprints?
+ When you spin a hard-boiled egg, it keeps on spinning. When you spin an uncooked egg, it falls over right away. Why?
+ Does a ball roll faster down a steeper hill? Why?
+ There are people all around the world. Why don't the people on the bottom fall off?
+ Why is it that you usually don't see the moon during the day but sometimes you can?
+ Why do we breathe more heavily when we run?
+ Why does our skin get darker in the summertime?
+ Why doesn't it hurt when your hair gets cut?
+ Why don't oil and water mix?
+ Why are things different colors?
+ Why does your breath turn to fog in the winter?
+ There are two high tides a day. One happens when the earth turns so the water is nearest to the moon. What causes the other high tide?
+ Why are there little hairs in your ears?
+ Why do we have two ears? Two eyes?
+ Why do squirrels have tails?
+ Why do people have eyebrows?
+ Why are dogs' noses moist and cool?
+ Why do dogs pant?
+ Why do rubber bands exercise force? Where do they get that energy from?

+ When you let air out of a bicycle tire, why does it feel cold?
+ Why does 70-degree ocean water feel cold when 70-degree air doesn't?
+ Why does a ball bounce but not a brick?

There are thousands of questions like this that you could ask. All you need to do is start observing things around you.

Another way to encourage your child's interest in science is to take them to science and natural history museums. One of Eric's earliest memories is seeing a demonstration at Boston's museum of science in which a feather and a ball were dropped in a vacuum. Both objects fell equally fast, which demonstrates that the only reason that heavier objects fall more quickly than light objects is wind resistance. Actually seeing a feather plummet to the ground before your eyes conveys this in a way that words or even video can't.

Feynman describes an early memory of a trip with his father to a museum of natural history where he saw rocks with grooves that had been made by a glacier:

> I remember the first time going there, when he stopped there and explained to me about the ice moving and grinding. I can hear the voice, practically. Then he would tell me, "How do you think anybody knows that there were glaciers in the past?" He'd point out, "Look at that. These rocks are found in New York. And so there must have been ice in New York. . . ." A thing that was very important about my father was not the facts but the process. How we find out.[4]

You can also develop your child's scientific talents by performing experiments. At Success Academy, we do science experiments five days a week beginning in kindergarten, and children love them. You don't need a lot of time or fancy equipment to do science experiments. They can be done in a few minutes with things around the house. Here are a few examples:

+ Put a plastic water bottle with a tablespoon of water in it into the microwave for a minute *with the cap off*; then using an oven mitt take the bottle out, put on the cap, and put it under cold water. The bottle will then collapse. What happened was that when you heated the bottle, the water turned into steam, which pushed out most of the air in the bottle. Then, when the bottle cooled, the steam turned back into water, which takes up less space than steam and therefore caused a vacuum. Given the vacuum inside the water bottle, the surrounding air pressure made the bottle collapse.

+ Place a lit match or tea candle on a plate and then cover it with an upside-down glass or Pyrex measuring cup. After a minute or so, the flame will go out. That is because fire is the process of combining carbon with oxygen to make carbon dioxide. When all of the oxygen underneath the glass has turned to carbon dioxide, the reaction stops. Through this experiment, your child can learn a great deal: that wood and wax have carbon in them; that air has oxygen in it; that fire occurs when oxygen combines with carbon; that this chemical reaction produces heat.

+ Put a tall glass sideways into a sink full of water, then turn it upside down underneath the water and pull it nearly out of the water. You will see the water doesn't fall down into the sink. That happens because the atmospheric pressure pushes down on the water in the sink, which pushes this water up into the glass.

There are many books on scientific experiments and activities for children but make sure the activities you choose are ones that really convey scientific information. Children don't learn much, for example, from making a vinegar and baking soda volcano. They find it cool, but it doesn't tell them anything about volcanoes. A better experiment is to combine a small amount of baking soda and vinegar in a measuring cup, and after the foam has subsided, pour out the invisible air onto a tea candle. The tea candle will go out because the baking soda and vinegar created carbon dioxide. The idea that there is this invisible substance that can extinguish a fire will fascinate a child.

Here are some books that have good experiments:

+ *201 Awesome, Magical, Bizarre, & Incredible Experiments* (Janice VanCleave)
+ *Chemistry for Every Kid: 101 Easy Experiments That Really Work* (Janice VanCleave)
+ *Awesome Science Experiments for Kids: 100+ Fun STEAM Projects & Why They Work* (Crystal Chatterton)
+ *The Everything Kids' Science Experiments Book: Boil Ice, Float Water, Measure Gravity—Challenge the World Around You!* (Tom Robinson)

While you can do experiments with things around the house, you may also wish to buy some scientific equipment. Einstein said that one of the things that sparked his interest in physics was a compass that was given to him when he was five years old. He found it fascinating that there was some invisible force that made the arrow point north no matter how much he turned the compass.

Here are some scientific tools I'd recommend you purchase for your child:

+ A microscope
+ USB microscope attachment (for looking at and taking pictures of insects)
+ A magnifying glass

+ Magnets
+ Loupe magnifier (for looking at insects)
+ Snap Circuits (electrical experiment kits)
+ Arduino kit (to build simple computers)

Beyond a few basic scientific instruments, I'd be cautious about buying many science "kits." Many of them aren't really educational. Solar car kits, for example, have become ubiquitous because kids like cars and parents like the idea of kids learning about solar energy, but unfortunately the child doesn't learn much. All that happens is that the child assembles a few pieces and wires and sees the car move. One simply can't learn much about a solar chip from looking at it. Many science kits have descriptions like this: "Bright colorful experiments to maintain engagement." The "engagement," however, should flow from the fact that the experiments teach you something about science, not that they are "bright" and "colorful." You are better off just doing the experiments in the books listed above, which often require only ordinary household items.

Here are a few science kits that are unusually good because they really focus on helping children understand scientific concepts:

+ Thames & Kosmos Physics Workshop
+ Thames & Kosmos Electricity & Magnetism Science Kit
+ Thames & Kosmos Motors & Generators
+ Thames & Kosmos Structural Engineering: Bridges & Skyscrapers
+ Thames & Kosmos Architectural Engineering, Science Experiment & Model Building Kit
+ Educational Insights Sprout & Grow Window Plant Growing Kit
+ EUDAX School Physics Labs Basic Electricity Discovery Circuit and Magnetism Experiment Kits
+ Makeblock mBot Coding Robotic Kit

Another way for your children to learn about science is to have them spend time in nature, particularly when they are quite young. Encourage them to pick up a decaying log and examine the bugs underneath with a magnifying glass, look at pond water under a microscope, or see how many different types of leaves they can gather. Try to avoid worrying about kids getting too dirty—the dirt is usually where the fun stuff can be found!

Feynman was particularly fascinated with how ants managed to establish straight lines to food so he did an experiment in a bathtub to find out:

> *I put some sugar on the other end of the bathtub. . . . The moment the ant found the sugar, I picked up a colored pencil . . . and behind where the ant went, I drew a line so I could tell where his trail was. The ant wandered a little bit wrong to get back to the hole, so the line was quite wiggly, unlike a typical ant trail.*
>
> *When the next ant to find the sugar began to go back, I marked his trail with another color. . . . This second ant was in a great hurry and followed, pretty much, the original trail, but because he was going so fast, he would go straight out, as if he were coasting, when the trail was wiggly. Often, as the ant was "coasting," he would find the trail again. Already it was apparent that the second ant's return was slightly straighter. With successive ants the same improvement of the trail by hurriedly and carelessly following it occurred. I followed eight or ten ants with my pencil until their trails became a neat line right along the bathtub.[5]*

Feynman did this experiment not when he was a child but when he was an adult! If you have an image of Feynman drawing colored lines in his bathtub as essentially an overgrown kid, you're not far off the mark.

Another way to nurture your child's scientific interests is to give them scientific books, and there have never been so many good ones available. The British publisher DK has long put out wonderful nonfiction books for children that are getting better and better. In 2017, DK came out with a new book called *Human Body*, one of the Knowledge Encyclopedias it is producing in conjunction with the Smithsonian Institution. These newer books use computer technology to develop images that are far more realistic looking and detailed than the images in its *Visual Dictionary*, which was published a quarter of a century earlier. The *Human Body*'s section on the circulatory system, for example, has striking images of an artery in which you can see its many different layers, the valve that prevents blood from flowing backward, and the three different types of blood cells. A child could spend hours poring over a book like this, and there are already several books in this Knowledge Encyclopedias series including a book on space. DK's Eyewitness books are also wonderful.

The National Geographic Society has also produced fantastic children's books that combine photographs from their enormous catalog with quite informative text. Take, for example, their book on sharks. On one page is a striking photograph of a hammerhead shark viewed from below with an arrow pointing to the clearly visible teeth. The text states, "If a shark loses a tooth, a new one moves forward to take its place." It also notes:

[A] shark is a fish. But a shark is not like other fish. Sharks do not have bones. They have soft cartilage instead. . . . Cartilage is light, strong and rubbery. The tip of your nose is cartilage. Can you feel how soft it is?[6]

The books in the National Geographic Readers and Little Kids First Big Books series cover innumerable topics, including the solar system, the ocean, and of course, animals. An advantage of the books in the Readers series is that they are "leveled," so you can pick a book at your child's reading level. Kids will also love the *Ultimate Bugopedia: The Most Complete Bug Reference Ever.* All these books have such strong visual elements that a child may be willing to stretch themselves to tackle more complicated texts than they otherwise would.

The Max Axiom, Super Scientist series is a collection of comic books that give excellent introductions to various scientific topics such as chemical reactions, states of matter, genes, and bacteria.

A good test for whether your child will learn something from a science book is whether you do. For example, here's a passage from a terrific book that tells me several things about birds I didn't know:

> *All raptors come with three features as standard equipment: powerful vision, sharp talons to grasp and kill prey, and a hooked beak to kill prey and tear it apart. . . .*
>
> *Each type of bird has evolved with a beak that helps it do special jobs. Osprey beaks have a hook to help them grip the fish the Ospreys eat. A Prairie Falcon has a notch in its beak, called a falcon tooth, which slips neatly between the neck bones of its prey. The bird kills its prey by breaking its neck. The Snail Kite's slender beak ends in a long hook, perfect for pulling snails out of their shells. . . . Just like our fingernails, raptors beaks constantly grow, but they have a razor-sharp edge from constant use.*[7]

This text is just chock-full of information as well as wonderful vocabulary and good turns of phrase ("evolved," "grip," "slips neatly," "slender," "razor-sharp edge").

Because science books typically don't have a narrative, kids can read them a few pages at a time. For this reason, these would be great books to leave in the back of your car or at the breakfast table and to bring with you when you are taking a bus or visiting the doctor's office.

There are many wonderful texts out there, but to get you started, here are a few more especially strong books in addition to those listed above:

+ *Start Exploring: Gray's Anatomy: A Fact-Filled Coloring Book* (Fred Stark)
+ *Encyclopedia Prehistorica Dinosaurs: The Definitive Pop-Up* (Matthew Reinhart and Robert Sabuda)
+ *Encyclopedia Prehistorica: Sharks and Other Sea Monsters* (Matthew Reinhart and Robert Sabuda)
+ *Bugs: A Stunning Pop-Up Look at Insects, Spiders, and Other Creepy-Crawlies* (George McGavin)
+ *The Way Things Work Now* (David Macauley)
+ *National Geographic Kids Why?: Over 1,111 Answers to Everything* (Crispin Boyer)
+ *What If?: Serious Scientific Answers to Absurd Hypothetical Questions* (Randall Munroe)
+ *A Little History of Science* (William Bynum)

As your child gets older, there are many texts written for adults that are readable by high school students or gifted middle school students. These include:

+ *Sapiens: A Brief History of Humankind* (Yuval Noah Harari)
+ *The Immortal Life of Henrietta Lacks* (Rebecca Skloot)
+ *A Short History of Nearly Everything* (Bill Bryson)
+ *The Martian: A Novel* (Andy Weir). A work of science fiction that is long on science.
+ *The Selfish Gene* (Richard Dawkins)
+ *Einstein: His Life and Universe* (Walter Isaacson)

Many science channels on YouTube are also a terrific resource for high school and gifted middle school students. These include:

+ **VERITASIUM:** A physicist addresses a broad variety of scientific topics such as the world's lightest solid, gravitational waves, and the reverse Leidenfrost effect.

+ **REAL ENGINEERING:** Addresses contemporary engineering challenges and successes with an emphasis on airplanes, spaceships, civil engineering, and material sciences.

+ **IT'S OKAY TO BE SMART:** A channel by PBS Digital Studios on a variety of scientific topics.

+ **PHYSICS GIRL:** This channel's name evokes its lighthearted presentation, but the content is quite sophisticated.

+ **THE ROYAL INSTITUTION:** Lectures and videos that are particularly entertaining on topics such as how we know that the earth's magnetic poles have flipped, whether viruses are alive, and how the ancient Greeks shaped modern mathematics.

+ **CLOSER TO TRUTH:** Interviews with leading thinkers about physics, philosophy, and religion, addressing topics such as how our universe began, how multiple universes are generated, whether the cosmos is a computer, and whether consciousness is an illusion.

+ **THE COMPLETE FUN TO IMAGINE WITH RICHARD FEYNMAN:** This is a single video in which Richard Feynman explains the origins of his interest in science.

There are also many worthwhile science programs that can be streamed. These are included in the back of the book, beginning on page 216.

14

MATH ENRICHMENT

When my dad was in middle school, he noticed from the times table that the square of a number (e.g., 4 times 4, which equals 16) was always 1 greater than the product of two numbers that are 1 less and 1 more (e.g., 5 times 3, which equals 15). He asked his teacher about whether this pattern was true not only of the numbers on the times table but of all numbers. My father's teacher made it clear to him that he viewed his question as an annoying distraction since it didn't pertain to the lesson. While this reaction was plainly wrong, the truth is that even a good teacher may find it hard to help children pursue their own mathematical intuitions since the class needs to cover certain material together. As a parent, you are in a far better position to help your children develop their mathematical intuition since you don't have to worry about dozens of kids at the same time.[*]

---

[*] The answer to my father's question, incidentally, is that this pattern does hold and the proof is fairly simple: $(x+1) \times (x-1) = x^2 + 1x - 1x - 1 = x^2 - 1$.

Every child has the capacity for mathematical intuition, but they are more likely to develop it if they are encouraged. Just as the Wizard of Oz helped Dorothy understand that she already had the power to return to Kansas by clicking her heels, you can help your children discover and develop the mathematical intuition they already possess.

I realize that many parents are intimidated by math because they haven't had good experiences with it themselves. If that's true in your case, it's probably because you weren't taught in a way that helped you access your mathematical intuition. If there were other students in your classes who, like my father, had such strong mathematical intuition that they were able to access it no matter how poorly they were taught, that may have led you to feel that you lacked mathematical talent but that doesn't follow. It simply demonstrates that, like most of us, you needed good instruction to access your mathematical intuitions.

Here is the most important thing to understand about math in particular and learning in general. For many people, the experience of struggling to understand something makes them feel stupid, but it's actually a sign that you are learning. If you go to the gym and you don't breathe heavily and feel your heart beating, that's not a good thing. Sure, it may be a sign that you're in good shape, but the point of going to the gym isn't to prove that you are in good shape but to get in better shape. The same is true of intellectual struggle. Struggling is not a sign that there is something wrong with you but rather that you are doing something that is good for you. So if something feels like it's hard to understand, just remember what Success Academy's chess teacher said: It's supposed to be hard. If you can have that attitude yourself and impart it to your children, it will immeasurably improve your ability to enjoy learning math.

To start your child on their mathematical journey, you can familiarize them with numbers and basic mathematical operations by playing games such as Sorry!, backgammon, and Monopoly. In addition, here are some games that are specifically designed to teach math skills:

+ **SUM SWAMP:** Teaches addition and subtraction.
+ **24:** Players are required to reach the number 24 by using addition, subtraction, multiplication, and division on the numbers they are given. More fun than it sounds.
+ **SUMOKU:** A crossword-style board game for kids ages six to ten.
+ **MATH FOR LOVE: PRIME CLIMB:** A board game for children around ten years old and up.
+ **PROOF!:** Game for children eight and older. Children compete to be the first to make an equation out of nine numbers.

Once your child has the basics down, they will be in a position to understand more advanced concepts such as fractions. Parents and educators owe a debt of gratitude to whoever came up with cutting pizzas into eight slices since it greatly helps with teaching fractions. Moreover, since your child is a captive audience when they're eating pizza, it can be a great time to ambush them with some math instruction. Here is a conversation you might have with them:

YOU: How many slices are there in a pizza?

CHILD: Eight.

YOU: Right. We call those eighths. When you cut something up into eight pieces, we call each piece an eighth. Suppose that instead of cutting a pizza into eight slices, we cut it into four big slices. What do you think you'd call those?

CHILD: I don't know.

YOU: I think you can figure it out. If you cut a pizza into eight pieces, we call those pieces eighths. If we cut them into four pieces, then we'd call them . . . .

CHILD: I don't know. Fourths?

YOU: Exactly. Sometimes people also call them quarters but it's the same thing. Quarters are fourths. Suppose you cut a fourth into two pieces, what would you get?

CHILD: I don't know.

YOU: Okay, let me draw it for you. Here's my pizza pie. Now, I'm cutting it like this into four pieces. What are those pieces called?

CHILD: Fourths.

YOU: Right. Very good! Now, I'm going to draw a line down the middle of each of these four pieces to cut them in half. How many pieces do we have now?

CHILD: Eight.

YOU: Right. So what do you get when you cut a fourth into two pieces?

CHILD: Eighths?

YOU: Very good! Now, there's something very strange about fractions. What's bigger, four or eight?

CHILD: Eight.

YOU: Right. Now, what's bigger, a fourth or an eighth?

CHILD: An eighth.

YOU: Well, let's look at the picture we drew. What's the fourth?

CHILD: This.

YOU: And what's the eighth?

CHILD: This.

YOU: Right, so which is bigger?

CHILD: The fourth.

YOU: Right. So let me ask you this. If four is smaller than eight, how come a fourth is bigger than an eighth?

CHILD: I don't know.

YOU: Well, tell me, how do you make a fourth?

CHILD: You cut the pizza into four pieces.

YOU: Right. And how do you make an eighth?

CHILD: You cut the pizza into eight pieces.

YOU: So can you tell me why an eighth is smaller than a fourth?

CHILD: Because the more pieces you cut the pizza into, the smaller the pieces get.

YOU: Exactly. That's why even though eight is bigger than four, an eighth is smaller than a fourth.

A child probably won't make all of this progress in a single sitting, but they don't have to. If you just take a few minutes to cover even a bit of this material, your child will make a lot of progress. That's because you are planting seeds in the fertile soil of your child's mind. The next time your child sees a pizza pie, they may remember what you said about fourths and eighths and even start making observations themselves.

Schools often teach children "procedural" math, meaning that they teach children to memorize the procedures for performing mathematical operations rather than helping them understand why those procedures work. The problem with this approach is that children often forget these procedures or confuse them with one another. Your child will be much better off if you can help them understand why these procedures work. One of the best ways to do that is to substitute simpler numbers for more complex ones. Suppose, for example, that your child gets the problem $3/7 + 3/14$. If they don't remember how to solve this problem, they probably won't have much intuition about what the solution will be. However, suppose that instead of $3/7 + 3/14$, they now add $\frac{1}{4}$ and $\frac{1}{2}$ of a pizza. They can probably visualize the fact that $\frac{1}{2}$ of a pizza plus $\frac{1}{4}$ of a pizza is equivalent to $\frac{3}{4}$ of a pizza. If you ask them what happened to the $\frac{1}{2}$ of a pizza, they can likely tell you that they turned it into $\frac{2}{4}$. Once they understand that, then it shouldn't be too hard for them to realize that just as they turned the half into fourths, they can turn the sevenths into fourteenths by splitting the sevenths in half. Thus $3/7$ becomes $6/14$, which, added together with $3/14$, equals $9/14$.

Similarly, suppose they are given the problem $11/13 \times 49/83$. Again, your child can try to do simpler problems such as $1/2 \times 3/4$. Imagine that you had to split $3/4$ of a pizza with a friend. How many slices would you each get? Hopefully, you (and your child) will realize that $3/4$ of a pizza is the same as 6 slices (since each quarter has 2 slices), so if you split them, you will each get 3 slices, which is $3/8$. So now you know that $1/2 \times 3/4 = 3/8$. Now think about that intuitively. What's happening is that you have the same number of pieces but each of those pieces is half as big because the denominator is twice as large. And once they know that, they can hopefully see that they can get this answer ($3/8$) by multiplying the numerators ($1 \times 3 = 3$) and denominators ($2 \times 4 = 8$). Now they can perform that procedure on the problem $11/13 \times 49/83$. Once your child gets used to that technique, it can be applied surprisingly often.

When children get beyond these basics, many become interested in very large numbers. For example, because your child knows that 1 million is a very large number, they will probably be interested to hear that the sun is 93 million miles away.[1] If they want to understand what 1 million is, you could explain it to them by asking them to imagine 1,000 rows of 1,000 pennies. They might also be interested to know that the closest star, Alpha Centauri, is 25 trillion miles away.[2] You can explain that 1 trillion pennies would be 1 million piles of 1 million pennies. You could also explain to your child that the ocean contains 352 quintillion gallons of water[3] and that 1 quintillion is 1 million times 1 million times 1 million. Understanding these large numbers is a way for your child to understand our base 10 system with numbers that interest them. One trillion is a lot more interesting than 100!

Children are also fascinated by the concept of infinity. To introduce your child to one of the most famous mathematical paradoxes involving infinity, tell them to stand across the room from something, say a couch, and then to walk halfway toward it. Ask them whether they've reached the couch. (No, obviously.) Then ask them to walk half of the remaining distance and ask them whether they've reached the couch now. (Again, no.) Do this a couple more times and then ask them how long it will take them to reach the couch. The answer is forever.

You might also ask your child whether there are more whole numbers or odd numbers. On the one hand, it seems like there are twice as many whole numbers as odd numbers; on the other hand, there are infinitely many whole numbers and infinitely many odd numbers, so it would seem like there should be the same number of odd numbers as whole numbers. There is no "right" answer to this question because it depends on how you define "more." Galileo thought it was meaningless to say that one infinity could be larger than another, but more recently, mathematicians recognize one infinity can be larger than another.

If you expose children to mathematical ideas like this, it will get them to start thinking about math. Ironically, what interests kids is much closer to what professional mathematicians do than what children learn in school. Real mathematicians don't sit around doing long division and multiplying fractions. Rather, they think creatively about mathematical problems. One of the most famous unsolved problems is known as the twin prime problem. Prime numbers that are two numbers apart—such as 5 and 7, 11 and 13, and 41 and 43— are known as twin primes. They become increasingly rare as you go farther along the number line. For example, there are four sets of twin primes between 1 and 20 (3 and 5, 5 and 7, 11 and 13, 17 and 19) but only one between 20 and 40 (29 and 31). The twin prime problem is whether there is an infinite number of twin primes or whether there is some number beyond which twin primes simply no longer exist. It is believed that the twin primes go on forever—that there is an infinite number of them—but nobody has yet been able to prove this.

Another fascinating problem is called Hilbert's Hotel after the mathematician who came up with it. Imagine that you are the desk clerk at a hotel with an infinite number of rooms, each of which is numbered (1, 2, etc.) and has a guest in it. A bus shows up with 100 more guests. You need to assign rooms to each of the new guests while ensuring that all the existing guests also have rooms. You can't assign Room 1 to the first new guest unless you find a new room for the guest who was previously in Room 1, and then you'd need to find a new room for the guest in that room. You need to come up with a system to ensure that if any guest comes up to the desk and asks for their room number, you can tell them what room they are in and be sure that no other person is in that room. Can you figure out a way to do that? And if you can figure that out, can you figure out a way to accommodate an additional infinity guests? And if you can figure that out, can you figure out what to do if an infinite number of busses suddenly shows up, each of which has an infinite number of passengers? (FYI: If you figure that one out, consider a career in mathematics.)

The point of explaining something like this is to get your kids to think about math and realize how interesting it is. Humor is another tool for helping kids appreciate math.

Here, for example, is a joke that sheds light on the mathematical concepts of rounding and approximation:

> *A museum visitor who was admiring a Tyrannosaurus rex fossil asked a museum employee how old it was. "That skeleton's sixty-five million and three years, two months, and eighteen days old," the employee replied. "How can you be so precise?" asked the visitor. "Well, when I started working here, I asked a scientist the exact same question, and he said it was sixty-five million years old—and that was three years, two months, and eighteen days ago."*

One of Abbott and Costello's most famous skits is about math:

ABBOTT: Pretend you're forty years old and you're in love with this little girl that's ten years old. . . . You're four times as old as that girl, and you can't marry her, so you wait five years. Now you're forty-five. The little girl is fifteen. Now, you're only three times as old as that little girl. So you wait fifteen years more. Now, the little girl is thirty, you're at sixty. Now, you're only twice as old as that little girl.

COSTELLO: She's catching up.

ABBOTT: Yes, yes. Now here's the question. How long do you have to wait until you and that little girl are the same age? . . .

COSTELLO: If I keep waiting for that girl, she'll pass me up. She'll wind up older than I am.

ABBOTT: What are you talking about?

COSTELLO: She'll have to wait for me!

ABBOTT: Why should she wait for you?

COSTELLO: I was nice enough to wait for her![4]

As your kids get older, you can start asking them some more complicated math riddles or questions to encourage their math abilities. Here are a few suggestions:

+ A boy says: "Two years ago, I was three times as old as my brother. In three years, I will be twice as old as him." How old is he?

+ There are three positive numbers that, when you multiply them together, you will get the same result as when you add them. What are they?

+ Suppose you took a bottle of water and made it twice as big in every direction. How much more water would it hold?

+ If you drop a penny from a building, it will travel 16 feet in 1 second. How far will it fall in 2 seconds?

+ My twin lives at the reverse of my house number. The difference between our house numbers ends in 2.

What are the lowest possible numbers for our houses?

+ Two trains are on the same track a distance 100 kilometers apart heading toward one another, each at a speed of 50 kilometers per hour. A fly starting out at the front of one train flies toward the other at a speed of 75 kilometers per hour. Upon reaching the other train, the fly turns around and continues toward the first train. How many kilometers does the fly travel before getting squashed in the collision of the two trains?

If you'd like more suggestions for how to teach your children math, here are two wonderful books on this topic:

+ *Let's Play Math: How Families Can Learn Math Together—and Enjoy It* (Denise Gaskins)
+ *Math You Can Play Combo: Number Games for Young Learners* (Denise Gaskins)

In addition, here are some fun math texts for kids:

+ *Primary Grade Challenge Math* (Edward Zaccaro)
+ *Challenge Math: For the Elementary and Middle School Student* (Edward Zaccaro)
+ *What's the Point of Math?* (DK): A wonderful illustrated book that looks at how math is used in everyday life.

Here are two fun math books that could be read by gifted middle school or high school students:

+ *The Magic of Math: Solving for x and Figuring Out Why* (Arthur Benjamin)
+ *Mathematics: A Human Endeavor* (Harold Jacobs)

Finally, here are three internet resources of great value for your child:

+ **BRILLIANT.ORG:** This website provides online instruction in math, science, and computer programming. It is in a class by itself. Rather than teaching through videos or written explanations, Brilliant.org uses interactive problems to help children learn intuitively. If your child has the discipline to work independently, they'd probably learn more about math, science, and computer programming if they dropped out of school and spent time using this website.

+ **3BLUE1BROWN:** This YouTube channel is somewhat like Khan Academy, but it has better production values and higher overall quality. It primarily focuses on high-level math although it also covers some other STEM topics. The math is at the level of a somewhat gifted high school student.

+ **VSAUCE:** This YouTube channel covers a variety of scientific and mathematical topics such as how to count past infinity and the famous and dastardly counterintuitive Monty Hall Problem.

15

POETRY

The poem "A Visit from St. Nicholas" begins:

'Twas the night before Christmas, when all through the
*   house*
Not a creature was stirring, not even a mouse;
The stockings were hung by the chimney with care,
In hopes that St. Nicholas soon would be there;
The children were nestled all snug in their beds;
While visions of sugar-plums danced in their heads;
And mamma in her 'kerchief, and I in my cap,
Had just settled our brains for a long winter's nap,
When out on the lawn there arose such a clatter,
I sprang from my bed to see what was the matter.

Think of how much less amusing this poem would be if it were written in prose: if it were stripped of its wonderful rhymes—of "beds" and "heads," of "cap" and "nap," and of "clatter" and "matter"—and of its ingenious waltz-like meter in which every third syllable is stressed:

> '*Twas the* **night** *before* **Christ***mas, when* **all** *through the* **house**
> *Not a* **crea***ture was* **stir***ring, not* **even** *a* **mouse***;*

Imagine it without its creative use of language: if the children had been "tucked in" bed rather than "nestled all snug in their beds"; if they had "dreamt of presents" rather than having "visions of sugar-plums danc[ing] in their heads"; if the parents had "slept" rather than "settled [their] brains for a long winter's nap"; if the father had heard a "noise" rather than a "clatter"; or if he had "risen" from bed rather than "sprang" from it.

Consider for a moment what an incredible feat a poem like this is. The author is telling a good story and deploying creative language while simultaneously obeying the poem's strict meter and coming up with nifty rhymes. That's why I find that reading a good poem is like watching somebody juggle while riding a unicycle.

I particularly enjoy it when humor is combined with poetry. Often the humor derives from the author's ingenuity in meeting the demands of the poetic form. For example, take this limerick in which the author begins with a word for which it would seem virtually impossible to find a rhyme—Nantucket—but manages to find a way to squirm out of the trap he has set for himself:

> *There once was a man from Nantucket*
> *Who kept all his cash in a bucket.*
> *But his daughter, named Nan,*
> *Ran away with a man*
> *And as for the bucket, Nan took it.*

Similarly notice the ingenious way in which the great comedic poet Ogden Nash manages to come up with a rhyme for "Sahara":

The ostrich roams the great Sahara.
Its mouth is wide, its neck is narra'.
It has such long and lofty legs,
I'm glad it sits to lay its eggs.

Not surprisingly, there are many funny children's poems. For example, the great Shel Silverstein wrote a poem called "Sick," which begins:

"I cannot go to school today,"
Said little Peggy Ann McKay.
"I have the measles and the mumps,
A gash, a rash and purple bumps.
My mouth is wet, my throat is dry,
I'm going blind in my right eye."

Fortunately, despite a truly astonishing set of maladies, including a bent spine, shrunken brain, and a temperature of 108, Peggy manages to make a miraculous recovery—when she learns it's Saturday!

Another great children's poet is Jack Prelutsky, whose poem "Be Glad Your Nose Is on Your Face," begins:

Be glad your nose is on your face,
not pasted on some other place,
for if it were where it is not,
you might dislike your nose a lot.
Imagine if your precious nose
were sandwiched in between your toes.

Notice how Prelutsky makes his poem more interesting by using words like "pasted" and "sandwiched" rather than simply "placed." A poem like this teaches children how using good vocabulary can improve their writing. So does this stanza from a poem by Bill Watterson:

My mother has eyes in the back of her head!
I don't quite believe it, but that's what she said.

. . .

I think she must also have eyes on her rear.
I've noticed her hindsight is unusually clear.

Virtually every line of this stanza is a gem. First, Watterson makes fun of a child's literal interpretation of the phrase "eyes in the back of her head," but the best joke of all is that "hindsight" suggests that one literally has eyes on one's behind. This joke encourages a child to recognize that words with a common root such as "hind" have related meanings.

I'd recommend giving your children poetry in small doses. Instead of saying, "We're going to read poetry for the next hour because it's educational," tell them that you found this really funny poem and read it to them at breakfast. If they want to hear another one right away, great. If not, well, Rome wasn't built in a day.

Here are some of my favorite poems for kids:

+ "Daddy Fell into the Pond" (Alfred Noyes)
+ "The Pig" (Roald Dahl)
+ "Bleezer's Ice Cream" (Jack Prelutsky)
+ "Mother Doesn't Want a Dog" (Judith Viorst)
+ "Paul Revere's Ride" (Henry Wadsworth Longfellow)
+ "How Doth the Little Crocodile" (Lewis Carroll)
+ "Casey at the Bat" (Ernest Thayer)
+ "Macavity: The Mystery Cat" (T. S. Elliot)
+ "Dream Deferred" (Langston Hughes)
+ "If—" (Rudyard Kipling)

Here are some wonderful collections of poetry for children:

+ *Read-Aloud Rhymes for the Very Young* (Jack Prelutsky and Marc Brown)

+ *Poetry Speaks to Children* (Elise Paschen)
+ *Where the Sidewalk Ends* (Shel Silverstein)
+ *Revolting Rhymes* (Roald Dahl)
+ *The Random House Book of Poetry for Children* (Jack Prelutsky)
+ *The Oxford Illustrated Book of American Children's Poems* (Donald Hall)

I would suggest you encourage your child to recite poetry as a present for your birthday or for Father's or Mother's Day since the process of committing a poem to memory allows one to understand it better. If your child finds memorizing too onerous, a dramatic reading is also quite nice.

You should also encourage your children to write their own poetry. In high school, Culver wrote a terrific rap that explains the Big Bang. It began:

Where do we come from, why do we exist?
How did the universe come from the abyss?
A dot exploded into everything—
today it's referred to as the Big Bang.
13.8 billion years ago
all energy and matter was set to blow.
It was all contained in a unitary dot
and when it blew up it was incredibly hot:
approximately 10 billion degrees.
The fundamental forces included gravity,
strong force, weak force, electromagnetism.
The universe complete? No atoms missing!
Particles called quarks were the sole matter
but then they combined, matter got fatter.
Electrons, neutrons, protons, these form atoms.
Hydrogen was the first element formed but it certainly wasn't
the last one.

I'd encourage you to listen to this rap on YouTube because it's even better with the accompanying music.[1]

One year, Culver and Eric collaborated on a poem they read at a family camp named Sandy Isle. People who'd been going to Sandy Isle the longest got first pick in choosing their cabins. One of the nicest, called Buena Vista, was assigned to a man named Larry Koff, who had been going for decades. Our family was assigned to a cabin named Wee Hoose. The camp's system for assigning cabins inspired Culver and Eric to write a poem that they performed at the camp's talent show, which purported to tell the story of what happened when Eric visited Koff's cabin:

> *Wee Hoose had seemed so nice, so quaint,*
> *but Buena Vista made me faint.*
> *With envy now my heart was full,*
> *injustice rank and horrible.*
> *Then I learned the awful truth,*
> *first pick went to the long in tooth.*
> *Right then I formed an evil plot:*
> *to stay in Wee Hoose, I would not.*
> *Larry Koff, Larry Koff!*
> *I'd find a way to knock him off.*
> *"Larry," I said, "you like to sail?"*
> *"Let's grab a boat, and bring some Ale."*
> *The wind blew strong, so when I jibed*
> *The boom knocked Larry over the side*
> *Soon the water was over his head.*
> *It seemed his jacket was full of lead.*

In the poem, Eric proceeds to knock off others who have seniority, then ends as follows:

> *One by one, they met their fate,*
> *All because I could not wait.*

Then at last, I was first in line.
Buena Vista now was mine.
I loved my home, I loved my view,
I held a party for everyone new
There was a guest who stayed awhile,
a young man new to Sandy Isle.
I asked which house he'd been assigned.
Wee Hoose, he answered; he seemed resigned.
And that would be the end of our tale
but then, he said, "You like to sail?"

The following year, Eric collaborated with Hannah on a sequel that they performed in which Eric gets Buena Vista but is haunted by the ghost of Larry Koff. Both of these poems were big hits, not because they were the most original or brilliant poems in the history of the English language but rather because people really appreciate poems that relate to their individual situations. If you can get your child to write a poem for your spouse's birthday, it will be appreciated even if it's pretty corny.

If the idea of poetry made your eyes glaze over before you read this chapter, I hope that you now realize how much fun it can be!

16

CORE KNOWLEDGE

n 1988, two psychology professors performed an experiment in which they measured how well children understood a passage narrating a half inning of a particular baseball game. After assessing the students' reading skills and baseball knowledge, the professors asked the students to read the passage about baseball and reenact it by moving toy baseball players around a board. The researchers found that poor readers who knew a lot about baseball did better than strong readers who knew very little about baseball.[1]

This study illustrates the importance of knowledge in comprehension. It isn't sufficient for children merely to learn how to read or even to become "critical thinkers"; rather, they must also learn a body of knowledge that will allow them to understand what they read and, more generally, to function in society. The most prominent advocate of this idea is Professor E. D. Hirsch, who has dubbed the information people are expected to know "core knowledge."

Since people will take for granted that you have core knowledge, it typically won't be explained to you and it's difficult to function well without it. To illustrate this point, consider the following lead sentence from an article published shortly after Syria had used nerve gas on its own citizens:

> *Defense Secretary Jim Mattis sought on Thursday to slow*
> *down an imminent strike on Syria, reflecting mounting*
> *concerns at the Pentagon that a concerted bombing*
> *campaign could escalate into a wider conflict between*
> *Russia, Iran and the West.*[2]

Suppose you're a congressional aide and your boss hands you this article and asks you to assess the validity of the Pentagon's concerns. Even understanding the above sentence at its most basic level requires you to know several facts: what a defense secretary is; what the Pentagon is; what the "West" and a "strike" refer to in this context; and why bombing Syria would affect our country's relationship with Russia and Iran. And to go beyond a mere literal understanding toward a more nuanced and critical assessment of the Pentagon's concerns, you'd need far more information. You'd need to understand that Russia and the United States are both nuclear powers and that nuclear bombs have immense destructive capacity; that the U.S. and Russia were in a cold war for the last half of the twentieth century and still have fraught relations; that Iran has aligned itself with Russia and has had a troubled relationship with the United States ever since the shah of Iran was overthrown in 1979; that Syria's current government has a history of human rights violations; that there is a principle of international law known as sovereignty, which generally prohibits countries from interfering with one another's internal affairs but that human rights violations are considered a sufficient justification for doing so; and that the question of whether the United States should place its concerns for the human rights of other countries' citizens ahead of its own national interests is hotly debated. It would also be helpful to think about the Syrian situation against a variety of historical precedents such as the genocides in Germany, Cambodia, Rwanda, and Yugoslavia and perhaps to think about this within the context of our country's historical flirtation with isolationism beginning with George Washington's warning against foreign entanglements. And I could go on and on.

An opponent of Hirsch might argue that a person who is a literate critical thinker can simply look up all the relevant information, but that isn't realistic. To obtain a solid background in everything I've listed above and all the other points I haven't would take months of research and study. Whether you are a congressional aide advising your boss, a journalist writing a story, or simply a citizen trying to decide whether the president you elected is doing a good job, you won't have months to do research every time you read an article. Moreover, even if you did, you wouldn't know where to start looking because you wouldn't know what you needed to understand. Yes, you could ask somebody else to guide you, but that's just passing the buck because you'd be relying upon somebody else to have the relevant knowledge.

In short, to function in a modern society, you need to master a body of knowledge, not just learn how to read and think. Your child's home life influences this. In fact, researchers have found that children from underprivileged homes who read at grade level through third grade often suffer a fourth grade slump, which is likely due to a lack of core knowledge. To get to a second grade level, children need to learn to decode, but beginning around third grade, books become more complicated and require more background knowledge and more advanced vocabulary.

Unfortunately, many children fail to pick up background knowledge because they learn things in such a superficial way that they don't retain them. That reality is captured by the proposal once made by the *Saturday Night Live* character Father Guido Sarducci for a "five-minute university" at which you'd only learn what students typically remember five years after they graduate from college.

In Spanish, for example, you'd learn, "*¿Como esta usted? Muy bien.*"
Economics? Supply and demand. Business? Buy and sell for more.

Sadly, there is considerable truth to Sarducci's joke. Some students don't retain much of what they learn in school because they learn it in such a superficial way that it becomes meaningless. For example, one popular American history textbook devotes one paragraph each to the Mayans and the Incas. The former, the text notes, built "pyramids, large stone temples, palaces, and bridges" while the latter built "massive buildings and forts . . . made of huge stone blocks." So little context is given that the information is virtually meaningless and impossible to remember. Imagine taking a test a month later in which you had to remember whether the Mayans were the ones who built "massive buildings" or the ones who built "large stone temples."

By contrast, Hirsch's Core Knowledge Foundation has a 65-page booklet just on the Mayan, Aztec, and Incan civilizations.[3] Because the author has more space to work with and assumes a higher reading level, the text is more interesting. Take, for example, the following excerpt:

> *The largest buildings in Maya cities were pyramids that*
> *also served as temples. . . . From their size, it is clear that*
> *religion was a key part of Maya life. Maya pyramids rose*
> *high above the surrounding treetops. Maya pyramids were*
> *some of the tallest structures in the Americas until 1902.*
> *That year, the twenty-two-story Flatiron Building was*
> *constructed in New York City.*

This text is better because it communicates how large Mayan pyramids were with an image (taller than the treetops), how remarkable this was historically (nothing taller was built until 1902), and the broader significance of this for the Mayans (religion was important to them).

E. D. Hirsch has a very specific program for precisely what facts your child should learn at what age. While his books are a great resource, parents should not feel they have to follow his guidelines methodically. If your children read a variety of good nonfiction books, their knowledge will eventually add up. Moreover, if you choose books that your children like, it will be a lot easier to get your children to read them. For example, take this passage from Howard Zinn's *A People's History of the United States*:

> *Arawak men and women, naked, tawny, and full of wonder, emerged from their villages on the island's beaches and swam out to get a closer look at the strange big boat. When Columbus and his sailors came ashore carrying swords, speaking oddly, the Arawak ran to greet them, brought them food, water, gifts. He later wrote of this in his log:*
>   *"They . . . brought us parrots and balls of cotton and spears and many other things. . . . They willingly traded everything they owned. . . . They do not bear arms and do not know them, for I showed them a sword, they took it by the edge and cut themselves out of ignorance. They have no iron. Their spears are made of cane. . . . They would make fine servants. . . . With fifty men we could subjugate them all and make them do whatever we want."*
>   *These Arawak of the Bahama Islands were much like Indians on the mainland, who were remarkable . . . for their hospitality and their belief in sharing. These traits did not stand out in the Europe of the Renaissance, dominated as it was by the religion of popes, the government of kings, the frenzy for money that marked Western civilization and its first messenger to the Americas, Christopher Columbus.*

Zinn's text puts you in the moment with its terrific descriptions, allows you to read Columbus's original words, and has a strong anecdote about the Arawaks injuring themselves on a sword that will help the reader remember that the Arawaks didn't have swords or iron.*

Some children find it hard to enjoy reading nonfiction because they don't view the people they are reading about as real. There are ways to overcome this obstacle. When I was a child, I greatly enjoyed coloring books because they helped me begin to imagine what it was like to live in an earlier age. Coloring in the outlines felt like I was bringing the images alive. Here are some historical coloring books:

+ *Ancient Egypt Coloring Book* (Peter Der Manuelian)
+ *Life in Ancient Rome Coloring Book* (John Green and William Kaufman)
+ *Life in Ancient Greece Coloring Book* (John Green and Stanley Appelbaum)
+ *A Coloring Book of Tutankhamun* (Cyril Aldred)
+ *A Coloring Book of Queen Nefertiti* (Bellerophon Books)
+ *Life in Old Japan Coloring Book* (John Green and Stanley Applebaum)
+ *The Medieval Castle* (A. G. Smith)
+ *Life in a Medieval Castle and Village Coloring Book* (John Green)
+ *Castles of the World Coloring Book* (A. G. Smith)
+ *Historic American Landmarks* (A. G. Smith)
+ *Life in Colonial America* (Peter F. Copeland)
+ *Story of the American Revolution Coloring Book* (Peter F. Copeland)
+ *Western Pioneers Coloring Book* (Peter F. Copeland)
+ *Story of the American Revolution Coloring Book* (Peter F. Copeland)

---

* *Some historians are critical of the views Zinn expresses in his book so I'm not necessarily endorsing it, but there's no contesting that it's well written.*

+ *Great African Americans Coloring Book* (Taylor Oughton)
+ *Story of the Civil War Coloring Book* (Peter F. Copeland)

In all of these books, the images have accompanying descriptive text. By taking a few minutes to read aloud the text accompanying a picture, you can make the experience of coloring more meaningful for your child.

When your child gets to around the third grade, they can start reading What Was? and Who Was? books, which are both engaging and informative. For example, the book *What Were the Salem Witch Trials?* begins:

> *In the winter of 1692, trouble came to the Village of Salem in the Massachusetts Bay Colony. Witch trouble!*
> *Suddenly, two girls got a strange illness. Their bodies twitched and shuddered. They spoke nonsense and seemed to be choking. They said they were being pinched by something invisible. Soon more girls in Salem began acting strangely, too. If this was an illness no one could find a cure.*[4]

This is pretty nifty writing and certainly far more engaging than most history textbooks!

For a large series of books, the What Was? and Who Was? books have surprisingly high standards for writing. To catch children's attention, they typically begin with a particularly interesting anecdote. For example, *What Was the Age of Exploration?* begins with a nice scene in which Vasco Núñez de Balboa escapes his creditors by sneaking aboard a ship inside a barrel. Similarly, *What Was the Gold Rush?* begins with a true story about a boy who finds a seventeen-pound rock that his family uses as a doorstop for several years until someone figures out that it's a gold nugget worth nearly half a million dollars. The books in these series cover many historical events and periods such as the Battle of Gettysburg, Pearl Harbor, the

Underground Railroad, and the Great Depression, as well as various important historical figures. Hannah tells me that she really enjoyed reading these books.

When students reach the fourth grade, they can start to read Eyewitness books, which address such topics as the American Revolution, the Civil War, and ancient Egypt. Children like these books because they are heavily illustrated. I would especially recommend *History of the World Map by Map* (DK) because it can help children learn geography while they are learning history.

In addition, David Macauley has many strong, well-illustrated books, including:

+ *City: A Story of Roman Planning and Construction*
+ *Castle*
+ *Pyramid*
+ *Underground*
+ *Cathedral: The Story of Its Construction*

If your child has a particularly strong interest in history, they may also wish to read *Story of the World: History for the Classical Child*, a four-volume set. These books are well written and can be read by elementary school children, although some children may be intimidated by their size.

As your child gets older, they can read many longer nonfiction books such as *Claudette Colvin: Twice Toward Justice,* a favorite of students at Success Academy, which tells the story of a girl who refused to give up her seat on a bus before Rosa Parks did. Many young adult books use a specific historical incident as an opportunity to give children a lot of information about the surrounding historical events. For example, in the wonderful book *Torpedoed: The True Story of the World War II Sinking of "The Children's Ship,"* the author includes much more background information about World War II than she would have included if she'd written it for an adult audience.

Here are some additional suggestions for nonfiction books for the middle school grades:

+ *Charles and Emma: The Darwins' Leap of Faith* (Deborah Heiligman)
+ *Carry On, Mr. Bowditch* (Jean Lee Latham)
+ *Unbroken: An Olympian's Journey from Airman to Castaway to Captive* (Young Readers Edition) (Laura Hillenbrand)
+ *The Boys Who Challenged Hitler: Knud Pedersen and the Churchill Club* (Phillip Hoose)
+ *Behind Rebel Lines: The Incredible Story of Emma Edmonds, Civil War Spy* (Seymour Reit)
+ *Chasing Lincoln's Killer* (James L. Swanson)

In 1935, E. H. Gombrich, who went on to become a famous art historian, wrote *A Little History of the World*, a book that has become a classic. In recent years, Yale University has commissioned a series of Little Histories texts in the spirit of Gombrich's book. They cover a variety of topics including religion, U.S. history, economics, archaeology, literature, and philosophy. Most of these books are quite good.

By the time your children reach high school, they will hopefully be able to start reading adult nonfiction. This is very important because high schools tend to neglect teaching children more contemporary information. For example, people should understand at least in general terms what mutual funds are or how sports teams increasingly use complex statistical analysis or how modern political campaigns are run. Fortunately, many lively and informative nonfiction books have been written in recent years. These include books about finance (*The Big Short*; *Too Big to Fail*); business (*The House of Morgan*; *Steve Jobs* by Walter Isaacson); politics (*All the President's Men*; *Parting the Waters: America in the King Years 1954–63*); science (*A

Short History of Nearly Everything; *What's Gotten Into You: The Story of Your Body's Atoms from the Big Bang Through Last Night's Dinner*); and economics (*Thinking, Fast and Slow*; *Freakonomics: A Rogue Economist Explores the Hidden Side of Everything*). And, of course, there has been an avalanche of great historical books in recent years, including Ron Chernow's biographies of George Washington and Alexander Hamilton, David McCullough's *John Adams* and *1776*, Doris Kearns Goodwin's *Team of Rivals: The Political Genius of Abraham Lincoln*, Mary Beard's *SPQR: A History of Ancient Rome*, and Tom Wolfe's *The Right Stuff*. My children particularly enjoyed the books *Freakonomics* by Steven D. Levitt and Stephen J. Dubner, *Bad Blood* by Michael Carreyrou, and *Elon Musk: Tesla, SpaceX, and the Quest for a Fantastic Future* by Ashlee Vance. I have recommended nonfiction books your child may wish to read in the list that starts on page 233.

I realize that your children may have difficulty finding the time to do reading outside of school, particularly when they reach high school, but you should urge them to make some time for it even if it's only a couple of hours a week. It's important that your children get in the habit of independent reading so they can become lifelong learners.

Obviously, there are other activities in which your child can engage that will increase their knowledge. They include many activities described elsewhere in this book, such as involving your child in dinnertime conversation and watching documentaries. In addition, your children may wish to consider joining their school's debate team if it has one. Both Hannah and Dillon did so, and I was amazed at how much they learned from it.

17

SCHOOL

n fifth grade, Supreme Court Justice Sonia Sotomayor decided that she wanted to get better grades but didn't know how. As she describes in her autobiography:

> *[S]ome kids were smarter than others; some kids worked harder than others. But as I also noticed, a handful of kids, the same ones every time, routinely got the top marks. That was the camp I wanted to join. But how did they do it?*
>
> *I decided to approach one of the smartest girls in the class and ask her how to study. Donna Renella looked surprised, maybe even flattered. In any case, she generously divulged her technique: how, while she was reading, she underlined important facts and took notes to condense information into smaller bits that were easier to remember; how, the night before a test, she would reread the relevant chapter. Obvious things once you've learned them, but at the time deriving them on my own would have been like trying to invent the wheel.[1]*

Unfortunately, most students are passive learners. Rather than figuring out what they need to do to learn the material, they simply do what their teachers require. This is unfortunate not only because children learn less this way but also because they don't learn how to become masters of their own fate. School is preparation for life. Children shouldn't wait until they graduate to start learning how to pursue their goals.

As Justice Sotomayor suggests, many of the things that will help a student learn better are quite obvious. Take math class. If your child is studying for a unit test, they should focus on the problems they got wrong on their homework. If they don't, they'll probably make the same mistakes again. After figuring out where they went wrong, they should do similar problems. Likewise, when they are studying for a final, the best place to start is with the problems they got wrong on the unit tests. This is all pretty obvious, but it's amazing how many students simply go over everything they've learned rather than focusing on their weaknesses. Just a modest amount of strategically focused effort can produce far better results.

Another good technique is outlining. Eric and I learned this technique from a high school teacher we both had named Elaine Grist, who required that students outline the material in the textbook they were using. This technique has two benefits. First, it reduces the material to a shorter form that is easier to study. Second, organizing the material logically forces the student to engage with the text in a way that helps them understand it better. Here is what an outline of George Washington's biography might look like:

GEORGE WASHINGTON

I. Military Service
   A. French and Indian War (1755–1758)
      1. Part of Seven Years War between Britain and France
      2. Promoted to Brigadier General

   B. Continental Army (1775–1783)
      1. Commander in Chief
      2. Major Battles
         a. Siege of Boston
         b. . . .
II. Presidency
  A. . . .
  B. . . .

Organizing material in this way is a much better technique than simply underlining passages.

It's also important that your child plan their time, which you should help them with. For example, they should look at their calendar to see if they are going to have several things due around the same time. Waiting until the end of the semester to finish a term paper is a bad idea if they'll also need time to study for finals.

Try to get your children into the habit of doing their work efficiently. When they are young, it may be a good idea to use a timer. The point isn't for your child to rush but rather to focus their attention on getting the work done. They will ultimately find their work much more tolerable if they can get it out of the way. You also want to encourage your children to do their work when they have energy. If your child waits until Sunday night to do their homework for the weekend, it will take them twice as long because they'll be tired. It's far better to do their work on Saturday and Sunday mornings when they are full of energy. For this reason, it's also wiser for them to tackle harder assignments and longer-term projects on the weekends than after school on weekdays.

I also think that your children should have specific goals for the grades they will get at school. Some people think grades are a distraction because students should be focused on learning for its own sake. While I appreciate that philosophy, I don't think it reflects human nature. People work best if they are striving for results, and it's hard for a child to strive for an abstract goal like becoming a better writer. It's easier for them to strive for a specific goal such as getting a particular grade on an assignment or in a class. Therefore, you should tell your children that it's important that they get good grades in school and that you will work with them to set goals for themselves. At the beginning of the year, ask them how well they think they can do in each class if they give it their best effort. You want them—not you—to set the goals, so they have bought into what they think they can reasonably do. If you think that goal is low, you may want to wait until a subsequent semester to push them to set a higher goal. Once your child has set their goal, you should talk with them regularly about whether they are achieving it.

How hard you want to push your children to do well is in part a matter of personal philosophy, but let me give you something to compare it to. When I visited a boarding school in China a few years ago, I saw that the children worked virtually all day every day. Hour after hour, they attended classes and did their homework. They got virtually no time off during the day besides the time for eating meals and bathing. When it was time for lights out, they went to bed and started it all over again the next day.

While I don't believe that children should be subjected to this type of regimen, the standard for work in the United States is pretty low: 70 percent of thirteen-year-olds do less than one hour of homework per evening.[2] That wouldn't trouble me if they were spending the rest of their time productively by writing software (as Bill Gates did when he was a child), making home movies (as Steven Spielberg did), or starting businesses (as Warren Buffett did), but most aren't. Instead, research shows, most children are spending their spare time on social media, watching television, and playing video games.

So you should push your child to do well in school in part because schools in America just don't require that much work. In addition, academic success is important for your child's future. Some teenagers will argue that they intend to work in fields that don't require conventional academic credentials but doing poorly in school can close off a lot of potential options. For example, since the odds of becoming a professional athlete are so slim, children who aspire to this profession should have a plan B. Earning a college degree will ensure that their plan B is a job that provides them with a decent income and that is at least related to their interests such as becoming a coach or working in a team's back office.

In all likelihood, you already know that your children should do well in school, but I'm telling you this in case you have a child who is claiming that school is irrelevant to their plans and you begin to doubt yourself. Don't! They are wrong.

Children won't always enjoy school, and that's something that they just need to accept. Life isn't always fun. It's important to gain the discipline of doing things you don't enjoy. However, there are limits. If your child truly hates school, that can be a sign that something is wrong, particularly if your child is intellectually engaged at home. One possibility is that your child's school isn't challenging enough. If so, your child may need to skip a grade. At Success, we skip many kids who are more advanced than their peers. Many schools resist this on the grounds that a child's "social-emotional development" needs to be considered. I think that should rarely be an obstacle. If it were really so critical that every child be at the exact same level of social-emotional development as their peers, then kids would often be left back or skipped based on that criterion since social-emotional development varies so much between children. Claims that a child shouldn't be skipped due to their social-emotional development are usually just an excuse for schools not to do something that is administratively inconvenient for them.

If your child's school won't skip them or it doesn't solve the problem, you may need to take a more radical tact. One possibility is a private school, but if you can't afford that or get a scholarship, consider homeschooling. If you're up for it, most homeschoolers have great success, but you'll need a bigger book! Fortunately, there are many out there from which to choose:

+ *Rethinking School: How to Take Charge of Your Child's Education* (Susan Wise Bauer)
+ *The Well-Trained Mind: A Guide to Classical Education at Home* (Jesse Wise and Susan Wise Bauer)
+ *Homeschooling Odyssey* (Matthew James)
+ *Teaching from Rest: A Homeschooler's Guide to Unshakable Peace* (Sarah Mackenzie)

There are also many good websites on homeschooling:

+ cathyduffyreviews.com: Reviews of books and educational resources including homeschooling curricula.
+ thehomeschoolscientist.com: Science experiments, activities and materials.
+ raisingupwildthings.com: Materials to help inspire children to appreciate nature.

I would also recommend these homeschooling resources even if you don't homeschool your children since homeschooling parents often have great ideas and insights into education.

18

LEARNING DISABILITIES

The actress Keira Knightley has a fascinating story about how she learned she had a learning disability:

[W]hen I was about five . . . I was absolutely [at the] top of my class and I was reading in front of people, and I thought of myself as being unbelievably intelligent. And then when I was six, [my teachers] realized that I hadn't been reading at all, and that my mum read to me all the time, we had lots of books at home, and I'd memorized them. And it was only when somebody finally gave me a book that my mum hadn't read me that they realized that I hadn't been reading at all and couldn't read at all. . . . I went from being at the top of the class to the absolute bottom of the class and I still remember what a shock that was and I still remember how I saw myself completely differently from that moment.[1]

It turned out that Knightley had dyslexia, a learning disability that makes it difficult to "decode" written words. Dyslexic children have trouble assembling individual letters into words and recognizing simple "sight words" such as "her" and "the" that most children can read without having to sound them out. Common symptoms of dyslexia are writing words or letters backward and confusing the letters "b" and "d." An estimated 20 percent of people have dyslexia, although most aren't diagnosed, particularly if their symptoms are mild.

Since decoding is a gateway skill for reading, it's easy for children with dyslexia to feel that they'll never learn how to read or that, even if they do, they'll never read well. With very rare exceptions, that simply isn't true. Some people may decode faster than others, but once a child gets to a certain foundational level of decoding, their progress in reading depends less on how well they can turn letters into words than on how well they can turn words into meaning. Take, for example, this Shakespearean couplet: "Love looks not with the eyes, but with the mind; and therefore is winged Cupid painted blind." Most third graders could decode this text, but few of them could understand it.

After a child learns to decode, progressing in reading depends on a child's vocabulary and their ability to untangle complex sentences and infer subtle meanings. For this reason, most dyslexics tend to catch up with their peers in the third or fourth grade. Eric had a typical case of dyslexia. He wrote his name backward and had great trouble learning to read, but once he got to third grade, he took off and was soon reading above grade level. While a small portion of dyslexics read more slowly even as adults, there are also positive benefits from dyslexia. Eric maintains that it has made him a better writer because he tends to read and write by hearing words in his head rather than going straight from sight to meaning. The director Steven Spielberg says that his tendency to read scripts slowly as a result of his dyslexia leads him to understand them better than most people.

The greatest danger from dyslexia isn't the intellectual impact but the emotional scars it can leave. The actor Henry Winkler said that as a result of his difficulty learning to read, "I felt horrible growing up. I always felt on the outside. I always felt like I was stupid, like I couldn't figure out concepts."[2] Winkler carried around this shame far into adulthood. Although he could read well enough to memorize scripts, he couldn't read out loud fluently at "table reads." He was so embarrassed by this that he would devise complex stratagems to cover up his difficulty with reading.

Many people of Winkler's generation felt this way because dyslexia was rarely diagnosed then. Winkler didn't learn that he had dyslexia until his stepson was diagnosed with it and Winkler realized that he had it, too. Interestingly, the exact same thing happened to the actress Cher when her son was diagnosed with dyslexia.

In recent years, schools have gotten much better at diagnosing dyslexia and it makes a huge difference. When Winkler was in school, he was told he was "stupid and lazy, and . . . that I was not living up to my potential." Compare this to Keira Knightley's experience many years later:

> *The teachers that I had recognized how important it was that I knew that the points that I was making and . . . the stories that I was telling were great and were valid and were interesting [so] they gave me a mark for that [and a separate mark for] spelling and the punctuation. . . . Because when you split them up, you're not saying you're not intelligent enough. What you're saying is . . . you may not be a brilliant speller, you may not be a very fast reader . . . but you'll be better at different things. And I think that's unbelievably important to know as a kid.[3]*

As a result of this more enlightened approach, Knightley didn't end up feeling a terrible sense of shame or inferiority.

The most important thing you can do for your child is to make sure that their dyslexia doesn't rob them of their confidence and self-esteem. If your child becomes discouraged or ashamed, it can lead them to dislike school and reading, which can then turn into a vicious cycle. To prevent this, you need to reassure your children that their dyslexia won't prevent them from succeeding in school and in life. You also need to let them know that they aren't defined by their ability to read, that there are many important intellectual skills such as the ability to tell a story or a joke, to play a game well, or to draw a picture.

Of course, your child is more likely to become anxious or embarrassed about their learning disability if you have those feelings yourself. To help you avoid having that happen, let me reassure you that there is very little correlation between children's learning disabilities and their long-term academic success as students, and even less with their success in life. This is true not only of dyslexia but of other disabilities such as Asperger syndrome and attention deficit hyperactivity disorder (ADHD). People suffering these learning conditions not only learn to compensate for them, they often have related intellectual gifts. Among the many gifted and successful people who have dyslexia, for example, are Steven Spielberg, Richard Branson, John Irving, Steve Jobs, Anderson Cooper, and Jay Leno. Those who have Asperger syndrome include Elon Musk, Dr. Michael Burry (the famed *Big Short* investor), actors Anthony Hopkins and Dan Akroyd, and singers David Byrne and Courtney Love.

So if your child is diagnosed with a learning disability, the first thing you should do is to take a deep breath. The second thing you should do is to ask for help. If your child has a learning disability, they are legally entitled to extra help, so don't hesitate to raise these issues with your child's school and ask for your child to be evaluated. Some parents are worried about their kids being labeled, but I truly believe those concerns are unfounded. Most educators really want to get children the resources they need, not to limit their opportunities. These resources can make a big difference for a child.

When you get help, don't expect immediate results. Helping a child with a learning disability isn't like fixing a car. A learning disabilities specialist won't change your child, they will help your child to change, and that takes time. A child won't learn to read ten times as fast if they see a learning disabilities specialist ten times as often. So you need to be patient. If you are too impatient, your child may start to feel more anxious about their disability.

Although you should get professional advice and help for your child, here are some ways you can help your child at home. Children with dyslexia may benefit from listening to audiobooks. This seems to have helped my daughter, Hannah, who inherited some of Eric's dyslexia. Part of the challenge for dyslexics is that reading requires that you do several things simultaneously: decode the words; turn those individual words into meaning (just as you would if you were listening to someone speak); and then analyze that meaning (e.g., figure out whether a character in a story who says that she really likes a scarf her grandmother has given her is being honest or just telling a white lie). In Hannah's case, she found it hard to enjoy reading when she was young because the extra intellectual energy she had to devote to decoding meant she had less left over for the other work that reading requires. She, therefore, preferred listening to audiobooks, which was very good for her intellectually because it allowed her to develop the other skills that reading requires: e.g., learning to understand complex sentences, building her vocabulary, and becoming an active reader who analyzes the text as they read it. Because Hannah continued to develop these skills as she learned to decode, she excelled at reading when she eventually overcame her problems with decoding.

In addition, Henry Winkler has cowritten a charming series of books for children with dyslexia that are based in part on his own experiences as a child. His Here's Hank series is printed in a font called Dyslexie that was designed to be easier for children with dyslexia to read. His Hank Zipzer series is for older children.

If your child is suffering from ADHD, you may want to consult a specialist about medication if other approaches don't work. I realize that many people are uncomfortable with the idea of using medication to change a child's behavior, but my experience is that some kids really need it. Here is what one woman who suffers from ADHD said about it:

> *The first time I took my medication, it was like putting on glasses and realizing I could see without squinting. I could focus. And without changing anything, my GPA went up a full point. Honestly, it was kind of miraculous. By 14, I had friends that liked me. By 15, I had published my first poem.*[4]

Some people have expressed concern that children are being overmedicated. They claim that medication can be avoided if you just use appropriate pedagogical techniques such as giving children gold stars for good behavior, allowing them to take breaks, and sitting them in the front of the classroom so the teacher can "redirect" them if they get "off task." We use these techniques at Success Academy and they work with most children who are overactive or fidgety, but some kids just don't respond to them. No amount of gold stars, redirection, and breaks gets them to a point where they can learn well and participate appropriately in a conventional classroom. We have found that medication can have a huge positive impact on these children. It doesn't make them docile or sleepy or rob them of their individuality. Instead, it helps them to focus the way that other children can. It's been said that for someone with ADHD, "it's like your brain keeps switching between 30 different channels and somebody else has the remote."[5] Giving a child medication gives them the remote.

As a result of a disability or any number of other factors, some children have difficulty keeping up with their classmates. For example, our older son's language skills developed more slowly than our other children's, and I suspect that was in part because he didn't have any older siblings with whom he could speak when he was young. Gender can also play a role. It is well known that boys tend to lag behind girls in language acquisition. If you divide children into "late talkers" and "early talkers," boys represent more than 70 percent of the late talkers and just 30 percent of the early talkers.[6] Not surprisingly, therefore, boys often lag behind girls in the early grades, particularly if they are relatively young for their class. If you have a boy who just barely made the age cutoff for kindergarten and who also happens to be delayed in his language acquisition by 6 months, he may enter kindergarten with language skills that are 18 months behind those of a girl in his class who just barely missed the age cutoff to enter kindergarten the prior year.

In the case of an individual child, their progress in school may be affected by any number of factors, including age, gender, home environment, and learning disabilities, whether obvious and diagnosed, or mild and undiagnosed. Whatever the reason for it, if a child falls so far behind their classmates that they can't understand the material the class is covering, this can lead to a vicious cycle since the student will fall even further behind and may develop a negative attitude toward school. When this happens, the best solution is often for the student to repeat a grade. This will allow the student to get back to a level at which they can follow the material and start learning again.

Unfortunately, some parents view a child's being held back as a punishment. It isn't. Instead, it's intended to allow the child to reset at a level where they can succeed academically. In my experience, the self-confidence children gain from succeeding academically every day far outweighs whatever disappointment and shame they may initially feel about being held back—particularly if you don't tell your child that being held back is shameful! At Success Academy, one of our students who was held back in his final year of elementary school spoke at his graduation ceremony the following year. This is what he said:

> *This time last year, I saw my class graduate without me, which made me feel disappointed, like I failed myself, but [this year] I read more, I asked my teachers more questions, and so with hard work, I was able to score a hundred percent on almost every math test and met my goals in [English]. When you fail, remember to be confident in yourself, ask teachers for help, and never think that you are a failure or that the game is over because of one setback. . . . As Vince Lombardi once said, it does not matter how many times you get knocked down but how many times you get back up.*

Think of how impressive it is that this ten-year-old boy was willing to publicly acknowledge, in front of all his classmates and their parents, that he'd been held back. Rather than being embarrassed by it, he beamed with pride at how he'd overcome this obstacle, and he was right to do so. I would bet my bottom dollar on this student becoming successful in life. Everybody encounters obstacles; what's important is having the bravery to face them and the work ethic to overcome them.

When parents are told their child needs to be held back, some have unrealistic ideas such as asking us to give their child tutoring. The problem with this is that we already have a long school day and assign a fair amount of homework. The idea that we can just pile on tutoring sessions for a child who is already struggling isn't always realistic. While tutoring can help children who have very specific issues such as dyslexia, some children just need more time to catch up with their peers. If you are told that your child needs to be held back, you should see it as an opportunity, not a failure. If you can bring yourself to do so, your child will have a chance to regain their footing in a way that may unlock their potential.

While you should accept the fact that your child may progress more slowly if they have a learning disability, make sure you don't let your child use their disability as an excuse for slacking off. While you shouldn't assume that a child with a learning disability who is progressing more slowly is being lazy, neither should you assume they aren't, since children with disabilities aren't immune from laziness. Keira Knightley says that while her parents made allowances for her disability, they nonetheless insisted that she work hard to keep up her grades. Since Knightley loved acting, they told her that they wouldn't let her act unless she kept up her grades. Similarly, Spielberg says that his parents were quite strict with him about finishing his homework and doing well in school. Like them, you need to make sure that your child is still applying themself in school and doing the best they can given their disability.

Some people prefer to call a learning disability a learning difference and I believe there is some truth to this—that it's not just a politically correct term to make people feel better. A mental condition that might make a child less able in one context may make them more able in another. However, since the world is largely designed for how the average child behaves, raising a child with a learning disability is usually more difficult. It's like being left-handed or seven feet tall in a world that is largely designed for right-handed people of average height. However, if you can learn to cope with any anxiety or disappointment you may have about your child being different, you may find that parenting a child with a learning disability can ultimately be satisfying. Your child will probably be able to accomplish just as much as a child without a learning disability, but they will need more help from you in finding their strengths and becoming comfortable with their differences. When they do, you will have even more reason to be proud of your parenting.

19

LEARNING BY DOING

As a young actor on *The Andy Griffith Show*, Ron Howard was privy to discussions in which the actors and writers would talk about ways to improve the script. Sometimes Howard himself made suggestions. Most were rejected, but when one was eventually accepted, it had a huge impact on him:

> *A rush of satisfaction coursed through me. I guess I didn't make any effort to hide it, because Andy looked straight at me and said, "What're you grinnin' at, young'un?" I said, "That's the first suggestion of mine that you've ever taken!" Andy, not missing a beat, said, "Well, it was the first one that was any damn good! Now let's get on with the scene." I doubt that Andy even remembered that moment. But I have carried this revelation, this discovery of my potential to influence others, ever since.*[1]

People often think that the only thing children really like to do is to play, but that simply isn't true. Just as adults gain satisfaction from fixing up a house, planting a garden, or doing their job, children enjoy accomplishing things. We view it quite differently when a child builds a sandcastle or a fort, but it stems from the same human desire to "work," to engage in labor to create something of value.

When I was growing up, I took great pleasure in making pottery and baking cakes. When I was a little older, I raised funds to repair a clock in the center of the rural town where my family lived for several years. I got my school to agree to use the proceeds from food sales at high school athletic events to fix the clock. When I took over, food was only being sold at a booth, which limited sales, so I had students start selling food in the stands, which increased sales dramatically.

My daughter, Hannah, has similar entrepreneurial instincts. She often set up lemonade stands when she was in middle school and, more recently, has created a free tutoring program at her school in which dozens of students participate.

As well as being fulfilling, work can be quite educational. When I took over food sales at athletic events, I was effectively running a small business. In her tutoring project, Hannah has learned a lot about using spreadsheets to keep track of the participants. Even activities like baking can be instructional because you need to learn how to follow directions carefully. You can ruin a cake if you skip one step or carelessly confuse tablespoons for teaspoons. Sometimes you need to convert measurements if you are doubling your recipe or if you need to convert a weight to a size (e.g., ounces to tablespoons). What's most important is that since you are trying to do something useful, it really matters how you do it.

One theme that emerges over and over in the biographies of successful people is early entrepreneurial activity. Ben Franklin began working as an apprentice printer at the age of twelve. By the age of thirteen, Thomas Edison was making $50 a week selling candy and newspapers on trains. As a teenager, Warren Buffett sold newspapers, golf balls, and stamps, and used the proceeds to invest in farmland that he rented out and a pinball machine that he placed in a local barbershop. Richard Branson dropped out of school at the age of sixteen and started various unsuccessful businesses, including selling Christmas trees and parakeets, before striking it big with a mail-order record business.

One of the reasons that entrepreneurial activities provide learning opportunities for children is that success is truly up to them. That isn't true in school. Rafe Esquith, a famously great teacher, tells a story about how he gave his class the assignment of building rockets:

> *The challenge for each team was to precisely measure, plan, and assemble their project. One group was trying hard but making mistakes in the placement of missile sections. Several of the teachers kept going over to the kids to show them how to build the rocket correctly. On a number of occasions, I had to politely but firmly ask the guests to leave the kids alone.*
>
> **GUEST:** (Whispering) *You don't understand, Rafe. They're doing it wrong.*
> **RAFE:** *I understand.*
> **GUEST:** *Their wings are crooked.*
> **RAFE:** *Yes, they are.*
> **GUEST:** *The launch lug is glued too close to the nose.*
> **RAFE:** *That's true.*
> **GUEST:** *And you're just going to sit there?*
> **RAFE:** *Yes, I am.*
> **GUEST:** *But their rocket won't fly! . . .*
> **RAFE:** *And then the group will have to figure out why their rocket won't fly. They'll have to come back to class and figure it out for themselves. It's what scientists do all the time.*[2]

Most teachers aren't as wise as Esquith, but even those who are can't let their students fail for long. The whole system of schooling is set up to ensure that students learn irrespective of their desire or commitment to doing so. Teachers check homework to make sure their students are doing it and, if they aren't, will talk to the students and, if necessary, to their parents. School must be this way because we can't just let kids go uneducated, but it deprives children of the sense of responsibility that comes with making decisions that can result in success or failure.

This is why it is important for children to work on their own projects. When a child works on their own project, they can fail without an adult intervening to save them. That experience of walking a tightrope without a safety net is invaluable. Moreover, children are more motivated when they are carrying out their own plans rather than somebody else's. That's human nature, and it's why children who engage in an entrepreneurial activity tend to be more invested in that activity than in their schoolwork.

Finding work one enjoys is a critical aspect of achieving happiness in life since one spends a good portion of one's life working. Moreover, one is more likely to be successful at work one enjoys. Many children graduate from college without any real sense of what type of work they enjoy. If your child can find out something that they like doing—whether it's computer programming, or working with people, or working with their hands—they are more likely to end up pursuing a career they enjoy. For that reason, I would recommend that you encourage and support your children's efforts to engage in an entrepreneurial activity even if it distracts them from their schoolwork.

It's also helpful for teenagers to have responsibility for younger children because it thrusts them into the role of acting more responsibly. When I was a teenager, I worked at two camps. At one, I led twelve-year-old girls on a two-week biking trip through Maine. The other counselor and I were responsible for making sure that all of these children were safe. It rained practically every day and we were camping each night. Since everyone was getting wetter and wetter, we had to improvise. In one town, we got the local firemen to allow us to spend the night in their firehouse. In another town, we knocked on someone's door and asked if we could take showers. They let us. All fourteen of us. These experiences helped me to learn to be resourceful and to get used to being responsible.

20

CHALLENGING YOUR CHILDREN

For a few years, my brother and I attended a socialist summer camp. My parents sent us there not for ideological reasons, but because it was cheap and we were pretty poor at the time. In keeping with the camp's socialist principles of equal distribution of wealth, my brother and I had to share the care packages our parents sent us with other students and we sang union and civil rights songs instead of traditional campfire songs. The camp's head, Morris Eisenstein, told me I was "bourgeois" but liked my enthusiasm for the civil rights and antiwar protests that he encouraged the campers to stage. I particularly endeared myself to him when I was discovered one night violating the camp's curfew to finish painting protest signs.

There was a fair amount of strife and conflict at the camp as many of the kids were rough and misbehaved. One year the kids acted so disrespectfully and made such a mess in the cafeteria that the kitchen staff went on strike. We learned this when we showed up for lunch one day and found there was no food. The campers held a meeting and we chose a delegation to negotiate with the kitchen staff. We struck a deal with them to resume lunch on the condition that the campers act more respectfully and help with cleanup.

I can imagine many parents viewing this experience as a disaster. Children are supposed to swim, make arts and crafts, tell ghost stories, and generally enjoy themselves at summer camp, not be forced to share their care packages and engage in labor negotiations to get their lunch. However, socialist camp was a real learning experience for me, and I mean that in all seriousness. The most comfortable childhood isn't the most educational childhood.

While the schools I attended weren't quite so adventurous, they were nonetheless quite socially challenging since I was always an outsider. At the first school I attended, my brother and I were the only white students, and this was the early 1970s, when there were a lot of racial tensions. We later moved to a rural community where none of the other children were Jewish or came from intellectual families like mine. Then I attended a public school in Paris when my father took a sabbatical there. And while we eventually returned to New York City for high school, by that time I'd gotten so used to hanging out with rural kids that returning to the city was an adjustment. When I sought to make friends on the first day of school by talking with a girl whose locker was near mine, she mentioned that she played in a punk rock band. I asked what its name was and she replied, "Steaming Vomit."

Being different can be hard for kids. For some reason, children seem to be obsessed with conforming and like to torment those who don't. Although I sometimes found it difficult to be out of step with my peers, I think that I ultimately benefited from the experience. As an adult, my professions as both an elected official and a school leader have required that I deal with an incredibly broad swath of humanity, ranging from billionaires to people getting by on public assistance. I'm comfortable with this because I've gotten used to dealing with people who are very different from me.

Many children interact with a fairly narrow range of humanity. Suburbs tend to be quite segregated economically since the cost of housing determines who can live where. There are middle-class suburbs, upper-middle-class suburbs, and wealthy suburbs. Children in these suburbs often attend local public schools with students largely of their same class—and often, largely of the same race—and then spend their summers at camps that serve a similarly monolithic constituency.

While cities tend to be more diverse, many children don't benefit from that diversity. For poor kids, that's involuntary since their families rarely have much choice in schools. However, the same is also true of wealthy children whose families do have a choice. They could send their children to a less affluent camp or a mixed-income school but they rarely choose to do so. Instead, their children spend almost all of their time with children of a similar class. For the quite wealthy, this can mean shuttling their children between fancy private schools, expensive camps, and luxurious summer homes.

I'm not blind to the advantages of sending one's children to an expensive private school or a suburban school in an affluent community. For obvious reasons, these schools are usually strong academically. That's why Eric and I sent our older son, Culver, to a private high school. However, even if your children do attend a school with wealthy children, you may want to consider ways in which you can expose them to people from different classes, cultures, and races. You may want to send your children to a less expensive camp than you could afford or encourage them to spend time in contexts that aren't so exclusive. Culver spent a lot of time playing basketball at the Martin Luther King Jr. housing projects, which happened to be across the street from our house. Working can also be a great experience for children.

In addition to challenging your kids socially, you also want them to have other experiences in which they are required to be resourceful. This can be tricky because one, of course, wants to protect one's children, which is nowadays referred to as "helicopter" parenting. I think that the use of this pejorative term is unfortunate. Life presents real dangers to children, and it isn't always easy to figure out where you should draw the line. If your children fall in with the wrong crowd, they can start doing drugs or get into legal trouble. Moreover, if a social situation gets too bad, students can become depressed or even suicidal. However, it is also true that being overprotective can deprive children of the challenges they need to mature.

One way to challenge a child is to send them to a more physically demanding or adventurous camp. When we were in France, my brother and I went to a camp for mountain climbing. We learned to scale up rock faces with ropes tied around our waists. Andre was brilliant at it; I wasn't. One day I fainted, developed a fever, and was taken to a hospital. Fortunately, I soon recovered, but again, it got me used to handling stressful experiences.

Eric and I began letting Culver travel alone in fifth grade. At that age, we generally told him to take a taxi if he was coming home after dark. One evening, he explained that he'd had some trouble getting home. He'd told the taxi driver to let him off at a subway station because he didn't have enough money to get all the way home and hadn't thought to save some for the subway. His solution was to ask someone for money. We asked him how he'd figured whom to ask and he said, "I asked someone who looked like they were rich."

While I wouldn't generally advocate sending children around town begging for money to get home, an experience like this does build character and resourcefulness. Culver had to come up with a plan for coming home (take a cab to a subway), find the courage to ask a complete stranger for money, and then figure out whom to ask for money (someone who had a lot of it!).

Where you draw the line is up to you, but it's important to remember that someday your children will leave the nest and they need to learn how to fly before they do!

21

HELPING YOUR CHILDREN
FIND THEIR TALENTS

According to Professor Amy Chua, the author of *Battle Hymn of the Tiger Mother*,

Western parents try to respect their children's individuality, encouraging them to pursue their true passions, supporting their choices, and providing positive reinforcement and a nurturing environment. By contrast, the Chinese believe that the best way to protect their children is by preparing them for the future, letting them see what they're capable of, and arming them with skills, work habits and inner confidence that no one can ever take away.[1]

I agree with Professor Chua that learning discipline and good work habits is important. Even if someone is lucky enough to spend most of their time pursuing something they are passionate about, they will inevitably have to do things they don't enjoy. Musicians have to practice; actors need to learn their lines; football players need to learn the playbook. Indeed, one of the ironies in life is that the more disciplined you are about doing the things you don't enjoy, the more likely you are able to choose a profession that you do enjoy.

However, what Chua seems to overlook is that a child who is pursuing their "true passions" may be more likely to develop discipline and good work habits. A child who forms a rock band with their friends may end up spending hour after hour practicing with their band. A child who starts a business may do a lot of mundane work to ensure that their business succeeds. The more motivated a child is, the more they will push themselves, which will lead them to develop a strong work ethic and sense of discipline. That's why I like to hire people with athletic experience. I find that serious athletes tend to have a strong work ethic because they understand the hard work that success requires. Similarly, one of Success Academy's best principals had previously trained as a dancer and I'm convinced that the discipline and hard work dancing requires was largely responsible for his success.

Another benefit to having a child pursue their interests is that it often leads to a permanent career. Spielberg began making films when he was in middle school. Warren Buffett began buying stocks when he was eleven years old. Bill Gates began programming in high school. Even if your child doesn't pursue a career that is directly related to their interests, they can nonetheless learn relevant skills. As editor-in-chief of the high school yearbook, I found out that I was very good at managing people.

So you should encourage your child to explore their interests. Sometimes children may need help recognizing that something interests them. When I noticed that my son Culver seemed to be a natural performer, I suggested he try out for the school play in his freshman year in high school. He did so and he was selected. It turned out to be one of his best experiences in high school. The teacher who directed it did a very good job of helping the students understand the play they were performing. After several weeks, Culver came home and said, "I love Shakespeare," which surprised me since Shakespeare can be a tough read for a fifteen-year-old. Culver continued to be interested in Shakespeare in particular and drama in general, and we encouraged that by taking him to plays and enrolling him in summer programs. My mother-in-law even took him to London to see some dramas on the West End.

So don't just let your children pursue their passions; help them find their passions. If they like music, sign them up for music classes. If they like playing chess, sign them up for chess classes and encourage them to participate in tournaments. If they like drawing, buy them some nice art materials and a book about learning to sketch. Look for every hint about their interests. When you see a six-year-old child's amateurish sketch, you don't necessarily think that they may someday become a great artist, but every artist was once a child who made childish art.

One challenge is figuring out whether to encourage your child to stick with something when they've lost interest in it. Some children flit from thing to thing. First, they want to play the guitar, then they want to learn karate, and then it's the next thing. The problem with this is that you don't necessarily enjoy something much until you've invested enough time into it to be good at it.

I had the opposite problem as a child. I was so determined to overcome challenges that I sometimes foolishly stuck at things at which I had no talent. With my parents' encouragement, I began studying the violin but I had no musical talent. I probably would have kept on, but my parents saw I was neither enjoying studying the violin nor making much progress so they let me know it would be all right to quit.

There is no secret formula for figuring out how long a child should stick with something before they give it up, but I'd suggest a few factors for your consideration. If your child says they want to quit something, first try to figure out whether or not they are getting any enjoyment at all from the activity in question and show any signs of talent. If the answer is no on both counts, let the child quit. If, however, it's not so clear, then you may want to encourage them to stick with it a little longer, particularly if they have a history of flitting from thing to thing. On the whole, however, I think it's better to let your child try lots of things and find what they like.

It's impossible to overestimate the importance of having experiences that allow one to find one's talents and enthusiasms. Colin Powell describes how this happened for him:

> *It was only once I was in college, about six months into college, when I found something that I liked, and that was ROTC, Reserve Officer Training Corps in the military. And I not only liked it, but I was pretty good at it. That's what you really have to look for in life, something that you like, and something that you think you're pretty good at. And if you can put those two things together, then you're on the right track, and just drive on.*[2]

If, like Colin Powell, your child can find something they like and are pretty good at, everything else will pale in comparison.

PART **III**

ESTABLISHING A POSITIVE RELATIONSHIP WITH YOUR CHILDREN

Much of this book is devoted to showing you how your children can learn through activities in which they'll want to engage, but inevitably, there will be times when your child needs to do things they don't want to do whether it's cleaning up their room, doing their homework, or going to the dentist. Many parents have trouble getting their children to do things they don't want to do. I see this all the time at Success Academy. Parents tell us they can't get their children to do an hour of homework a night even though we get these very same children to do many hours of schoolwork each day. You would think it would be the other way around. After all, our students' parents know them better than we do, only have to deal with one or two kids at a time instead of a classroom of thirty, and can exact punishments we can't such as taking away their child's smartphone or grounding them. So why do we often succeed where they fail?

Part of it is training. Before teachers at Success Academy are put in charge of a classroom, they get months of training. Parents get none. It's assumed that they learned how to parent from their parents, but that in turn assumes that those parents knew what they were doing, which they may not have.

In addition to a lack of training, parents are handicapped by their strong emotions. While emotions are also an asset in parenting, they are a double-edged sword since they can lead us to act in unhelpful ways. Parents who are embarrassed by their children can become hypercritical. Parents who are frustrated by their children can become belligerent or even violent. Parents who are defensive of their children can ignore their misbehavior. Often, teachers are more successful precisely because they aren't so emotional about their students, which allows them to be more objective about what will motivate their students to behave.

This part of the book is about that, how to parent your child in a positive and constructive manner. It's also about dealing with your aspirations for your children and teaching them a system of values that will help them become happy and productive.

22

ACCENTUATE THE POSITIVE

While you have the legal right to make your children do things, it can be difficult in practice. You can't call up the police and tell them to make your children clean up their rooms and do their homework. The truth is that, for better or worse, parenting depends in large measure upon the consent of the governed.

This presents a real challenge because children are often immune to reasoning. Benjamin Franklin once observed how "convenient a thing it is to be a reasonable creature since it enables one to find or make a reason for anything one has a mind to do," which is a pretty good description of most children. If you tell them they should study hard so they'll be able to go to college, they may respond that they don't have to because they plan to be a baseball player or a rock star. If you tell them that they need to clean their room, they'll say it's their room so nobody else should care about it.

If neither coercion nor reasoning works, you may be wondering what's left. The answer is that children have an instinct to please adults, particularly their parents, and you must use that instinct to your advantage by carefully doling out praise and disapprobation. At times, it may not seem as effective as punishment, but in the long term, it's actually the most effective way to parent, provided you are systematic and patient.

At Success Academy, we train teachers to celebrate our scholars' achievements. When an elementary school student answers a hard question correctly, their teacher will smile and say something encouraging such as "Kiss your brain." Children love this recognition and will strive to get more of it. The same thing can work for you. Don't reserve your praise for special occasions such as a stellar report card; incorporate it into your daily interactions. If you hear your child use some advanced vocabulary word, say, "Nice vocabulary word!" If your child shows you a drawing they've done, take the time to comment on its merits.

We also train our teachers that they need to focus on classroom management even when things are going well. Many teachers fail to acknowledge and appreciate student behavior when things are going well—they take their students' good behavior for granted. Then a student misbehaves so the teacher admonishes them. If this happens repeatedly, it sets up a bad dynamic. If a student hears only reprimands, they just develop a negative attitude toward the teacher as someone who can't be pleased or "has it in" for them. That's human nature. Since we want to feel good about ourselves, we naturally tend to discount the judgment of someone who is always critical of us. Conversely, since we tend to believe that someone who praises us a lot has good judgment, we'll take that person's criticisms more seriously.

The same dynamic applies to parenting. There's an old Jewish joke about a mother who gives her son two ties for Chanukah. The next time he goes over to his mother's home for dinner, he makes sure to wear one of the ties she gave him. Noticing this, the mother says, "What's the matter? You didn't like the other one?" If you are like this mother, your children will start to think that you can never be pleased so there's no point trying.

Some parents fall into the trap of thinking that getting angry at their kids can be an effective form of parenting. It happens like this: You are already tired or in a bad mood because of a long day at work or because of some other stresses in your life and your child does something annoying like failing to clean up their dishes at dinner or knocking something over because they're careless. Because you are already on edge, you overreact and scream at your child. The child, frightened by this strong reaction, starts to behave. This feels good. Not only were you able to work off some steam, but getting angry really seemed to work.

Except that it doesn't. Yes, your child will behave in the short term, but when this happens a few times, the message they will take away is that you tend to overreact when you are in a bad mood. They will, therefore, simply tailor their behavior to your mood, behaving well only when they think you are in a bad mood, so now you have to scream at them whenever you want them to behave. In effect, your strategy now requires you to get in a bad mood to make your children behave. Not only is this unhealthy for you, but it will undermine your relationship with your children since they will start to see you simply as a source of negativity.

Often, parents don't realize that they are approaching their parenting with a bad attitude. They think they are angry at their children because their children are particularly poorly behaved when, in fact, their children are just doing the types of things that children tend to do. I understand that parenting can be hard. Given the stresses of work, financial challenges, marital troubles, health problems, and any other number of issues, it can be hard to play the role of a calm, patient parent. However, the brutal truth is that if you allow the stresses of your life to undermine your relationship with your children, you will just end up with another source of unhappiness and stress in your life.

If this is happening to you, then you need to do what our teachers do, which is to make a point of giving positive feedback irrespective of your mood. Our teachers understand this is part of their job. Just as an actor can't decide to act pissy in a romantic scene because they are having a bad day, our teachers can't refrain from giving out praise just because they are in a bad mood. They need to force a smile on their face even if that's not how they feel. You will be a more effective parent if you take the same approach. This is particularly important if you've gotten into a negative cycle with your kids. When your children come home, try to look for something to praise as quickly as possible so you can dole out some praise before your child does something that annoys you.

Of course, you will naturally have emotions as a parent and your ability to draw upon them will ultimately make you a better parent, but you must listen to your own emotions judiciously. Sometimes your emotions will be helpful and sometimes they won't. For example, if your child happens to spill something on a brand-new white couch by accident, your anger may exceed what is appropriate, given your child's culpability. Rafe Esquith gives a great example of a man who had a prized baseball that was signed by members of the Red Sox. The man explained to his young son that he couldn't play with this ball because it had writing on it. One day, the man noticed that his ball was missing and spoke to his son, who cheerfully explained that he had solved the problem of being unable to play with the ball because it had writing on it by licking it off.

There will often be a gap between the emotions you are feeling at any given moment and those that it will be helpful for you to express. When you are in a good mood, you may wish to let some things slide when you shouldn't, and when you are in a bad mood, you may neglect to dole out praise when it is deserved. As much as possible, you should try to express helpful emotions. I realize that some may object that this sounds inauthentic, but I wouldn't agree. People try to adjust their expressions of emotion all the time. For example, if you are on a job interview, you may laugh at the interviewer's joke even if they aren't the greatest comedian in history. And if you are celebrating your spouse's birthday but you have a bad day at work, you may decide this isn't the moment to launch into a tirade about how much you hate your job. There are all sorts of contexts in which we try to adjust our emotional responses to people. Being a parent requires that you do so with your kids.

Now, of course, nobody is perfect. Even children realize that everyone can have a bad day. But if you develop a habit of lashing out at your child when you're in a bad mood, it will diminish your authority. Some parents mistakenly think that losing their temper is a good thing because their children tiptoe around afterward. That, however, is temporary. Your children will begin to see your reactions as those of an unjust person who is prone to flying off the handle at any moment.

So you need to be careful about how much negative feedback you give your children and also how you give it. I learned this in part from a great teacher named Paul Fucalaro, who was critical in helping me start Success Academy. If one of my schools was having trouble, I would send Paul to the school and he would ask to teach a class consisting only of the most difficult kids. Within days, he'd have them eating out of his hand. Interestingly, some teachers thought he was being too tough on the students, but the students seemed to love him. I came to understand that while he was demanding, he was very careful about how he expressed his criticism. He never seemed to be angry or frustrated with the students or said anything to demean or discourage them such as "Don't be stupid" or "With work like that, you'll never amount to anything." Instead, he would express *disappointment* and *sadness*. He would say, "I'm disappointed that you didn't do better on this assignment," or "You are such a smart kid that it makes me sad when I see you do work like this." Since Paul didn't get angry at the students, they didn't get angry at him. Instead, they felt bad that they'd made him sad and would try to figure out a way to make him happy again.

Listening to Paul, you would think that he regarded every child as a genius and an angel and that he was genuinely shocked when they strayed from the path. If you really think well of your children, you should hold them to a higher standard, not a lower one. And that's how you want your children to feel: that you think so highly of them that you are surprised when they misbehave. If you take this attitude, then your child is more likely to believe that they are fundamentally a well-behaved child who sometimes misbehaves. On the other hand, if you say to your child, "You're always getting in trouble!" then your child is more likely to believe that they are fundamentally a poorly behaved child who is destined to remain so.

When your children are young, it's best to be as positive as possible about their accomplishments, but as they get older, you should dole out your praise a little more strategically to set high expectations. Let's say that your child gets a 90 on their first test in algebra. Should you say "Great job!" or "That's okay, but you can do better," or "I'm disappointed; you can do better"? It's probably better not to say "great job" on the first test because then they've got nothing to strive for. If you think 90 is actually a pretty good score because last year your child got a 90 in math, then I'd say, "That's okay, but you can do better." If your child got a 95 in math last year, I'd say, "I'm disappointed; you can do better." Then your child will hopefully improve, and you can give them more positive feedback on their subsequent tests.

Above all, you need patience. Parents often make the mistake of thinking that they aren't making progress if they don't see immediate results. If that happens, reflect for a moment on the physical growth of your children. When your children come home from school at the end of the day, they don't look taller than when you sent them off to school. They are taller since they're growing all the time, but that growth is happening too slowly to be visible. Similarly, if you sit down with your child and explain how important it is that they study, they probably aren't going to say, "You're right, Mom, I realize that I've been slacking off, and I now understand that hard work and good study habits are critical to my future success and happiness." Instead, they may protest that homework is boring or that they are already working hard, or even if they do say the right things, their behavior may fail to match their words. When this happens, parents often get so frustrated that it leads to unproductive behavior. They get angry, give up, or berate their children. This is understandable, but it's unhelpful.

If you do lose your temper, consider apologizing to your child. Some parents feel that it undermines their authority, but I don't believe it does. You can apologize for losing your temper without admitting that your child was acting correctly. You can explain that what your child was doing was very frustrating but that you shouldn't have yelled at them. Your child may even be more open to your critique if you concede that it shouldn't have been delivered in such an intemperate manner.

Perhaps the best way to calm yourself is to arm yourself with the knowledge that if you are patient and persistent, you will succeed in the end. As someone who raised three children and has seen many others do so, I can assure you that it is true. I'm not promising perfection, but I've seen parents who are patient and persistent, and I've seen parents who give in to frustrations and anger, and in the long run, the former are always more successful than the latter.

Of course, the more you actually enjoy parenting, the easier it will be to be positive and patient, so you should make a real effort to find activities in which you can engage with your children that will bring you real pleasure.

23

SAYING NO TO YOUR CHILDREN

G uests at the childhood home of scientist Randy Pausch would often be shown his room. His parents had allowed his siblings and him to paint it and they used it as a marvelous creative exercise. They drew a silver metal elevator door and, above it, a panel with numbers 1 through 6 to indicate the floor number on which the imaginary elevator was located. Floor number 3 was illuminated, which they found amusing since they lived in a ranch house. On the ceiling, they wrote the words "I'm trapped in the attic!" backward so it would look like someone had scratched the letters out on the attic floor. Pausch also drew a representation of the myth of Pandora's box, a quadratic equation he liked, and a submarine lurking in a body of water behind a bunk bed with a periscope rising above the bedspread.

When Pausch's friends would see his room, they would express surprise that his parents had let him paint it since most parents wouldn't. Most of us would likely think of the potential damage from spilled paint and the work of repainting the room. When one has children, it can feel like it's a constant battle to prevent chaos from prevailing, so it's understandable that most parents wouldn't want to let their children use their room as a canvas for their artistic efforts, but Pausch was forever grateful to his parents for letting him do so.

You should take the same approach as much as possible. Suppose, for example, that your child wants to use bedsheets for the roof of some fort they are building outside. The sheets may, of course, be ruined but is that really so important? They probably cost less than a trip to the movies. Or suppose that your child is in the grocery store's meat section and sees something unusual such as beef tongue or tripe and wants to try it. You may object that they really won't like it and it will get thrown out in the end. Maybe you're right, but does it really matter?

You should be careful about saying no to children because you want to let them experiment and express themselves. In addition, it's easier to say no to your children about things that are important if you say yes to them about the things you can live with. That's the approach Eric and I took with our children, and I believe it's one of the reasons that our children rarely argued with us when we put down our feet about things we really cared about such as playing video games, whining, or insolence, none of which we tolerated.

Figuring out how strict to be about rules gets more challenging when your children become teenagers. Where you draw the line depends in part on your personal philosophy. No parent will tell their kid that it's all right to try opioids or take part in orgies, but people vary on whether they feel comfortable with their children having sex or having a beer at a party. What I can tell you is that I've seen parents who set such unrealistic expectations for their children's behavior that they lose all influence and ability to communicate with them. If that happens, then your child may engage in even riskier behavior and may not communicate with you if it gets them into trouble. So try to be thoughtful.

It's also important to deliver your no's carefully. Here is an example of how some parents respond to a request:

CHILD: Paul is having a party on Friday night. Can I go?
PARENT: No.
CHILD: How come?
PARENT: You're too young to go to parties.
CHILD: But all of my friends are going.
PARENT: They shouldn't be going either.
CHILD: But you never let me have fun. It's not fair. You're mean.
PARENT: Paul is bad news. You shouldn't be hanging out with him.
CHILD: But I really, really want to go, Mom. *Please* can I go?
PARENT: Okay, you can go, but I don't think it's safe. I better not find out that you were doing something there that you shouldn't have been.

This parent has made several mistakes. First, the parent (let's call her Jane) has made it clear that she thinks it's unsafe for her child (let's call him John) to go to Paul's house and that even when she relents, she still thinks it's a bad idea. That is not a great message because Jane appears to be implicitly admitting that her own fears are unfounded. After all, why would she relent if she truly thinks that going to the party is dangerous? In addition, John comes to learn that the way to get to a yes is just by being manipulative: first by attacking his mother ("You're mean") and then by trying to play on her sympathies ("*Please*"). If Jane really loves her child, then none of this should make any difference because her decision about whether to let her child go to the party shouldn't be influenced by this manipulation. In fact, at this point, John could reasonably conclude that he was right all along that she was just being mean since, by letting him go, Jane has implicitly acknowledged that her fears of danger must have been unfounded.

Try to avoid reflexively saying no and then giving in because it will lead to your child constantly trying to pressure you to change your mind under the theory that you will usually do so. In addition, it will undermine your authority because it will look like you don't really believe what you are saying. Instead, if you have concerns, express those concerns and have a conversation. This gives you a chance to figure out how strongly committed you are to saying no and how much your child cares about this particular activity. You may also find a way to address your concerns, such as having your child come home from a party by a certain time. But understand that the point isn't necessarily to convince your child that you are right, and it's unwise to give your child the sense that you feel you need their approval. In the end, you will need to make a decision and may decide to play your trump card of being a parent by either refusing permission or setting conditions. However, by engaging in this process, you can make sure that you only say no when you are really prepared to stick to your position. In addition, even if your child doesn't agree with your decision, they may nonetheless appreciate the fact that you are going through this process rationally and carefully, which may decrease their resentment at being told no. Even if your child doesn't accept your rationale in the heat of the moment, they may do so later.

Once you do reach a decision, you need to appear confident in that decision. This might seem contradictory to the idea of listening to your child's concerns but it isn't. A judge doesn't show they are indecisive or lack conviction because they listen carefully to the position of the parties before them. To the contrary, the fact that they listened carefully to each side's position is precisely what makes them confident. So listen carefully but then reach a decision, stick to it, and appear confident. Don't be defensive, don't be angry, and above all, don't make it apparent that you are troubled that your child doesn't agree with you because you doubt yourself. You've given the matter careful thought so simply hand out your judgment with confidence and equanimity. Of course, you will make some mistakes.

That's inevitable. All that anyone can expect you to do is to use your best judgment.

It's also unwise to lose your temper. If you get angry, your child may suspect that you made your decision not because you were thinking about their interests but because you were in a bad mood. It can be very hard to remain calm because your children can act quite unfairly and unkindly but you need to act like a parent. You need to make it clear that you are making your decisions calmly and rationally even when you are dealing with a child who is being intransigent and petulant. For example, if your child says you are being mean, say that you are sorry to hear that they feel that way. If your child says that they hate you, say that you are disappointed they are saying that but that you hope they'll feel differently when they've had a chance to calm down. You need to maintain your composure and your worldview. It isn't always easy, but in the long run, it will pay dividends.

One of the things that you need to understand and accept about children is that most have an instinct to test your limits. You can get the impression from this that your children don't believe there should be any limits but usually this isn't true. Most children accept that you must set limits but feel that it's fair for them to test those limits. So don't take it personally if your children do so as well.

24

DEALING WITH YOUR ASPIRATIONS
FOR YOUR CHILDREN

ordon Caplan, a New York City lawyer, was at the top of his profession. He had been elected as chairman of Willkie Farr & Gallagher, one of the country's best law firms, and named a Dealmaker of the Year by *The American Lawyer* magazine. Unfortunately, he was also so desperate to get his daughter into his alma mater, Cornell University, that he hired someone to correct his daughter's answers on a college admissions test. When he was caught, he lost his job, pled guilty to a felony, went to jail, and had his law license suspended.

Obviously, Mr. Caplan's actions were immoral but what astonishes me even more is how irrational they were. Mr. Caplan's daughter didn't need her father to cheat for her to get into a good college. When his scheme fell apart, she still managed to get into St. Lawrence University, the kind of excellent liberal arts college that many students prefer to a large university.

Moreover, until this misdeed, Mr. Caplan had been a law-abiding citizen who had made millions of dollars in charitable contributions and had done considerable pro bono work—most of it, ironically, in the field of education. So what explains his conduct? Here is what Mr. Caplan has said:

> *It was about me, not about my child. That took a lot of self-realization. It was deep insecurity, I think. I frankly think a lot of people in my former profession have this notion of having to prove yourself all the time. It overwhelmed me and it destroyed my life.*[1]

While few of us go to Mr. Caplan's lengths, many parents have similarly strong feelings about their children. Our children are virtually extensions of ourselves. When they misbehave, we're mortified; when they shine, we exult. Their successes are our successes; their failures are our failures. We care just as much about their fate as we do our own, perhaps even more so, but while we can control our own actions, or at least think we can, we have only limited control over theirs. And caring deeply about something you can't control is a recipe for anxiety.

Of course, having aspirations for one's children also has huge benefits since it's part of what motivates us to do so much for them, from reading to them after a long day's work to paying their college tuition. Moreover, since our children crave our approval, our capacity for taking pride in their accomplishments motivates them to succeed. It's this very fact that our desire for our children to do well can be positive that makes it hard for us to recognize when it isn't. Here are a few suggestions for telling the difference.

First, some parents make the mistake of seeing their children's lives as a chance to get a do-over on their own. They may think that they made some terrible mistake in their life and don't want their children to make the same mistake. They may regret that they abandoned their dream of becoming a doctor to start a family and may want their children to pursue that career. Or they may have been denied some opportunity that they want their child to have. A father may wish that his father had played baseball with him so he obsesses about his son's Little League career. Or a mother may wish that she'd gotten the opportunity to go to an Ivy League college like her best friend in high school so she is determined to see her daughter go to such a school.

You need to let your child live their own life, not to live the life you wish you'd had. Your child may not want to play baseball or go to an Ivy League school or become a doctor or a lawyer. You need to help them find their own path. This doesn't mean you need to refrain from giving them any advice or assistance. To the contrary, parents can have a lot of insight into their children and know a lot more than them about the career choices that are available. However, you will be most effective at helping your children if you remember that they aren't you.

Another mistake parents make is worrying too much about what other people will think of their children. They are eager to tell all their friends that their child got into Harvard or, alternatively, ashamed to admit that their child didn't. This seems to have been Mr. Caplan's problem. He was very focused on proving himself to other people, and one way of doing so was to get his daughter into a good college. If you are spending a lot of time worrying about what other people think of your children, that's not a good thing either for you or for your child. Your child may begin to feel bad about themself because they fail to live up to your aspirations or they may internalize your belief that they should focus all their energies on impressing other people rather than figuring out what interests them and what will be a meaningful use of their talents.

I realize that even if you agree with my advice, just telling you not to care so much about what other people think of your children doesn't mean you'll stop. I don't have some magic solution for stopping, but I'd nonetheless like to share my philosophy about this for what it's worth.

When your child is young, they may be one of the smartest children in their school, and if so, they may be admitted to some top high school, and if they do very well there, they may be admitted to some top college, and if they do well there, they may be admitted to some top graduate school, and if they do well there, they may end up at a top law firm or investment bank or hospital. However, unless your child is one out of a billion, they won't turn out to be the smartest person in the world, or the most talented athlete in the world, or the richest person in the world. Thus, if you focus on whether there are other children who are more successful than yours, you will always be dissatisfied unless your child happens to be the next Jeff Bezos, Michael Jordan, or Albert Einstein. For this reason, it's unwise to focus on comparing your children to other children. Instead, you should focus on helping them maximize their talents, develop their interests, and figure out how to live a productive, meaningful, and joyful life. Doing so not only will be more helpful for your child, but will also make you a happier parent.

25

TEACHING YOUR CHILDREN
HOW TO ENJOY LIFE

The idea that you might need to teach your children how to enjoy life may seem strange to you. After all, enjoying life seems to be the one thing that kids do naturally. What they need to learn, you may say, is not more ways to enjoy themselves but to clean their rooms, act responsibly, and do their homework. All of that is true, but many happy children grow up to be unhappy adults. There is a difference between enjoying life as a young child and being prepared to enjoy life as a teenager or an adult.

When John Adams was serving as ambassador to France, he wrote to his wife about the joys of seeing art in Paris:

I could fill volumes with descriptions of temples and palaces, paintings, sculptures, tapestry, porcelain, etc. . . . if I could have time. But I could not do this without neglecting my duty. . . . I must study Politics and War so that my sons may have liberty to study Mathematics and Philosophy. My sons

ought to study Mathematics and Philosophy, Geography,
Natural History, Naval Architecture, Navigation,
Commerce and Agriculture, in order to give their children
a right to study Painting, Poetry, Music, Architecture,
Statuary, Tapestry and Porcelain.[1]

Interestingly, history seems to be moving in the opposite direction. A hundred years ago, most college students would pursue a liberal arts education by studying topics such as English, art history, and classical languages. Today, they are more likely to pursue more practical studies such as economics, computer science, and engineering. In part, this reflects our increasingly competitive society. Merely graduating from a good college no longer ensures a good job. Instead, employers prefer candidates who graduate with specific skills that are relevant to the jobs they seek.

This development may well be a good thing for our economy, but students need to be prepared not just for their careers but for life beyond it. In fact, this need may become even more urgent in the decades to come since computers and robots are performing so much work that used to be performed by humans that there may soon be little left over for humans. A life of leisure may sound great in theory, but it actually presents a huge challenge. When you've had a hard day at work, it may be great fun to sit down to dinner with your family or watch a football game or go on a well-deserved vacation, but people may find permanent leisure far less appealing.

In my experience, people are happiest if their life includes some type of meaningful productive activity. For some, that may be a career. For others, it's raising children, volunteering, coaching a Little League team, or pursuing artistic endeavors. But unfortunately, we are constantly being bombarded with the message that happiness comes from consumption. When advertisers tell us to "treat" ourselves to their product or that we "deserve" their products, they are trying to make us believe that buying things is the ultimate reward, that we will be happy if only we buy a fancier car or a bigger house. The problem, as Oscar Wilde once said, is that there are two tragedies in life: not getting what you want and getting what you want. That is why those who seek happiness through the acquisition of material goods are chasing a mirage. Like an addict, they need more and more to make them happy, but it's never really enough.

None of this is intended as a judgment. We all like buying and having things we enjoy, and there's nothing wrong with that. Neither am I saying that money doesn't play a role in achieving happiness. It plainly does. If you can afford to live reasonably near where you work, your commute will be short enough that you can spend time with your family. If you can afford to own a car or to travel for your vacations, that will allow you to spend time doing things you like, whether it's lying on the beach, walking in the woods, or visiting foreign countries.

There is, however, an unhealthy tendency in this country to want to buy more and more things for the pure thrill of buying and own-ing. I don't believe this leads to happiness. Given that, it's important to teach your children not to make consumption the centerpiece of their life.

Unfortunately, doing this will require fighting corporate Amer-ica. Just like you, corporate America sees your child as a developing person with tremendous potential who can be molded and shaped, but they have a different aspiration for your child: to turn them into *Homo consumericus*, a creature that wants nothing more in life than to buy as many products as possible. To achieve that goal, compa-nies employ armies of experts to brainwash your child into thinking that their products will bring happiness. Of course, each individual company only cares about selling your child its particular product, but this symphony of appeals combines to send the message that happiness derives from consumption.

Eric and I thought that our children were largely immunized

from these influences because we didn't let them watch broadcast television, but we came to realize that corporations were finding other ways to influence them. The first is simply designing their products to be addictive. Human instincts that were formed when food was scarce have led us to like salt, fat, sugar, and carbohydrates. Manufacturers have figured out how to exploit those instincts to sell more junk food. Once kids start enjoying the sensory overload of eating Cheetos or a Big Mac, it's hard for them to appreciate the simpler pleasures of eating an apple or a baked potato. And the same is true for any number of other products. Video games are designed to give children constant stimulation. Movies are designed to exploit our instinctual attraction to sex and violence.

Moreover, even if your child isn't directly exposed to a lot of advertising, they are exposed to the culture that this advertising has created. Their friend shows them some incredible new toy they got that the friend will play with for the next week until they get another toy. They attend a birthday party at which a friend is showered with gifts, whose paper is ripped off in an orgy of acquisition.

There is an interesting example of this in the film *Back to the Future*. In the beginning of the film, Marty McFly's family is dysfunctional and unhappy. His father is underconfident, his mother is an alcoholic who no longer loves her husband, and the family members aren't supportive of one another. By the end of the film, when Marty's travel into the past has magically changed the present, the family is now happy. His mother is healthy and athletic, his father is an author, and they are both affectionately flirting with one another. In many respects, this is a wonderful film with many great messages about standing up for oneself, but there was another aspect of the ending to which the actor Crispin Glover had such a strong objection that he refused to participate in the sequels. The film makes clear that the family is now quite affluent. In particular, Marty's father owns a BMW and Marty himself owns a brand-new customized black pickup truck. As Mr. Glover explained:

I thought it was not a good idea for our characters to have monetary reward. Because it basically makes the moral of the film be that money equals happiness. . . . By having the son character cheer by having a truck in the garage—what I was arguing for was that the characters should be in love, and that the love should be the reward.[2]

While I don't think it's so terrible to acknowledge that money matters, Glover is right that Marty's discovery that he now owns a pickup truck seems to be the culmination of the film. Moreover, it's not just that he has a ride to allow him to take his girlfriend on a date. Instead, he has a tricked-out Toyota Xtra Cab SR5 with lights on the roof, large tires, and a lifted suspension. A re-created version of this vehicle later sold for $110,000.

Back to the Future came out just as product placements in films were becoming more common. Now, they are constant. Harley-Davidson paid $10 million to get its electric motorcycle featured in Marvel's *Avengers: Age of Ultron*. The James Bond franchise is particularly attractive to companies. BMW paid $150 million to have its cars featured in several Bond films, Aston Martin paid $140 million to have its cars featured in *Die Another Day*, and Heineken paid $45 million to have James Bond shown sipping on its beer.

Unfortunately, while the free market is a brilliantly efficient mechanism for producing and distributing products and services, it is also completely amoral. Companies are just as happy to sell your child a 1,300-calorie double cheeseburger with bacon as a healthy sandwich. They are just as happy to sell your child a violent video game as a well-written book. Companies don't want to make your child unhealthy and ignorant, but they don't really care if that happens and never will. Even if we could get all the existing fast-food companies to stop selling unhealthy food, others would arise to take their place as long as there was a buck to be made by doing so.

How do you fight back? Don't take your children to stores where they can go running around saying "I want this" and "I want that." Protect your children from commercials as much as possible. This goes back to watching less television but also to watching television without commercials. People in general and kids in particular end up getting all this stuff that they don't really need but that TV ads have told them will make them happy. Don't encourage your child to believe that having things brings happiness by giving them too many gifts. The concept that you express your love for somebody by giving them a gift is a nice idea that once worked pretty well, but many kids get so much stuff nowadays that it quickly becomes overkill.

Eric and I never gave our kids a lot of gifts, but even then, we came to realize that we were still giving them too many. The problem was that we'd buy bikes and sleds and other things when our children needed them so when our children's birthdays came around, we'd end up buying things they didn't need. Nowadays, when our kids need something expensive, they ask us for it and we'll agree we'll count it as their next birthday present.

If you want to get your children presents for their birthday, then I'd suggest that you and other family members give your child one or two good presents rather than several. Also, if you're having other children over for your child's birthday party, tell their parents not to bring birthday presents. Make birthday parties about having fun, not acquiring presents. One year, Eric created a kind of scavenger hunt game for the birthday of one of our children. Eric handed our children one clue that said something like "Brr, I'm freezing cold," which led them to look in the freezer, where they found one of those plastic Easter eggs that contained another clue that led them to the next Easter egg, and so on and so on. Many of the clues were obscure and based on inside jokes known only to us. Our kids loved this hunt so much that they asked Eric to do it again for their subsequent birthdays. Something like this can be a lot of fun, and it's much more personal than buying a toy.

As for your own birthday, use it as an opportunity to reinforce your values. Eric discourages gifts for his birthday and instead asks that our kids share with him a memory of something they enjoyed doing as a family. You can also help your children figure out gifts for your spouse that will be meaningful such as a home-made card, a home-baked cake, or reciting a poem.

Children need to understand that while money can give them the *opportunity* to be happy, they can't consume their way to happiness. The sooner a child learns this, the more likely that they will become happy. They need to understand that one can spend a wonderful day playing board games, reading a book, baking a cake, listening to some music, and having dinner with some friends. If you can teach your children how to do that, their chances of happiness will increase immeasurably, and the best way to teach them this is to show how it's done. Play games with your children to demonstrate how much fun can be had with a simple deck of cards. Make a treehouse or bake a cake with your children to show them the pleasure of productive activity. Read a book to your children to show them the pleasure of intellectual activity.

CONCLUSION

The Joy of Parenting

When Culver was four years old, Eric and I took him to the beach and we played a game with him in which we would follow a wave out as it receded and then, when the next wave came, turn and run as fast as we could to avoid it catching us. If we felt the water touch our feet as we ran, then we'd lost. Culver loved this game. He squealed with joy as he ran from the waves. And as I ran, I couldn't help but share in his joy. As silly as the game was, I got caught up in seeing how far we could follow the receding wave without the next one catching us and then running frantically, conscious of the sand underneath my feet as I waited to see if the cold foamy seawater would splash through our toes as we fled.

Parenting is perhaps most fundamentally about teaching our children to become adults, so it is one of its ironies that while we teach our children how to become adults, they remind us how to be children. Childhood can be such a joyful time and it gives parents an opportunity to share in that joy. It gives us an excuse to listen to silly songs and rewatch beloved movies, to look at insects and build sandcastles, to play board games and build tree houses, to do all those things that you may have enjoyed as a child.

Parenting can also be a chance to reestablish a better relationship with intellectual inquiry. Many people leave high school or college with a negative attitude toward learning because they were under a lot of pressure to do well academically and because their classes became increasingly technical and difficult. Instead of getting caught up in books like *Charlotte's Web* and *Charlie and the Chocolate Factory*, high school students plow through books that they find difficult to understand. Instead of learning how our heart keeps us alive, college students nervously study formulas in their organic chemistry class.

Having a child is a chance to rediscover the joy of learning. You can read about ancient civilizations without worrying about what will be on the test. You can listen to a book with your child without having to write a ten-page essay on what it means. You can learn about science without having to memorize the periodic table or the equation for velocity. You may find that you actually enjoy some subjects you recall disliking in school and that it's fun to share what you learned in school.

And perhaps it will be an opportunity for you to begin learning again. You can expand your intellectual horizons rather than just closing up shop. You can cite new facts and have new debates instead of just expressing the same old views and citing the same old facts that your spouse has gotten used to over the course of your marriage. Maybe you'll even change some of your views; it happens!

And here is the kicker: Not only is parenting an opportunity for you to rediscover the joy in learning, but the more you do so, the better you'll be as a parent. Joy is your parenting superpower. Like laughter, joy is infectious. The more you enjoy playing, learning, and living, the more your children will.

ACKNOWLEDGMENTS

Part of what has made writing this book such a joy is that it has allowed me to share the wonderful work that so many people have done to enrich the lives of children. Some of these people are famous, but there are so many others who toil away in relative obscurity but nonetheless make a tremendous contribution to our children's education. Take Joan Holub, a woman I'd never heard of until writing this book. Ms. Holub has written several books in the Who Was? and What Was? series, including *Who Was Marco Polo?*, *What Was the Gold Rush?*, and *What Were the Salem Witch Trials?* These are all wonderfully written books that manage to be both engaging and informative at the same time. I so much wish that these books had been available when I was a child as I'm sure I would have devoured them!

Or take the husband-and-wife team Bill Ritchie and Andrea Barthello. In 1985, they founded a company "to translate the brilliant ideas of the craziest mathematicians, engineers and inventors into simple toys that can be appreciated by boys and girls around the world." This company, now called ThinkFun, has created a wonderful collection of educational games, many of which are recommended in this book.

Or take Susan Hammond, a musician whose experience with her own children led her to the idea of combining classical music with the spoken word. This inspiration resulted in the marvelous Classical Kids concerts and recordings.

My point in highlighting these four individuals is not simply to celebrate their work but to point out just how many people are creating wonderful games, books, songs, and documentaries for your child to enjoy and learn from. I wish to acknowledge the contributions of these unsung heroes.

Thank you to Rachel Garlin, for allowing us to reprint the lyrics to her song "Broke Down House."

I am also grateful to the many educators with whom I've had the privilege to work at Success Academy. I have learned so much from them about educating children and parenting.

I would like to thank Ann Powell for her generous help in reviewing and revising this book and my assistants, Kori Kanaday and Daniel Kuk, who make it possible for me to juggle my many responsibilities.

I am also grateful to the many people at HarperCollins who worked on this book, in particular Sarah Pelz for championing it and Deborah Brody and Emma Peters for guiding it through the editorial process. Thanks also to Ben M. Gambuzza and to Jane Rosenman for her editorial suggestions.

Finally, I am grateful to my three children—Culver, Dillon, and Hannah—whose considerable accomplishments are in part what inspired Eric and me to write this book.

FOR PARENTS OF
PRESCHOOL CHILDREN

Since this book is primarily aimed at parenting school-age children, I've decided to gather my tips for preschool parents in a brief section here.

Babies learn things automatically by interacting with you, other children, and their physical environment. In the beginning, they are mastering the use of their senses and their bodies, such as how to focus their eyes so they can see and how to grasp and move objects. Your child will learn all of this in virtually any environment, but it's very easy to make your child's environment more stimulating by giving them toys they can manipulate such as these:

+ Rattles
+ Shape sorters
+ Stacking cups
+ Stacking rings
+ A pounding bench wooden toy
+ Maracas or egg shakers
+ Pull-along toys
+ Learning Advantage Go Wheelie
+ Dolls
+ Toy trucks

+ Soft books
+ Cardboard building blocks

Stay away from electronic toys. You don't want or need toys to do too much. Children may like getting a doll that talks or a fire engine that has lights and a working siren, but it's better if your child does the talking and makes the fire engine sounds. In this area, less is more.

When your child gets older, here are some slightly more complex toys:

+ Wooden standard unit building blocks
+ Play-Doh
+ Magnetic building block toys such as Elongdi, Goobi, Witka, or Picasso Tiles
+ Marble run sets
+ Plastic gear sets
+ Wooden train sets
+ Pattern blocks

When your child is ready to start designing things, give them Lego building blocks or, if they are under five years of age, Duplo blocks, which are larger and therefore easier to manipulate and less likely to be swallowed. Lego blocks make it easy for children to be creative. They can snap together a few pieces and create a car, a house, or a rocket ship of their own design in just a few minutes. Stay away from the kits that are designed to create a particular object such as a spaceship from *Star Wars*. Instead, get "classic Lego," which can be purchased on eBay by the pound and consists of various sizes and shapes of building blocks with a few more complex pieces such as wheels but that doesn't include single-purpose specialized pieces such as Lego Light Saber or the windshield for the *Millennium Falcon*.

If you want to give your child some inspiration, you might use books from Jennifer Kemmeter's Build It series, which has fairly simple Lego projects. There are some books with far more complicated Lego projects, which look incredibly cool but are too hard for most children.

As your child gets older (say four or five), you may wish to introduce them to puzzles to develop their logical and analytical skills. Here are some great ones:

+ Tangram puzzles
+ Katamino
+ Three Little Piggies (SmartGames)
+ Little Red Riding Hood (SmartGames)
+ Bunny Peek a Boo (SmartGames)
+ Color Code (SmartGames)

The first few board games listed in the games section of this book are also good for preschool children.

Stay away from toys that don't require creativity such as radio-controlled cars and drones and pretty much any electronic toy, including those that purport to be "educational." You should also resist your children's desire to constantly acquire new toys. Like adults do, children can fetishize their possessions. They start to love the experience of buying, owning, and showing off their toys. This human instinct can be useful in some contexts. For example, if you are proud of your house, car, or flower garden, that may lead you to enjoy taking care of it, which is a good thing. Similarly, it's great if your child spends hours building something with Legos because they have a cool idea for a spaceship to transport dinosaurs to Mars. It's not good, however, if your child is constantly wanting to buy things for the pleasure of acquisition: If they are begging for cool new sneakers when they have functional ones already; if they want to get a "Batman bike" when they already have a bike that is fine.

These are all perfectly natural instincts, but you should nonetheless strongly discourage them.

To develop your child's language, talk to them as much as possible. It may seem strange to say things to a child they can't understand but that's how they'll learn. In addition, as discussed above, you should also read to your child as much as possible.

Most children know their alphabet before they go to kindergarten so it's a good idea if your child does, too. Here are a few games that help with that.

+ Zingo
+ Peaceable Kingdom Alphabet Go Fish Letter Matching Card Game
+ Peaceable Kingdom Alphabet Bingo

As you are reading to your child, you may also wish to start explaining to them that certain letters have certain sounds associated with them. Some precocious children learn to read before going to kindergarten. If you want to try to teach your children to read, you may wish to consult *Teach Your Child to Read in 100 Easy Lessons* by Siegfried Engelmann or *The Ordinary Parent's Guide to Teaching Reading* by Jessie Wise. However, I wouldn't place much importance on your children learning to read before they go to school; none of mine did and it doesn't seem to have held them back academically.

With respect to math, it's also a good idea if your children have some basic numeracy before they go to kindergarten. Children have an intuitive sense of math. They understand, for example, that three cookies are more than two cookies. Your first task is to teach your child the names of these numbers and how to count. Here are some games to achieve that:

+ Zingo 1-2-3
+ Tiny Polka Dot
+ Hi Ho Cherry-O

In addition, the card games Uno, Go Fish, and War can reinforce basic number skills.

Math manipulatives such as the following can help your child understand more advanced math skills:

+ Cuisenaire Rods: addition
+ Base 10 Blocks: the base 10 system
+ Magnetic Fraction Tiles: fractions
+ Unifix Cubes: counting, addition, subtraction, multiplication, and division

That's all I have to say on the preschool years, but keep in mind that many of the other chapters here, such as those concerning music, science, and games, start to become relevant when your child is about four years old.

RECOMMENDED MOVIES
AND TELEVISION SHOWS

Below is a list of recommended movies and television shows. I've indicated the youngest age at which the average child might be able to appreciate these shows, but most of them can be enjoyed not only by older children but by adults as well.

AGE 6+

Walking with Dinosaurs (BBC, 1999): Six-part series on dinosaurs

Walking with Beasts (BBC, 2001): Prehistoric animals

Walking with Cavemen (BBC, 2003): Origins of man; evolution

Steamboat Bill Junior (1928): Buster Keaton silent film

The Gold Rush (1925): Charlie Chaplin silent film

Duck Soup (1933): A classic Marx Brothers film

AGE 7+

The General (1926): Buster Keaton silent film set in the Civil War

Mary Poppins (1964): The classic Disney musical

The Sound of Music (1965): Classical musical set in the years just before World War II

The Wizard of Oz (1939)

Mankind: the Story of All of Us (2012): A twelve-part miniseries that tells the story of mankind from the emergence of humans through the nineteenth century; very strong visuals

AGE 8 +

Ben Hur (1960): Drama set in Roman times

The Ten Commandments (1956): Set in Egyptian times

The Life of Mammals (BBC, 2002): David Attenborough

AGE 9 +

Planet Earth (BBC, 2006): David Attenborough

Africa (BBC, 2013): David Attenborough

Life (BBC, 2009): David Attenborough

The Great Human Odyssey (PBS, 2015): The emergence of *Homo sapiens*

The African Queen (1951): Terrific adventure story with Humphrey Bogart and Katherine Hepburn

Singin' in the Rain (1952): Classic musical

AGE 10+

Wonders of the Universe (BBC, 2011): Miniseries on physics narrated by rock star scientist Brian Cox

Wonders of Life (BBC, 2013): Origins of life; evolution; biology

Spartacus (1960): Drama set in Roman times

Wonders of Our Solar System (BBC, 2010)

West Wing (NBC, 1999–2006): TV series on American politics; extremely well written and informative

Charles Darwin and the Tree of Life (2009, BBC): David Attenborough documentary on evolution

Doctor Who (Ninth through Eleventh Doctors, 2005–2013): This series is surprisingly thought-provoking

Shane (1953): A classic Western

Captains Courageous (1937): A spoiled rich boy is picked up by a fishing vessel after falling off a large boat; based on a great Rudyard Kipling story

Mr. Smith Goes to Washington (1939): A sweet idealistic film that will teach children about politics

AGE 11+

The Crossing (A&E, 2000): Film on George Washington crossing the Delaware River during the Revolutionary War

Glory (1989): Film on U.S. Civil War's first all-Black volunteer company

Lincoln (2012): Film on Abraham Lincoln's presidency

The Civil War (1990): Ken Burns documentary

Sullivan's Travels (1941): Hilarious but touching film set in the Great Depression

1776 (1972): A musical about the American Revolution

The Treasure of the Sierra Madre (1948): Film about gold prospecting by John Huston with Humphrey Bogart

Mr. Smith Goes to Washington (1939): A Frank Capra film with Jimmy Stewart about an idealistic politician who goes to the Senate

Dial M for Murder (1954): Classic Hitchcock thriller based on a famous play

To Be or Not to Be (1942): An Ernst Lubitsch comedic masterpiece set in World War II

Monty Python and the Holy Grail (1975): A comedy set in the Middle Ages

To Kill a Mockingbird (1962): A lawyer defends a Black man against an undeserved rape charge

AGE 12+

High Noon (1952): One of the great Westerns

Quest for Fire (1981): Fictionalized story of prehistoric man

The Music Man (1962): Terrific musical

In Search of Giants (BBC, 2007): Science program about particle physics

Amadeus (1984): The life of Mozart; helps build an appreciation of his music

Selma (2014): Martin Luther King Jr.'s epic march from Selma to Montgomery, Alabama, to secure voting rights

Mandela (2013): The life of Nelson Mandela

Thirteen Days (2000): About the Cuban Missile Crisis

The Right Stuff (1983): Amusing historical drama on the U.S. space program

West Side Story (1961): Classic musical

Apollo 13 (1995): Docudrama on a lunar mission gone wrong

All the President's Men (1976): Covers the *Washington Post*'s investigation of Watergate

The Vietnam War (2017): Documentary by Ken Burns

The Post (2017): A film about the battle over publication of the Pentagon Papers during the Vietnam War

Witness for the Prosecution (1957): Classic murder mystery courtroom drama

Twelve Angry Men (1975): Famous courtroom drama with Henry Fonda

My Cousin Vinny (1992): A brilliant comedy that is actually surprisingly sophisticated about legal procedure

Groundhog Day (1993): A brilliant comedy with a profound moral

John Adams (HBO miniseries, 2008): Critical moments in the life of founding father John Adams

Inherit the Wind (1960): Classic film about the teaching of evolution in school.

AGE 13+

Elizabeth (1998): Film about Queen Elizabeth I of England

Good Night and Good Luck (2005): About journalist Edward R. Murrow standing up to Senator Joe McCarthy

Amistad (1997): A dispute about the mutiny of slaves on a Spanish ship and the resulting court case in the United States

The Pirates of Penzance (1983): Based on a Gilbert and Sullivan play and including the classic song "The Very Model of a Modern Major General"

Lawrence of Arabia (1962): Epic historical drama about an English officer's role in World War I

Doctor Zhivago (1965): Set in Russia during World War I and the Russian Revolution

The Grapes of Wrath (1940): Set in the Great Depression and based on the Steinbeck novel

Patton (1970): Epic biographical war film about General George Patton

Casablanca (1939): A classic love story set in World War II

My Fair Lady (1964): A British musical

Saving Private Ryan (1998): Film about D-Day

The Longest Day (1962): Film about D-Day

The Great Escape (1963): Set in World War II

The Pianist (2002): Jewish musician struggles to survive in Warsaw during World War II

Darkest Hour (2017): Winston Churchill in the early days of World War II

Letters from Iwo Jima (2006): Story of the battle of Iwo Jima from a Japanese perspective

The Bomb (PBS, 2014): Documentary about the creation and use of the nuclear bomb

Gandhi (1982): Brilliant epic film about the Indian leader

Agora (2009): Film about clash of Christians and pagans in the late Roman Empire

The Best Man (1964): Film adaptation of a Gore Vidal play about a presidential election; starring Henry Fonda

Romeo and Juliet (1968): Franco Zeffirelli's adaptation of the classic play

Master and Commander (2003): A film by Peter Weir that gives a fairly accurate depiction of eighteenth-century maritime warfare

Gettysburg (1993): A film about this critical battle in the American Revolution

The Brooklyn Bridge (1981): Ken Burns documentary about the construction of the Brooklyn Bridge

AGE 14+

Advise and Consent (1962): Sophisticated political drama by Otto Preminger about the confirmation of a nominee for secretary of state

An American in Paris (1951): Classic musical with great dancing

Frost/Nixon (2008): A dramatic retelling of the post-Watergate television interviews between British talk show host David Frost and former president Richard Nixon

Paths of Glory (1957): Set in World War 1

The Last of the Mohicans (1992): Epic historical drama set in 1757 during the French and Indian War

Schindler's List (1993): Film about a man's effort to save Jews from genocide

A Man for All Seasons (1966): The story of Thomas More, who
  stood up to King Henry VIII when the king rejected the Roman
  Catholic Church to obtain a divorce
The Man Who Would Be King (1975): Film by John Huston based on
  a short story by Rudyard Kipling
Sense and Sensibility (1995): Arguably the best film adaptation of a
  Jane Austen novel
Too Big to Fail (2011): Drama on the 2008 financial crisis
Dr. Strangelove (1964): A dark comedy on nuclear war
Margin Call (2011): Entertaining and surprisingly sophisticated film
  set amid the 2008 financial crisis
The Big Short (2015): A comedy about the 2008 financial crisis
Hamilton (2020): A film version of the groundbreaking musical on
  the life of Alexander Hamilton
Chernobyl (2019): This miniseries teaches both about nuclear power
  and about the Soviet Union
New York (1999–2003): A series of documentaries by Ric Burns on
  the history of New York City

AGE 15+

Twelve Years a Slave (2013): The story of a free-born Black man
  who is captured by slavers; based on a true story
Hotel Rwanda (2004): Film on genocide in Rwanda
Jazz (2001): The history of jazz in the United States by Ken
  Burns
Charlie Wilson's War (2007): About the United States' support for
  Afghan rebels against the Soviet Union
Much Ado About Nothing (1993): An approachable Shakespearian
  comedy with many great actors including several Hollywood
  stars
The Killing Fields (1984): British film about the Khmer Rouge regime
  in Cambodia as experienced by two journalists
Fog of War: Eleven Lessons from the Life of Robert S. McNamara
  (2003): Documentary on McNamara's reflections on war
  combined with archival footage
Rashomon (1950): Brilliant Japanese film
Downfall (2004): The final ten days of Hitler's rule

The Message (1976): Drama about the life of Muhammad and early
   Islamic history

Barry Lyndon (1975): A beautiful film based on a novel by Thackery

Henry V (1989): One of the greatest Shakespearian film adaptations,
   by Kenneth Branagh

The Last Emperor (1987): A film about China's last emperor

Reds (1981): A story about a journalist who witnessed the Russian
   Revolution

RECOMMENDED BOOKS

Below is a list of recommended books. I have categorized them by the earliest age at which most children will probably be able to read a book. For example, I've given an age range of eight to ten for the Harry Potter books because most children will first be able to read these books sometime between the ages of eight and ten. Some children may not be able to read Harry Potter books until they are older and some unusually precocious children may be able to read them at a younger age. Moreover, just because I indicate that a book can be read by children in a certain age range, that doesn't mean that older children will be unable to profit from reading these books. Many older children and adults enjoy reading the Harry Potter books. In addition, some of the books that I've listed, such as *Call of the Wild*, are, in fact, adult books.

I've also listed books for high school students. These are all adult books. I've chosen them because they are very good and cover a variety of topics.

Fiction

WORDLESS
    Chalk, Bill Thomson
    Creepy Castle, John S. Goodall

Flotsam, David Wiesner

Good Dog, Carl (Good Dog, Carl, #1), Alexandra Day

Good Night, Gorilla, Peggy Rathmann

Journey, Aaron Becker

Julián Is a Mermaid (Julián, #1), Jessica Love

Quest, Aaron Becker

Sector 7, David Wiesner

The Arrival, Shaun Tan

The Lion and the Mouse, Jerry Pinkney

The Snowman, Raymond Briggs

Tuesday, David Wiesner

Unspoken: A Story from the Underground Railroad, Henry Cole

AGES: 4–6

A Bad Case of Stripes, David Shannon

Are You My Mother?, P. D. Eastman

Bedtime for Frances, Russell Hoban

Bread and Jam for Frances, Russell Hoban

Brown Bear, Brown Bear, What Do You See?, Bill Martin Jr.

But Not the Hippopotamus, Sandra Boynton

Casey at the Bat: A Ballad of the Republic Sung in the Year 1888, Ernest Lawrence Thayer

Chicka Chicka Boom Boom, Bill Martin Jr.

Chicken Soup with Rice, Maurice Sendak

Don't Let the Pigeon Drive the Bus!, Mo Willems

Don't Let the Pigeon Stay Up Late!, Mo Willems

Dr. Seuss's ABC, Dr. Seuss

Five Little Monkeys Jumping on the Bed, Eileen Christelow

Fox in Socks, Dr. Seuss

Go, Dog. Go!, P. D. Eastman

Goodnight Moon, Margaret Wise Brown

Green Eggs and Ham, Dr. Seuss

Guess How Much I Love You, Sam McBratney

Harold and the Purple Crayon (Harold, #1), Crockett Johnson

Horton Hatches the Egg, Dr. Seuss

How Do Dinosaurs Say Good Night?, Jane Yolen

If You Give a Mouse a Cookie, Laura Joffe Numeroff

In the Night Kitchen, Maurice Sendak

Knuffle Bunny: A Cautionary Tale (Knuffle Bunny, #1), Mo
Willems

Little Blue Truck, Alice Schertle

Llama Llama Red Pajama, Anna Dewdney

Love You Forever, Robert Munsch

Madeline, Ludwig Bemelmans

Mel Fell, Corey R. Tabor

Mike Mulligan and His Steam Shovel, Virginia Lee Burton

Miss Nelson Is Missing! (Miss Nelson, #1), Harry Allard

No, David!, David Shannon

Oh, the Places You'll Go!, Dr. Seuss

Olivia (Olivia, #1), Ian Falconer

One Fish, Two Fish, Red Fish, Blue Fish, Dr. Seuss

Owl Moon, Jane Yolen

Press Here, Hervé Tullet

Richard Scarry's Best Storybook Ever!, Richard Scarry

Sisters First, Jenna Bush Hager, Barbara Pierce Bush, and Ramona
Kaulitzki

Stone Soup, Jon J. Muth

Sylvester and the Magic Pebble, William Steig

The Cat in the Hat, Dr. Seuss

The Complete Adventures of Curious George, Margret Rey

The Grouchy Ladybug, Eric Carle

The Gruffalo, Julia Donaldson

The Little Engine That Could, Watty Piper

The Little House, Virginia Lee Burton

The Mitten, Jan Brett

The Monster at the End of This Book, Jon Stone

The Night Before Christmas, Clement C. Moore

The Paper Bag Princess, Robert Munsch

The Poky Little Puppy, Janette Sebring Lowrey

The Polar Express, Chris Van Allsburg

The Rainbow Fish, Marcus Pfiste

The Runaway Bunny, Margaret Wise Brown

The Snowy Day (Peter, #1), Ezra Jack Keats

The Story of Babar (Babar, #1), Jean de Brunhoff

The Tale of Custard the Dragon, Ogden Nash
The Three Billy Goats Gruff, Paul Galdone
The True Story of the 3 Little Pigs!, Jon Scieszka
The Ugly Duckling, Hans Christian Andersen
The Velveteen Rabbit, Margery Williams Bianco
The Very Busy Spider, Eric Carle
The Very Hungry Caterpillar, Eric Carle
There Was an Old Lady Who Swallowed a Fly, Pam Adams
There's a Wocket in My Pocket!, Dr. Seuss
We're Going on a Bear Hunt, Michael Rosen
What Do People Do All Day?, Richard Scarry
Where the Wild Things Are, Maurice Sendak
Yertle the Turtle and Other Stories, Dr. Seuss

AGES: 6–8

A Light in the Attic, Shel Silverstein
Aesop's Fables: The Classic Edition, Aesop and Charles Santore
Alexander and the Terrible, Horrible, No Good, Very Bad Day, Judith
    Viorst
Amelia Bedelia (Amelia Bedelia, #1), Peggy Parish
And to Think That I Saw It on Mulberry Street, Dr. Seuss
Astérix and Cleopatra (Astérix, #6), René Goscinny
Astérix and the Golden Sickle (Astérix, #2), René Goscinny
Astérix and the Goths (Astérix, #3), René Goscinny
Astérix and the Normans (Astérix, #9), René Goscinny
Astérix at the Olympic Games (Astérix, #12), René Goscinny
Astérix in Britain (Astérix, #8), René Goscinny
Astérix the Gaul (Astérix, #1), René Goscinny
Astérix the Gladiator (Astérix, #4), René Goscinny
Astérix the Legionary (Astérix, #10), René Goscinny
Blueberries for Sal, Robert McCloskey
*Caps for Sale: A Tale of a Peddler, Some Monkeys and Their Monkey
    Business*, Esphyr Slobodkina
Chrysanthemum, Kevin Henkes
Cigars of the Pharaoh (Tintin, #4), Hergé
Click, Clack, Moo: Cows That Type, Doreen Cronin
Clifford the Big Red Dog, Norman Bridwell

Cloudy with a Chance of Meatballs (Cloudy with a Chance of
    Meatballs, #1), Judi Barrett
Corduroy, Don Freeman
Danny and the Dinosaur, Syd Hoff
Days with Frog and Toad (Frog and Toad, #4), Arnold Lobel
Destination Moon (Tintin, #16), Hergé
Elmer and the Dragon (My Father's Dragon, #2), Ruth Stiles Gannett
Eloise, Kay Thompson
Extra Yarn, Mac Barnett
Falling Up, Shel Silverstein
Fantastic Mr. Fox, Roald Dahl
Frog and Toad All Year (Frog and Toad, #3), Arnold Lobel
Frog and Toad Are Friends (Frog and Toad, #1), Arnold Lobel
Frog and Toad Together (Frog and Toad, #2), Arnold Lobel
Horton Hears a Who!, Dr. Seuss
How the Grinch Stole Christmas!, Dr. Seuss
I Want My Hat Back, Jon Klassen
If You Give a Moose a Muffin, Laura Joffe Numeroff
Jabari Jumps, Gaia Cornwall
Just So Stories, Rudyard Kipling
Last Stop on Market Street, Matt de la Peña
Little Bear (Little Bear, #1), Else Holmelund Minarik
Little Red Riding Hood, Trina Schart Hyman
Lyle, Lyle, Crocodile, Bernard Waber
Make Way for Ducklings, Robert McCloskey
Matilda, Roald Dahl
Mouse Soup, Arnold Lobel
My Father's Dragon (My Father's Dragon, #1), Ruth Stiles Gannett
Pierre: A Cautionary Tale in Five Chapters and a Prologue, Maurice
    Sendak
Red Rackham's Treasure (Tintin, #12), Hergé
Rikki-Tikki-Tavi, Rudyard Kipling
Sadako and the Thousand Paper Cranes, Eleanor Coerr
Small Pig, Arnold Lobel
Stellaluna, Janell Cannon
Strega Nona, Tomie dePaola
The 500 Hats of Bartholomew Cubbins, Dr. Seuss

The Black Island (Tintin, #7), Hergé

The Blue Lotus (Tintin, #5), Hergé

The Children's Book of Virtues, William Bennett

The Crab with the Golden Claws (Tintin, #9), Hergé

The Dragons of Blueland (My Father's Dragon, #3), Ruth Stiles Gannett

The Emperor's New Clothes, Hans Christian Andersen

The Five Chinese Brothers, Claire Huchet Bishop

The Giving Tree, Shel Silverstein

The Jungle Books, Rudyard Kipling

The Little Match Girl, Hans Christian Andersen

The Lorax, Dr. Seuss

The Secret of the Unicorn (Tintin, #11), Hergé

The Sneetches and Other Stories, Dr. Seuss

The Stinky Cheese Man and Other Fairly Stupid Tales, Jon Scieszka

The Story of Ferdinand, Munro Leaf

The Twits, Roald Dahl

The World of Winnie-the-Pooh (Winnie-the-Pooh, #1–#2), A. A. Milne

There Is a Bird on Your Head! (Elephant & Piggie, #4), Mo Willems

Tikki Tikki Tembo, Arlene Mosel

Tintin in Tibet (Tintin, #20), Hergé

Where the Sidewalk Ends, Shel Silverstein

AGES: 8–10

Because of Winn-Dixie, Kate DiCamillo

Beezus and Ramona, Beverly Cleary

Bone: The Complete Edition, Jeff Smith

Bridge to Terabithia, Katherine Paterson

Charlie and the Chocolate Factory (Charlie Bucket, #1), Roald Dahl

Charlotte's Web, E. B. White

Crown: An Ode to the Fresh Cut, Derrick Barnes

D'Aulaires' Book of Greek Myths, Ingri and Edgar d'Aulaire

Danny the Champion of the World, Roald Dahl

From the Mixed-Up Files of Mrs. Basil E. Frankweiler, E. L. Konigsburg

Hansel and Gretel, Neil Gaiman

Harriet the Spy, Louise Fitzhugh

Harry Potter and the Sorcerer's Stone, J. K. Rowling

James and the Giant Peach, Roald Dahl

Little House on the Prairie, Laura Ingalls Wilder

Mr. Popper's Penguins, Richard Atwater

Mrs. Frisby and the Rats of NIMH (Rats of NIMH, #1), Robert C. O'Brien

Mrs. Piggle-Wiggle (Mrs. Piggle Wiggle, #1), Betty MacDonald

My Name Is Yoon, Helen Recorvits

Peanuts Treasury, Charles M. Schulz

Peter Pan, J. M. Barrie

Pippi Longstocking (Pippi Långstrump, #1), Astrid Lindgren

Ramona the Pest, Beverly Cleary

Sideways Stories from Wayside School, Louis Sachar

Stuart Little, E. B. White

Superfudge, Judy Blume

Tales of a Fourth Grade Nothing, Judy Blume

The Authoritative Calvin and Hobbes: A Calvin and Hobbes Treasury, Bill Watterson

The Bad Beginning (A Series of Unfortunate Events, #1), Lemony Snicket

The Battle of the Labyrinth (Percy Jackson and the Olympians, #4), Rick Riordan

The BFG, Roald Dahl

The Boxcar Children (The Boxcar Children, #1), Gertrude Chandler Warner

The Calvin and Hobbes Lazy Sunday Book, Bill Watterson

The Complete Fairy Tales, Hans Christian Andersen

The Cricket in Times Square (Chester Cricket and His Friends, #1), George Selden

The Essential Calvin and Hobbes: A Calvin and Hobbes Treasury, Bill Watterson

The Lightning Thief (Percy Jackson and the Olympians, #1), Rick Riordan

The Little Prince, Antoine de Saint-Exupéry

The Lost Hero (The Heroes of Olympus, #1), Rick Riordan

The Miraculous Journey of Edward Tulane, Kate DiCamillo

The Mouse and the Motorcycle (Ralph S. Mouse, #1), Beverly Cleary

The Sea of Monsters (Percy Jackson and the Olympians, #2), Rick
    Riordan
The Season of Styx Malone, Kekla Magoon
The Secret Garden, Frances Hodgson Burnett
The Tale of Despereaux, Kate DiCamillo
The Tale of Peter Rabbit, Beatrix Potter
The Titan's Curse (Percy Jackson and the Olympians, #3), Rick Riordan
The Trumpet of the Swan, E. B. White
The Wind in the Willows, Kenneth Grahame
The Witches, Roald Dahl
Wayside School Is Falling Down, Louis Sachar

AGES: 10–12

A Swiftly Tilting Planet, Madeleine L'Engle
A Wind in the Door, Madeleine L'Engle
A Wrinkle in Time, Madeleine L'Engle
Alice's Adventures in Wonderland / Through the Looking-Glass, Lewis
    Carroll
Are You There God? It's Me, Margaret, Judy Blume
Ender's Game (Ender's Saga, #1), Orson Scott Card
Front Desk (Front Desk, #1), Kelly Yang
Ghost, Jason Reynolds
Holes, Louis Sacha
Maniac Magee, Jerry Spinelli
My Brother Sam Is Dead, James Lincoln Collier
New Kid (New Kid, #1), Jerry Craft
Old Yeller, Fred Gipson
Other Words for Home, Jasmine Warga
Roller Girl, Victoria Jamieson
Sounder, William H. Armstrong
The Crossover, Kwame Alexander
The Devil's Storybook, Natalie Babbitt
The Fellowship of the Ring, J. R. R. Tolkien
The Golden Compass (His Dark Materials, #1), Philip Pullman
The Hobbit, J. R. R. Tolkien
The Indian in the Cupboard (The Indian in the Cupboard, #1),
    Lynne Reid Banks

The Legend of Sleepy Hollow, Gris Grimly

The Lord of the Rings, J. R. R. Tolkien

The Mysterious Benedict Society (The Mysterious Benedict Society, #1),
    Trenton Lee Stewart

The Phantom Tollbooth, Norton Juster

The Wonderful Wizard of Oz (Oz, #1), L. Frank Baum

Tuck Everlasting, Natalie Babbitt

Watership Down, Richard Adams

Wonder, R. J. Palacio

AGES: 12–14

A Christmas Carol, Charles Dickens

A Separate Peace, John Knowles

A Tree Grows in Brooklyn, Betty Smith

Anne of Green Gables (Anne of Green Gables, #1), L. M. Montgomery

Carry On, Mr. Bowditch, Jean Lee Latham

Childhood's End, Arthur C. Clarke

Flowers for Algernon, Daniel Keyes

Hatchet, Gary Paulsen

Johnny Tremain: The Story of Boston in Revolt Against the British,
    Esther Forbes

Little Women, Louisa May Alcott

Mary Poppins (Mary Poppins, #1), P. L. Travers

Messenger, Lois Lowry

Number the Stars, Lois Lowry

The Absolutely True Diary of a Part-Time Indian, Sherman
    Alexie

The Adventures of Huckleberry Finn, Mark Twain

The Adventures of Tom Sawyer, Mark Twain

The Book Thief, Markus Zusak

The Call of the Wild, Jack London

The Chronicles of Narnia, C. S. Lewis

The Complete Persepolis, Marjane Satrapi

The Curious Incident of the Dog in the Night-Time, Mark Haddon

The Diary of a Young Girl, Anne Frank

The Fault in Our Stars, John Green

The Giver, Lois Lowry

The Hitchhiker's Guide to the Galaxy (The Hitchhiker's Guide to the
  Galaxy, #1), Douglas Adams
The House on Mango Street, Sandra Cisneros
The Invention of Hugo Cabret, Brian Selznick
The Outsiders, S. E. Hinton
The Princess Bride, William Goldman
The True Confessions of Charlotte Doyle, Avi
The Watsons Go to Birmingham—1963, Christopher Paul Curti
To Kill a Mockingbird, Harper Lee
White Fang, Jack London

AGE: HIGH SCHOOL

1984, George Orwell
And Then There Were None, Agatha Christie
Animal Farm, George Orwell
Beloved, Toni Morrison
Brave New World, Aldous Huxley
Catch-22, Joseph Heller
Do Androids Dream of Electric Sheep?, Philip K. Dick
Fahrenheit 451, Ray Bradbury
Of Human Bondage, W. Somerset Maugham
Pride and Prejudice, Jane Austen
Song of Solomon, Toni Morrison
Stranger in a Strange Land, Robert A. Heinlein
The Catcher in the Rye, J. D. Salinger
The Color Purple, Alice Walker
The Great Gatsby, F. Scott Fitzgerald
The Green Mile, Stephen King
The Handmaid's Tale (The Handmaid's Tale, #1), Margaret Atwood
The Help, Kathryn Stockett
The Hound of the Baskervilles (Sherlock Holmes, #5), Arthur Conan
  Doyle
The Killer Angels (The Civil War Trilogy, #2), Michael Shaara
The Kite Runner, Khaled Hosseini
The Martian, Andy Weir
The Martian Chronicles, Ray Bradbury
The Metamorphosis, Franz Kafka

Nonfiction

AGES: 6–8

DKfindout! Ancient Egypt, DK Publishing

DKfindout! Stone Age, DK Publishing

DKfindout! Vikings, DK Publishing

DKfindout! World War I, DK Publishing

DKfindout! World War II, DK Publishing

First History Encyclopedia: A First Reference Book for Children (DK First Reference), DK Publishing

Hidden Figures: The True Story of Four Black Women and the Space Race, Margot Lee Shetterly

The History of Pearl Harbor: A World War II Book for New Readers (The History Of: A Biography Series for New Readers), Susan B. Katz

The History of the Civil Rights Movement: A History Book for New Readers (The History Of: A Biography Series for New Readers), Shadae Mallory MA

The History of the Civil War: A History Book for New Readers (The History Of: A Biography Series for New Readers), Susan B. Katz

The House That Jane Built: A Story About Jane Addams, Tanya Lee Stone

The Story of Anne Frank: A Biography Book for New Readers (The Story Of: A Biography Series for New Readers), Emma Carlson Berne

The Story of Barack Obama A Biography Book for New Readers (The Story Of: A Biography Series for New Readers), Tonya Leslie

The Story of Benjamin Franklin: A Biography Book for New Readers (The Story Of: A Biography Series for New Readers), Shannon Anderson

The Story of Ella Fitzgerald: A Biography Book for New Readers (The Story Of: A Biography Series for New Readers), Kathy Trusty

The Story of Gandhi: A Biography Book for New Readers (The Story Of: A Biography Series for New Readers), Susan B. Katz

The Story of Harriet Tubman: A Biography Book for New Readers (The Story Of: A Biography Series for New Readers), Christine Platt

The Story of Helen Keller: A Biography Book for New Readers (The Story Of: A Biography Series for New Readers), Christine Platt

The Story of Leonardo da Vinci: A Biography Book for New Readers (The Story Of: A Biography Series for New Readers), Ciara O'Neal

The Story of Marie Curie: A Biography Book for New Readers (The Story Of: A Biography Series for New Readers), Susan B. Katz

The Story of Martin Luther King Jr.: A Biography Book for New Readers (The Story Of: A Biography Series for New Readers), Christine Platt

The Story of Nelson Mandela: A Biography Book for New Readers (The Story Of: A Biography Series for New Readers), Floyd Stokes

The Story of the Wright Brothers: A Biography Book for New Readers (The Story Of: A Biography Series for New Readers), Annette Whipple

Timelines of Everything, DK Publishing

AGES: 8–10

Castle, David Macaulay

Cathedral: The Story of Its Construction, David Macaulay

DK Eyewitness Books: Ancient Egypt, George Hart

DK Knowledge Encyclopedia: Human Body!, DK IMPULSE

Knowledge Encyclopedia History!: The Past as You've Never Seen It Before, DK Publishing

Kokoda: Younger Readers, Peter FitzSimons

The Way Things Work, David Macaulay

What Is the Declaration of Independence?, Michael C. Harris

What Is the Panama Canal?, Janet B. Pascal

What Was the Age of Exploration?, Catherine Daly

What Was the Alamo?, Pam Pollack

What Was the Battle of Gettysburg?, Jim O'Connor

What Was the Berlin Wall?, Nico Medina

What Was the Bombing of Hiroshima?, Jess M. Brallier

What Was the Boston Tea Party?, Kathleen Krull

What Was the Gold Rush?, Joan Holub

What Was the Great Depression?, Janet B. Pascal

What Was the Harlem Renaissance?, Sherri L. Smith

What Was the Holocaust?, Gail Herman

What Was the Lewis and Clark Expedition?, Judith St. George

What Was the March on Washington?, Kathleen Krull

What Was the Plague?, Roberta Edwards
What Was the Underground Railroad?, Yona Zeldis McDonoug
What Was the Vietnam War?, Jim O'Connor
Where Are the Great Pyramids?, Dorothy Hoobler
Where Is the Great Wall?, Patricia Brennan Demuth
Who Was Abraham Lincoln?, Janet B. Pascal
Who Was Anne Frank?, Ann Abramson
Who Was Ben Franklin?, Dennis Brindell Fradin
Who Was Betsy Ross?, James Buckley Jr.
Who Was Franklin Roosevelt?, Margaret Frith
Who Was Gandhi?, Dana Meachen Rau
Who Was Harriet Beecher Stowe?, Dana Meachen Rau
Who Was Harriet Tubman?, Yona Zeldis McDonough
Who Was Henry Ford?, Michael Burgan
Who Was Louis Armstrong?, Yona Zeldis McDonough
Who Was Marco Polo?, Joan Holub
Who Was Marie Antoinette?, Dana Meachen Rau
Who Was Mark Twain?, April Jones Prince
Who Was Martin Luther King, Jr.?, Bonnie Bader
Who Was Paul Revere?, Roberta Edwards
Who Was Rosa Parks?, Yona Zeldis McDonough
Who Was Theodore Roosevelt?, Michael Burgan
Who Was Thomas Alva Edison?, Margaret Frith
Who Was Thomas Jefferson?, Dennis Brindell Fradi
Who Was William Shakespeare?, Celeste Davidson Mannis
Who Was Winston Churchill?, Ellen Labrecque
Who Were the Wright Brothers?, James Buckley Jr.

AGES: 10–12

A Short History of the Civil War, DK Publishing
A Short History of World War II, DK Publishing
Ancient Egypt: The Definitive Visual History, DK Publishing
Ancient Times: From the Earliest Nomads to the Last Roman Emperor
    (The Story of the World #1), Susan Wise Bauer
Artists: Their Lives and Works, DK Publishing
Early Modern Times: From Elizabeth the First to the Forty-Niners
    (The Story of the World, #3), Susan Wise Bauer

History of the World in 1,000 Objects, DK Publishing
History of the World Map by Map, DK Publishing
Sapiens: A Graphic History, Volume 1—The Birth of Humankind,
    David Vandermeulen
Sapiens: A Graphic History, Volume 2—The Pillars of Civilization,
    David Vandermeulen
The Arts: A Visual Encyclopedia, DK Publishing
The Civil War: A Visual History, DK Publishing/Smithsonian
*The Illustrated Story of Art: The Great Art Movements and the
    Paintings That Inspired Them*, DK Publishing
The Middle Ages: From the Fall of Rome to the Rise of the Renaissance
    (The Story of the World, #2), Susan Wise Bauer
The Modern Age: From Victoria's Empire to the End of the USSR (The
    Story of the World, #4), Susan Wise Bauer
*Timelines of History: The Ultimate Visual Guide to the Events That
    Shaped the World*, DK Publishing
Train: The Definitive Visual History, DK Publishing
World History: From the Ancient World to the Information Age, DK
    Publishing
World War II: Visual Encyclopedia, DK Publishing

AGES: 12–14

A Little History of the World, E. H. Gombrich
All the President's Men, Carl Bernstein
Moneyball: The Art of Winning an Unfair Game, Michael Lewis
Narrative of the Life of Frederick Douglass, Frederick Douglass
Shoe Dog: A Memoir by the Creator of Nike, Phil Knight
The Girl with Seven Names: A North Korean Defector's Story,
    Hyeonseo Lee
*The Hot Zone: The Terrifying True Story of the Origins of the Ebola
    Virus*, Richard Preston
The Middle Passage: White Ships/ Black Cargo, Tom Feelings
The Right Stuff, Tom Wolf

AGE: HIGH SCHOOL

1493 for Young People: From Columbus's Voyage to Globalization,
    Charles C. Mann

1776, David McCullough

A Civil Action, Jonathan Harr

A Little History of Economics, Niall Kishtainy

A Little History of Religion, Richard Holloway

A Little History of the United States, James West Davidson

A People's History of the United States, Howard Zinn

Alexander Hamilton, Ron Chernow

Bad Blood: Secrets and Lies in a Silicon Valley Startup, John Carreyrou

Band of Brothers: E Company, 506th Regiment, 101st Airborne from Normandy to Hitler's Eagle's Nest, Stephen E. Ambrose

Benjamin Franklin: An American Life, Walter Isaacson

Black Boy, Richard Wright

Bury My Heart at Wounded Knee: An Indian History of the American West, Dee Brown

Einstein: His Life and Universe, Walter Isaacson

Elon Musk: Tesla, SpaceX, and the Quest for a Fantastic Future, Ashlee Vance

Endurance: Shackleton's Incredible Voyage, Alfred Lansing

Freakonomics: A Rogue Economist Explores the Hidden Side of Everything, Steven D. Levitt and Stephen J. Dubner

Guns, Germs, and Steel: The Fates of Human Societies, Jared Diamond

Into Thin Air: A Personal Account of the Mount Everest Disaster, Jon Krakauer

John Adams, David McCullough

Lincoln, David Herbert Donald

Long Walk to Freedom, Nelson Mandela

Master of the Senate, Robert A. Caro

Maus I: A Survivor's Tale: My Father Bleeds History (Maus, #1), Art Spiegelman

Means of Ascent, Robert A. Caro

Mutiny on the Bounty: A Saga of Sex, Sedition, Mayhem and Mutiny, and Survival Against Extraordinary Odds, Peter FitzSimons

Night (The Night Trilogy, #1), Elie Wiesel

No Ordinary Time: Franklin and Eleanor Roosevelt: The Home Front in World War II, Doris Kearns Goodwin

Outliers: The Story of Success, Malcolm Gladwell

Parting the Waters: Martin Luther King and the Civil Rights Movement 1954–63, Taylor Branch

SPQR: A History of Ancient Rome, Mary Beard

Steve Jobs, Walter Isaacson

Survival in Auschwitz, Primo Levi

Team of Rivals: The Political Genius of Abraham Lincoln, Doris Kearns Goodwin

The Autobiography of Benjamin Franklin, Benjamin Franklin

The Autobiography of Malcolm X, Malcolm X

The Big Short: Inside the Doomsday Machine, Michael Lewis

The Boys in the Boat: Nine Americans and Their Epic Quest for Gold at the 1936 Berlin Olympics, Daniel James Brown

The Devil in the White City, Erik Larson

The Great Bridge: The Epic Story of the Building of the Brooklyn Bridge, David McCullough

The House of Morgan: An American Banking Dynasty and the Rise of Modern Finance, Ron Chernow

The Immortal Life of Henrietta Lacks, Rebecca Skloot

The Last Lion: Winston Spencer Churchill: Alone, 1932–40, William Manchester

The Law Book: Big Ideas Simply Explained, DK Publishing

The Making of the Atomic Bomb, Richard Rhodes

The Nine: Inside the Secret World of the Supreme Court, Jeffrey Toobin

The Path to Power, Robert A. Caro

The Power Broker: Robert Moses and the Fall of New York, Robert A. Caro

The Power of Babel: A Natural History of Language, John McWhorter

The Rise and Fall of the Third Reich: A History of Nazi Germany, William L. Shire

The Shortest History of China, Linda Jaivin

Too Big to Fail: The Inside Story of How Wall Street and Washington Fought to Save the Financial System from Crisis—and Themselves, Andrew Ross Sorkin

Truman, David McCullough

Unbroken: A World War II Story of Survival, Resilience and Redemption, Laura Hillenbrand

Washington: A Life, Ron Chernow

SCIENCE

AGES: 6–8

Dinosaur!: Over 60 Prehistoric Creatures as You've Never Seen Them Before (Knowledge Encyclopedias), DK Publishing

Encyclopedia Prehistorica: Dinosaurs, The Definitive Pop-Up, Robert Sabuda

Encyclopedia Prehistorica Mega-Beasts Pop-Up, Robert Sabuda

Encyclopedia Prehistorica: Sharks and Other Sea Monsters, Robert Sabuda

Inside the Human Body (The Magic School Bus, #3), Joanna Cole

Lost in the Solar System (The Magic School Bus, #4), Joanna Cole

On the Ocean Floor (The Magic School Bus, #5), Joanna Cole

The Human Body Coloring Book: The Ultimate Anatomy Study Guide, DK Publishing

The Magic School Bus at the Waterworks (The Magic School Bus #1), Joanna Cole

The Magic School Bus Gets Baked in a Cake: A Book About Kitchen Chemistry, Joanna Cole

The Magic School Bus Going Batty: A Book About Bats, Joanna Cole

The Magic School Bus Inside Ralphie: A Book About Germs, Joanna Cole

The Magic School Bus Inside the Earth (The Magic School Bus #2), Joanna Cole

The Magic School Bus Makes a Rainbow: A Book About Color, Joanna Cole

The Magic School Bus Sees Stars: A Book About Stars, Joanna Cole

AGES: 8–10

A Crash Course in Forces and Motion with Max Axiom, Super Scientist, Emily Sohn

A Journey into Adaptation with Max Axiom, Super Scientist, Agnieszka Biskup

A Journey Through the Digestive System with Max Axiom, Super Scientist, Emily Sohn

A Refreshing Look at Renewable Energy with Max Axiom, Super Scientist, Katherine E. Krohn

Adventures in Sound with Max Axiom, Super Scientist, Emily
   Sohn
An Anthology of Aquatic Life, Sam Hume
An Anthology of Intriguing Animals, Ben Hoare
Animal!: The Animal Kingdom as You've Never Seen It Before
   (Knowledge Encyclopedias), John Woodward
Animals: A Visual Encyclopedia, Carrie Love
*Crossing on Time: Steam Engines, Fast Ships, and a Journey to the
   New World*, David Macaulay
Decoding Genes with Max Axiom, Super Scientist (Graphic Science),
   Amber J. Keyser
Human (DK/Smithsonian Institution), Robert Winston
Human Body! (Knowledge Encyclopedias), DK Publishing
Knowledge Encyclopedia, DK Publishing
Micro Life: Miracles of the Miniature World Revealed, DK
   Publishing
Ocean: A Visual Encyclopedia, John Woodward
Ocean!: Our Watery World as You've Never Seen It Before (Knowledge
   Encyclopedias), DK Publishing
Oceanology: The Secrets of the Sea Revealed, DK Publishing
Science! (DK/Smithsonian Institution) DK Publishing
Space!: The Universe as You've Never Seen It Before (Knowledge
   Encyclopedias), DK Publishing
Space: A Visual Encyclopedia, DK Publishing
The Attractive Story of Magnetism with Max Axiom, Super Scientist,
   Andrea Gianopoulos
The Basics of Cell Life with Max Axiom, Super Scientist, Amber J.
   Keyser
*The Basics of Cell Life with Max Axiom, Super Scientist: 4D An
   Augmented Reading Science Experience* (Graphic Science 4D),
   Amber J. Keyser
*The Dynamic World of Chemical Reactions with Max Axiom, Super
   Scientist*, Tammy Enz
The Illuminating World of Light with Max Axiom, Super Scientist,
   Emily Sohn
The Incredible Work of Engineers with Max Axiom, Super Scientist,
   Tammy Enz

The Mysteries of the Universe: Discover the Best-Kept Secrets of Space, DK Publishing

The Mystery of Metal: The Fascinating Story of a Discovery That Changed the Course of History, Eric Grannis

The Planets: The Definitive Visual Guide to Our Solar System, DK Publishing

The Powerful World of Energy with Max Axiom, Super Scientist, Tammy Enz

The Science of Basketball with Max Axiom, Super Scientist (Science of Sports), Nikole Brooks Bethea

The Science of Steam Engines, Eric Grannis

The Shocking World of Electricity with Max Axiom, Super Scientist, Liam O'Donnell

The Solid Truth About States of Matter with Max Axiom, Super Scientist, Tammy Enz

The Surprising World of Bacteria with Max Axiom, Super Scientist, Agnieszka Biskup

The Wonders of Nature, Ben Hoare

The World of Food Chains with Max Axiom, Super Scientist, Liam O'Donnell

Understanding Photosynthesis with Max Axiom, Super Scientist, Liam O'Donnell

Understanding Viruses with Max Axiom, Super Scientist, Tammy Enz

Viruses and Vaccines: Smallpox to COVID-19, Eric Grannis

What Was the Age of the Dinosaurs?, Megan Stine

What Was the Ice Age?, Nico Medina

Who Was Galileo?, Patricia Brennan Demuth

Who Was Isaac Newton?, Janet B. Pascal

Zoology: Inside the Secret World of Animals, DK Publishing

AGES: 10–14

How Technology Works: The Facts Visually Explained, DK Publishing

Scientists Who Changed History, DK Publishing

The Elements Book: A Visual Encyclopedia of the Periodic Table, DK Publishing

The Science of Animals: Inside Their Secret World, DK Publishing

AGE: HIGH SCHOOL

A Brief History of Time, Stephen Hawking

A Short History of Nearly Everything, Bill Bryson

Big Bang: The Origin of the Universe, Simon Singh

Black Holes & Time Warps: Einstein's Outrageous Legacy, Kip S. Thorne

Sapiens: A Brief History of Humankind, Yuval Noah Harari

"Surely You're Joking, Mr. Feynman!": Adventures of a Curious Character, Richard P. Feynman

The Emperor of All Maladies: A Biography of Cancer, Siddhartha Mukherjee

The Flamingo's Smile: Reflections in Natural History, Stephen Jay Gould

The Selfish Gene, Richard Dawkins

The Third Chimpanzee: The Evolution and Future of the Human Animal, Jared Diamond

What If? Serious Scientific Answers to Absurd Hypothetical Questions (What If?, #1), Randall Munroe

What's Gotten Into You: The Story of Your Body's Atoms, from the Big Bang Through Last Night's Dinner, Dan Levitt

RECOMMENDED AUDIOBOOKS

Below is a list of recommended audiobooks. As with my list of printed books, I have categorized these audiobooks by the earliest age at which most children will probably be able to listen to them. In some cases, a book is listed for a younger age here than it is for the printed version on the theory that it is easier to listen to a book than it is to read it. I've selected books based on both the quality of the text and the quality of the performance. Note that the names given are the narrators of these books rather than the authors.

AGES: 4–6

A Visit from St. Nicholas: 'Twas the Night Before Christmas, Christian Andrade

A Weekend with Wendell, Melissa Leebaert

Blueberries for Sal, Melba Sibrel

Burt Dow: Deep Water Man, Tim Sample

Caps for Sale, Owen Jordan

Clementine, Jessica Almasy

Corduroy Audiobook Collection, Viola Davis

Doctor De Soto, Ian Thomson

Don't Let the Pigeon Stay Up Late!, Mo Willems

Frog and Toad Audio Collection, Arnold Lobel

Goggles!, Geoffrey Holder

Goldilocks and the Three Bears: Special Edition, Kat Marlowe
Hansel and Gretel, Kathy Bates
Horton Hears a Who!, Dustin Hoffman
Lon Po Po, B. D. Wong
Mike Mulligan and His Steam Shovel, Rod Ross
Mufaro's Beautiful Daughters, Terry Alexander
Nate the Great, John Lavelle
Peter and the Wolf, Jim Dale
Stone Soup, Rodd Ross
Stone Soup, B. D. Wong
The 500 Hats of Bartholomew Cubbins, Don Butler and Chas Butler
The Amazing Bone, Meryl Streep
The Cat in the Hat, Kelsey Grammer
The Eloise Audio Collection: Four Complete Eloise Tales: Eloise, Eloise in Paris, Eloise at Christmastime, and Eloise in Moscow, Bernadette Peters
The Gigantic Turnip, Ellen Verenieks
The Gruffalo, Imelda Staunton
The Little Engine That Could, Mike Ferreri
The Lorax, Ted Danson
The Tale of Peter Rabbit, Pauline Brailsford
The Three Billy Goats Gruff, Stephen Mangan
The True Story of the Three Little Pigs, Paul Giamatti
The Very Hungry Caterpillar, Kevin R. Free and Eric Carle
Three Tales of My Father's Dragon: My Father's Dragon, Elmer and the Dragon, and The Dragons of Blueland, Robert Serva
Tikki Tikki Tembo, Peter Thomas
Where the Wild Things Are, Peter Schickele
Why Koala Has a Stumpy Tail, Martha Hamilton and Mitch Weiss
Why Mosquitoes Buzz in People's Ears, James Earl Jones
Yertle the Turtle—Dr. Seuss, John Lithgow

AGES: 6–8

A Snicker of Magic, Cassandra Morris
Brave Irene, Meryl Streep
Catwings, Ursula K. Le Guin
Charlotte's Web, Meryl Streep

Classic Poems for Boys, Rachel Bavidge, Jasper Britton, Roy McMillan,
    Benjamin Soames, Anton Lesser, and Michael Caine

Classic Poems for Girls, Roy McMillan, Laura Paton, Anne-Marie
    Piazza, and Benjamin Soames

Danny the Champion of the World, Peter Serafinowicz

Fairy Stories, Roy Macready

Fantastic Mr. Fox and Other Stories, Quentin Blake, Hugh Laurie,
    Stephen Fry, and Chris O'Dowd

Framed, Brian Holden

Freckle Juice, Laura Hamilton

How to Train Your Dragon, David Tennant

How to Train Your Dragon: A Hero's Guide to Deadly Dragons, David
    Tennant

How to Train Your Dragon: How to Ride a Dragon's Storm, David
    Tennant

Little House in the Big Woods, Book 1, Cherry Jones

Matilda, Kate Winslet

Nelson Mandela's Favorite African Folktales, Samuel L. Jackson,
    Whoopi Goldberg, Matt Damon, and Alan Rickman

Otherwise Known as Sheila the Great, Judy Blume

Peter Pan, Lily Collins

Princess Cora and the Crocodile, Davina Porter

Revolting Rhymes & Dirty Beasts, Stephen Mangan, Tamsin Greig,
    and Miriam Margolyes

Rikki Tikki Tavi, Emma Lysy

Stuart Little, Julie Harris

The BFG, David Walliam

The Brave Tin Soldier and Other Fairy Tales, David Tennant,
    Anne-Marie Duff, Sir Derek Jacobi, and Penelope Wilton

The Emperor's New Clothes and Other Fairy Tales, Anne-Marie Duff,
    Penelope Wilton, and Sir Derek Jacobi

The Henry Huggins Audio Collection, Neil Patrick Harris and William
    Roberts

The Jungle Book, Benjamin May

The Last of the Dragons, Emma Gregory

The Ramona Quimby Audio Collection, Stockard Channing

The Twits, Richard Ayoade, Bill Bailey, and Kate Winslet

The Witches, Lolly Adefope
Upside-Down Magic, Rebecca Soler
What's The Big Idea, Ben Franklin?, Jean Fritz
Who Was Harriet Tubman?, Adenrele Ojo
Wilfrid Gordon McDonald Partridge, Mem Fox

AGES: 8–10

Because of Winn-Dixie, Jenna Lamia, Ann Patchett, and Kate
    DiCamillo
Bloody Jack, Katherine Kellgren
Charlie and the Chocolate Factory, Douglas Hodge
Chitty Chitty Bang Bang, David Tennant
Coraline, Neil Gaiman
Crenshaw, Kirby Heyborne
D'Aulaires' Book of Greek Myths, Paul Newman, Sidney Poitier,
    Kathleen Turner, and Matthew Broderick
Freddy and the Bean Home News, John McDonough
From the Mixed-Up Files of Mrs. Basil E. Frankweiler, Jill Clayburgh
Harry Potter and the Sorcerer's Stone, Book 1, Jim Dale
I Survived the Sinking of the Titanic, *1912, Book 1*, Lauren Fortgang
James and the Giant Peach, James Acaster
Mrs. Frisby and the Rats of NIMH, Barbara Caruso
Old Yeller, Peter Francis James
Percy Jackson's Greek Gods, Jesse Bernstein
Spy School, Book 1, Gibson Frazier
Tales of a Fourth Grade Nothing, Judy Blume
The 39 Clues, Book 1: The Maze of Bones, David Pittu
The Bearskinner, Richard Ferrone
The Explorer, Peter Noble
The Mysterious Benedict Society, Del Roy
The Mysterious Howling, Katherine Kellgren
The One and Only Ivan, Adam Grupper
The Railway Children, Virginia Leishman
The Secret Garden, Carrie Hope Fletcher
The Tale of Despereaux, Graeme Malcolm
The Wind in the Willows, Chris MacDonnell
The Wonderful Wizard of Oz, Anne Hathaway

Tuck Everlasting, Peter Thomas

Wonder, Kaya McLean, Lila Sage Bromley, Dariana Alvarez, Santino Barnard, Ry Chase, and Madeleine Curry

AGES: 10–12

Alice's Adventures in Wonderland, Scarlett Johansson

Ghost, Guy Lockard

Number the Stars, Blair Brown

Peter and the Starcatchers, Jim Dale

The Chronicles of Narnia Complete Audio Collection, Kenneth Branagh, Alex Jennings, Michael York, Lynn Redgrave, Derek Jacobi, Jeremy Northam, and Patrick Stewart

The Fellowship of the Ring, Rob Inglis

The Golden Compass, Philip Pullman, Joanna Wyatt, Rupert Degas, Alison Dowling, Douglas Blackwell, Jill Shilling, Stephen Thorne, Sean Barrett, Garrick Hagon, John O'Connor, Susan Sheridan and Full Cast

The Hitchhiker's Guide to the Galaxy, Stephen Fry

The Hobbit, Andy Serkis

NOTES

1: BOARD GAMES

1. Chris Stormont, "Famous People Who Play or Played Chess." The Stormont Kings, 2017. https://www.stormontkingschess.com/famous -people-who-play-or-played-chess/.
2. Karin, "Jamaica Produces a Chess-Master, Maurice Ashley." https:// yardedge.net, 2012. https://www.yardedge.net/jamaicans-on-the-edge /jamaica-produces-a-chess-master-maurice-ashley.
3. Benjamin Franklin, "The Morals of Chess [before 28 June 1779]." Founders Online, National Archives, n.d. https://founders.archives.gov /documents/Franklin/01-29-02-0608.
4. Learners Chess, "Why Chess?" Learners Chess Academy, 2021. https://learnerschess.org/articles-research/.
5. Karin, "Jamaica Produces a Chess-Master, Maurice Ashley." https:// www.yardedge.net/jamaicans-on-the-edge/jamaica-produces-a-chess -master-maurice-ashley.
6. John Dewey, *Democracy and Education*, 1916. https://www.gutenberg .org/files/852/852-h/852-h.htm.

5: MOVIES AND TELEVISION

1. "Kalahari," *Africa*. Season 1, Episode 1, BBC, 2013. https:// subslikescript.com/series/Africa-2571774/season-1/episode-1-Kalahari.
2. National Geographic, "Dawn of Darkness," *Savage Kingdom*. YouTube, 2021. https://youtu.be/3rHxgKI97s4?t=63.
3. picsandportraits, "1970s Nature Documentaries: Sleepcore Stream." YouTube, June 20, 2018. https://www.youtube.com /watch?v=mPhuvAhqJak&list=PLMZBpWb9dbDR9DL1h3hyvm9xe 9d5AYjEw.
4. Kirk Ellis, "Unite or Die," *John Adams*. Season 1, Episode 5, HBO, 2008, at 11:56. https://www.hbo.com/john-adams/season-1/5-unite-or-die.
5. Henry Fielding, *Tom Jones*. Book XV, Chapter i, 1749. https://www .gutenberg.org/cache/epub/6593/pg6593-images.html.

6: ART

1. Steve Jobs, "Stay Hungry. Stay Foolish." Stanford Commencement Address, 2005. https://fs.blog/steve-jobs-stanford-commencement /#:~:text=None%20of%20this%20had%20even,first%20computer%20 with%20beautiful%20typography.

7: ASKING QUESTIONS

1. Randy Pausch, *The Last Lecture*. Kindle Edition. Hachette Books, 2008, p. 22.

8: EXPOSING KIDS TO ADULT CONVERSATIONS

1. George Orwell, "The Principles of Newspeak," *Nineteen Eighty-Four*. Appendix, 1949. https://orwell.ru/library/novels/1984/english/en_app.
2. Ron Howard, *The Boys*. Kindle Edition. William Morrow, 2021, pp. 94–95.

10: COMEDY

1. Bud Abbott and Lou Costello, "Who's on First?" *The Naughty Nineties*. Filmsite, 1945. https://www.filmsite.org/whosonfirst.html.
2. Jackie Mason, "The World According to Me." YouTube, 1988. https:// www.youtube.com/watch?v=n3ZDslOxPhI.
3. Lewis Carroll, "The Garden of Live Flowers," *Through the Looking-Glass*. Chapter II, 1871. Alice-in-Wonderland.net. https://www.alice-in -wonderland.net/resources/chapters-script/alice-in-wonderland-quotes/.
4. Lewis Carroll, "A Mad Tea-Party," *Alice's Adventures in Wonderland*. Chapter VII, 1865. https://www.cs.cmu.edu/~rgs/alice-VII.html.
5. Andy Quick, "Argument." YouTube, 2016. https://www.youtube.com /watch?v=xpAvcGcEc0k&t=155s. Excerpt condensed for space.
6. Browingate, "Monty Python—Constitutional Peasants Scene." YouTube, 2014. https://www.youtube.com/watch?v=t2c-X8HiBng.
7. Cinematheia, "Monty Python Dead Parrot." YouTube, 2014. https:// www.youtube.com/watch?v=vZw35VUBdzo.
8. Ronald Reagan, "Reagan Joke—Soviet Union and Getting a New Automobile." YouTube, 2013. https://youtu.be/CLW7r4o2_Ow?t=32.
9. "Remarks of Senator John F. Kennedy at the Gridiron Club, Washington, D.C., March 15, 1958." JFK Library, n.d. https://www .jfklibrary.org/archives/other-resources/john-f-kennedy-speeches/ washington-dc-19580315.
10. "Debate Between the President and the Former Vice President

Walter F. Mondale, in Kansas City, Missouri." Reagan Foundation, October 21, 1984. https://www.reaganfoundation.org/ronald-reagan /reagan-quotes-speeches/debate-between-the-president-and-former -vice-president-walter-f-mondale-in-kansas-city-missouri/.

11: CHEAP THRILLS

1. Linda Lee Graham, "An Eighteenth Century Luxury: Books." Voices from the Eighteenth Century, n.d. https://www.lindaleegraham.com /an-eighteenth-century-luxury-books/.
2. Benjamin Franklin, "The Autobiography of Benjamin Franklin." Frank Woodworth Pine (ed.). Project Gutenberg, 2008. https://www .gutenberg.org/files/20203/20203-h/20203-h.htm.
3. Katherine Schaeffer, "Among Many U.S. Children, Reading for Fun Has Become Less Common, Federal Data Shows." Pew Research Center, November 11, 2021. https://www.pewresearch.org/fact -tank/2021/11/12/among-many-u-s-children-reading-for-fun-has -become-less-common-federal-data-shows/.
4. Facts for Families, "Screen Time and Children," No. 54. American Academy of Child & Adolescent Psychiatry, updated February 2020. https://www.aacap.org/AACAP/Families_and_Youth/Facts_for _Families/FFF-Guide/Children-And-Watching-TV-054.aspx.
5. Matthew James, *Homeschooling Odyssey*. JR Books Online, 1998. http:// www.jrbooksonline.com/PDF_Books/Homeschooling_Odyssey -Matthew_James-1998-131pg-EDU.pdf.
6. James, *Homeschooling Odyssey*.
7. James, *Homeschooling Odyssey*.
8. Katie M. Palmer, "Movie Trailers Are Getting Insanely Fast. Trust Us, We Counted the Cuts." *Wired*, June 10, 2013. https://www.wired.com /2013/06/online-trailers-cuts/.
9. D. A. Christakis, "The Effects of Infant Media Usage: What Do We Know and What Should We Learn?" *Acta Paediatrica*, Wiley Online Library, 2009. https://onlinelibrary.wiley.com/doi/abs/10.1111/j.1651 -2227.2008.01027.x.

12: READING

1. "Learning to Read: Excerpt from the Autobiography of Malcolm X." English 2150: Language as Power, Baruch College, 2023. https://blogs .baruch.cuny.edu/eng2150fall2017/?page_id=301.

2. Jane Austen, *Northanger Abbey*, 1803. Project Guttenberg. https://www.gutenberg.org/files/121/121-h/121-h.htm.
3. Stacey Conradt, "10 Stories Behind Dr. Seuss Stories." Mental Floss. Reprinted by CNN, updated January 23, 2009. http://www.cnn.com/2009/LIVING/wayoflife/01/23/mf.seuss.stories.behind/index.html.

13: SCIENCE

1. Big Think, "Neil deGrasse Tyson: Want Scientifically Literate Children? Get Out of Their Way." YouTube, 2014. https://www.youtube.com/watch?v=AIEJjpVlZu0.
2. Richard Feynman, "The Making of a Scientist." *Cricket Magazine*, Vol. 23, No. 2, October 1995.
3. Chris Higgins, "Video Premiere: Richard Feynman on Understanding." Mental Floss, March 31, 2015.https://www.mentalfloss.com/article/62611/video-premiere-richard-feynman-understanding.
4. Lori Dorn, "Legendary Scientist Richard Feynman Opens Up About His Relationship with His Father in an Animated 1966 Interview." Laughing Squid, March 31, 2015. https://laughingsquid.com/legendary-scientist-richard-feynman-opens-up-about-his-relationship-with-his-father-in-an-animated-1966-interview/.
5. "Feynman's Ants." mathpages.com, n.d. https://www.mathpages.com/home/kmath320/kmath320.htm.
6. Anne Schreiber, *National Geographic Readers: Sharks.* National Geographic Kids, 2011. https://www.amazon.com/National-Geographic-Readers-Anne-Schreiber-ebook/dp/B008OI576W.
7. Charles W. G. Smith and Christyna Laubach, *Raptor! A Kid's Guide to Birds of Prey.* Storey Publishing, 2002.

14: MATH ENRICHMENT

1. Phil Davis, "How Big Is the Solar System?" NASA—SOLAR SYSTEM EXPLORATION: Our Galactic Neighborhood, February 1, 2020. https://solarsystem.nasa.gov/news/1164/how-big-is-the-solar system/#:~:text=As%20noted%20earlier%2C%20Earth's%20average,That's%201%20AU.
2. Lee Mohon (ed.), "Alpha Centauri: A Triple Star System About 4 Light Years from Earth." NASA, June 6, 2018. https://www.nasa.gov/mission_pages/chandra/images/alpha-centauri-a-triple-star-system-about-4-light-years-from-earth.html.

3. Ocean Exploration Trust, "How Much Water Is in the Ocean? And 20 More Must-Know Sea Stats." Nautilus Live, December 4, 2020. https://nautiluslive.org/blog/2020/12/04/how-much -water ocean#:~:text=The%20ocean%20contains%20352%20 quintillion,into%20the%20atmosphere%20through%20evaporation.

4. Abbott and Costello, "How Old Will He Be When SHE Catches Up?" YouTube, 2014. https://www.youtube.com/watch?v=FvbKp57lVeU.

15: POETRY

1. Culver Moskowitz, "Big Bang Rap." YouTube, 2016. https://www .youtube.com/watch?v=kvJZBV6gx0E&feature=youtu.be.

16: CORE KNOWLEDGE

1. D. R. Recht and L. Leslie, "Effect of Prior Knowledge on Good and Poor Readers' Memory of Text." *Journal of Educational Psychology*, Vol. 80, No. 1, 1988, p. 16.

2. Helene Cooper, Thomas Gibbons-Neff, and Peter Baker, "Mattis Tries to Put Brakes on Possible Syria Strike, to 'Keep This from Escalating,' " *New York Times*, April 12, 2018. https://www.nytimes.com/201/04/12 /us/politics/trump-syria-attack.html.

3. Core Knowledge Foundation, "Maya, Aztec, and Inca Civilizations." Core Knowledge: History and Geography, 2016. https://www .coreknowledge.org/wp-content/uploads/2017/03/CKHG_G5_U2_ MayaAztecInca_Student-Reader.pdf.

4. Joan Holub, *What Were the Salem Witch Trials?*. Penguin Workshop, August 11, 2015.

17: SCHOOL

1. Sonia Sotomayor. *My Beloved World*. Kindle Edition. Knopf Doubleday Publishing Group, 2013, p. 72.

2. Tom Loveless, "Homework in America." The Brown Center Report on American Education. Brookings Institution, March 18, 2014. https:// www.brookings.edu/research/homework-in-america/.

18: LEARNING DISABILITIES

1. Made By Dyslexia, "Keira Knightley OBE—Made By Dyslexia Talk." YouTube, 2019. https://www.youtube.com/watch?v= OLb6ehPPc4E.

2. CosmicRuss, "Henry Winkler Talks About Dyslexia, June 2012." YouTube, 2012. https://www.youtube.com/watch?v=zYBZeJGm_hw.

3. Made By Dyslexia, "Keira Knightley." https://www.youtube.com/watch?v=OLb6ehPPc4E.

4. Jessica McCabe, "Understanding ADHD, Failing at Normal: An ADHD Success Story." TEDxBratislava. YouTube. October 9, 2017. Link to Segment 3: https://www.youtube.com/watch?v=JiwZQNYlGQI&t=456s.

5. McCabe, "Understanding ADHD, Failing at Normal." Link to entire talk: https://www.youtube.com/watch?v=JiwZQNYlGQI.

6. Shir Adani and Maja Capanec. "Sex Differences in Early Communication Development: Behavioral and Neurobiological Indicators of More Vulnerable Communication System Development in Boys." National Library of Medicine, National Center for Biotechnology Information. PubMed Central. *Croatian Medical Journal*, Vol. 60, No. 2, April 2019. https://www.ncbi.nlm.nih.gov/pmc/articles/PMC6509633/.

19: LEARNING BY DOING

1. Ron Howard, *The Boys,* Kindle Edition, William Morrow, 2021. p. 96.

2. Rafe Esquith, *Teach Like Your Hair's on Fire*. Kindle Edition. Penguin Publishing Group, 2007, pp. 104–5.

21: HELPING YOUR CHILDREN FIND THEIR TALENTS

1. Amy Chua, *Battle Hymn of the Tiger Mother*. Bloomsbury Publishing, 2012, p. 63.

2. "General Colin L. Powell, USA on Passion." Academy of Achievement, n.d. https://achievement.org/video/colin-powell-1/.

24: DEALING WITH YOUR ASPIRATIONS FOR YOUR CHILDREN

1. Debra Cassens Weiss, "'I Destroyed My Life': Former Willkie Co-Chair Suspended for Paying $75K to Boost Daughter's ACT Score." *ABA Journal*, February 19, 2021. https://www.abajournal.com/news/article/former-willkie-co-chair-gets-suspension-after-paying-75k-to-boost-daughters-act-score-i-destroyed-my-life-he-said.

25: TEACHING YOUR CHILDREN HOW TO ENJOY LIFE

1. "John Adams to Abigail Adams, 12 May 1780." *Founders Online,* National Archives. https://founders.archives.gov/documents /Adams/04-03-02-0258.

2. SiriusXM, Crispin Glover: "Zemeckis Got Really Mad at Me: Opie and Anthony." YouTube, 2014. https://youtu.be/lcG61w474zY?t=119.

INDEX

popular psychology, 62–63
Porter, Davina, 99
positive, accentuating the, 183–89
Powell, Colin, 180
praise, effectiveness of, xv, 184, 186,
    188
Prelutsky, Jack, 138
preschool parents, tips for, 211–15
presents, 204–5
prime numbers, 12–13, 131
private schools, 157, 175
probability, concept of, 7
problem-solving habits, 33–34
"procedural" math, 129
product placements in films, 203
Proof! game, 127
psychology, popular, 62–63
punishment, 184
puzzles, 34–35, 213
Python, Monty, 65–67

Q
questions, asking, 46–49

R
ratios, concept of, 113
reading. *See also* books
    becoming an active reader, 107–8
    classic children's literature, 102–3
    comic books, 95–96
    decoding while, 97
    developing imagination through, 91
    Dr. Seuss, 101–2
    with dyslexia, 159–64
    graphic novels, 94–95
    at high school level, 104–5
    impact on intellect, 92
    learning English as spoken language
        through, 97–98
    learning grammar through, 89
    learning vocabulary through, 89
    levels, determining, 106

making time for, 92
nurturing interest in, 100
picture books, 93–94
at right difficulty level, 103–4, 106
statistics on, 78
summer, 60
teaching children to, 214
wordless or nearly wordless books,
    92–93
Reagan, Ronald, 71, 72–73
Real Engineering (science channel),
    124
"real me," searching for the, 62–63
recorded books. *See* audiobooks
repeating a grade, 165–66
rhetorical techniques, 104–5
riddles, math, 133–34
The Right Stuff (Wolfe), 152
Risby, Bonnie, 34
Rock, Chris, 3
Roosevelt, Theodore, 3
Rowling, J. K., 102
The Royal Institution (science
    channel), 124
rules and boundaries, 191–94

S
sadness, expressing, 187
Salinger, J. D., 91
Sarducci, Guido, 145–46
Sartre, Jean-Paul, 3
Savage Kingdom (documentary),
    37–38
Scales and Three Balls, 30
Schickele, Peter, 22, 26
schools, 153–58, 175
science, 109–24
    books about, 121–23, 239–42
    buying scientific equipment,
        118–19
    encouraging child's interest in,
        109–18

ABOUT THE AUTHORS

Eva Moskowitz and Eric Grannis began dating as students at Stuyvesant High School. They married in 1989 and have had three children together: Culver, who graduated from Columbia University; Dillon, who attends the University of Chicago; and Hannah, who attends the Wharton School at the University of Pennsylvania.

Eva earned a Ph.D. in American history from Johns Hopkins University in 1991. After teaching at several universities, including Vanderbilt and the University of Virginia, she entered politics and became a member of the New York City Council, where she became chair of the council's education committee, which oversees the city's public school system.

After leaving the council in 2005, Eva founded Harlem Success Academy with 165 students. In the years that followed, Eva has turned Success Academy Charter Schools into one of the fastest-growing, highest-performing public charter school networks in the nation, with more than 50 schools enrolling over 20,000 students. Success's students regularly outperform students from New York's most affluent neighborhoods and go on to attend leading universities.

Eva has shared her expertise with thousands of educators and visitors from around the world, testified before Congress, and worked with political leaders from both parties to advance educational reform. Her memoir, *The Education of Eva Moskowitz*, details her relentless efforts to advance educational equity.

Eric is an attorney in private practice. Prior to that, he taught middle school math and science. Eric has also been instrumental in founding several charter schools both as a board member and attorney.